W9-AKA-992

DISCARD

¡CUBA LIBRE!

ALSO BY TONY PERROTTET

Off the Deep End:
Travels in Forgotten Frontiers

The Naked Olympics:
The True Story of the Ancient Games

Pagan Holiday:
On the Trail of Ancient Roman Tourists

Napoleon's Privates:
2,500 Years of History Unzipped

The Sinner's Grand Tour:
A Journey through the Historical Underbelly of Europe

¡CUBA LIBRE!

Che, Fidel, and
the Improbable Revolution
That Changed World History

TONY PERROTTET

BLUE RIDER PRESS

blue
rider
press

An imprint of Penguin Random House LLC
penguinrandomhouse.com

Map illustration by Jennifer May Reiland

Photo page 9 is courtesy of Oficina de Asuntos Históricos, Havana. Photo
page 103 is from Andrew St. George Papers (MS 1912), Manuscripts &
Archives, Yale University. Photo page 193 is courtesy of Cuban revolution
collection, 1955–1970 (inclusive), Manuscripts & Archives, Yale University.
Photo page 293 is from the collection of the author; photographer unknown.

Library of Congress Cataloging-in-Publication Data
Names: Perrottet, Tony, author.
Title: Cuba libre! : Che, Fidel, and the improbable revolution that changed
world history / Tony Perrottet.
Description: New York, New York : Blue Rider Press, 2019.
Identifiers: LCCN 2018045143 | ISBN 9780735218161 (hardback) |
ISBN 9780735218185 (ebook)
Subjects: LCSH: Castro, Fidel, 1926–2016. | Guevara, Che, 1928–1967. |
Cuba—History—Revolution, 1959. | BISAC: HISTORY / Modern /
21st Century. | HISTORY / Caribbean & West Indies / Cuba. |
HISTORY / United States / 20th Century.
Classification: LCC F1788 .P474 2019 | DDC 972.9106/40922—dc23
LC record available at https://lccn.loc.gov/2018045143

Printed in the United States of America
1   3   5   7   9   10   8   6   4   2

BOOK DESIGN BY KATY RIEGEL

FOR HENRY, SAM,
Y LOS OLVIDADOS DE LA HISTORIA

Contents

PART TWO

The Amateur Guerrillas

PART THREE

Revolutionary Road

PART FOUR

Honeymoon with Che

¡CUBA LIBRE!

Prologue:
Fidelmania

THE WORLD'S MOST notorious guerrilla leader was about to invade their living rooms, and Americans were thrilled. At 8:00 p.m. on Sunday, January 11, 1959, some 50 million viewers tuned their television sets to *The Ed Sullivan Show*, the trendsetting variety revue that had introduced them to Elvis Presley a few years earlier and would bring them the Beatles several years later. On this winter's evening the avuncular Sullivan was hosting a Latin celebrity who had aroused intense curiosity across the United States: Fidel Castro, a charming thirty-two-year-old lawyer-turned-revolutionary, known for his unkempt beard and khaki patrol cap, who had against all odds overthrown a bloodthirsty military regime in Cuba.

For America's most beloved entertainment program, it was a rare excursion into politics. Earlier in the hour, Sullivan had presented a more typical array of artistic offerings for the staid Eisenhower era. Four acrobats leapt and gamboled around the stage (two of them wearing ape costumes). The Little Gaelic Singers crooned soothing Irish harmonies. A stand-up comic performed a cheesy routine about suburban house parties. Finally, Sullivan cut to the main attraction: his friendly interview with Fidel at the very cusp of the rebels' victory.

The segment had been filmed at 2:00 a.m. on January 8 in the provincial outpost of Matanzas, 60 miles east of Havana, using the town hall as an improvised TV studio. Only a few hours after the interview, Fidel would make his triumphant entrance into the Cuban capital, his men riding on the backs of captured tanks in euphoric scenes that evoked the liberation of Paris. It was the electrifying climax of history's most unlikely revolution: a scruffy handful of self-taught insurgents—many of them kids just out of college, literature majors, art students, and engineers, including a number of trailblazing women—had somehow defeated 40,000 professional soldiers and forced the sinister dictator, President Fulgencio Batista, to flee from the island like a thief in the night.

Given the animosity that sprang up between the US and Cuba soon after, the chummy atmosphere of the conversation today seems closer to *The Twilight Zone*. On-screen, Sullivan and his guest could hardly look more incongruous. Trying to look casual as he leans against a table, the thickset fifty-seven-year-old *yanqui* impresario appears to have just walked out of a Brooks Brothers ad in his tailored suit and tie, his helmet of dyed hair neatly combed and brilliantined. (He was often parodied as a "well-dressed gorilla.") Fidel, by contrast, was already a fashion icon for rebellious American youth, his olive-drab uniform, martial kepi, and raffish facial hair instantly recognizable. Clustered around the pair are a dozen equally shaggy young rebels who were known in Cuba simply as *los barbudos*, "the bearded ones," all cradling weapons—"a forest of tommy guns," Sullivan later said. Fidel's lover and confidante, Celia Sánchez, who often appeared by his side in press interviews, was this time standing off-camera, wearing specially tailored fatigues and balancing a cigarette in her finely manicured fingers. The most efficient organizer of the Rebel Army, she had brokered the media event and now dedicated herself to keeping the male guerrillas, who were as excitable as schoolboys, from wandering across the set or talking.

With his first breath, Sullivan assures CBS viewers that they are about to meet "a wonderful group of revolutionary youngsters," as if they are the latest pop music sensation. Despite their unwashed appearance, Fidel's followers are a far cry from the godless Communists depicted by the Cuban military's propaganda machine, he adds; in fact, they are all wearing Catholic medals and some are even piously carrying copies of the Bible. But Sullivan is most interested in Fidel himself. The sheer improbability of his victory over the thuggish strongman Batista had bathed him in a romantic aura. US magazines openly described Fidel as a new Robin Hood, with Celia as his Maid Marian, robbing from the rich to give to the poor.

Sullivan's first questions are not the most hard-hitting:

"Now, in school," he chortles in his distinctively nasal voice, "I understand you were a very fine student and a very fine athlete. Were you a baseball pitcher?"

"Yes," Fidel replies in the halting English learned at his Jesuit high school and several visits to New York City. "Baseball, basketball, softball. Every kind of sport."

"Undoubtedly all of this exercise you did at school prepared you for this role?"

"Yes. I found myself in good condition to exist in the mountains..."

The hardened celebrity hound Sullivan is clearly starstruck by his guest, and his delivery is far more animated than his usual monotonous drone back in the New York studio. Comandante en Jefe Castro, meanwhile, comes across as earnest, sweet-natured, and eager to please, furrowing his brow with effort as he grasps for his English vocabulary. It's hard not to feel for the rebel leader as he struggles gamely with the half-remembered tongue.

Some of the interview is haunting in retrospect. "I'd like to ask you a couple of questions, Fidel," Sullivan says, serious for a moment. "In Latin American countries over and over again, dictators [have] stolen millions and millions of dollars, tortured and killed people. How do you propose to end that here in Cuba?"

Fidel laughs. "Very easy. By not permitting that any dictatorship come again to rule our country. You can be sure that Batista . . . will be the last dictator of Cuba."

In 1959, Sullivan saw no reason to argue.

The lovefest now proceeds to its crescendo. "The people of the United States, they have great admiration for you and your men," the host advises Fidel. "Because you are in the real American tradition—of a George Washington—of any band who started off with a small body [of men] and fought against a great nation and won." Fidel takes the compliment in stride; after all, the US press had been idolizing him for nearly two years as a citizen-soldier in the very spirit of 1776.

"What do you feel about the United States?" Sullivan asks.

"My feeling to the people of the United States is a feeling of sympathy," Fidel says evenly, "because they are a very worker people . . ."

("They work hard," Ed interprets.)

"They have founded that big nation, working very much . . ."

("That is right . . ." Ed nods.)

"United States is not one race [of] people, [they] came from every part in the world . . . That is why the United States belong[s] to the world, to those who were persecuted, to those who could not live in their own country . . ."

"We want you to like us." Sullivan glows. "And we like you. You and Cuba!"

The show then cuts back to Sullivan in CBS's Manhattan studio, where the arbiter of middle-class American taste lavishes Fidel with the same magnanimous praise he had heaped on Elvis.

"You know, this is a fine young man and a very smart young man," he pronounces, squeezing his arms together in his famous hunched stance. "And with the help of God and our prayers, and with the help of the American government, he will come up with the sort of democracy down there that America should have."

And then the show rolled on to its next variety segment: a fashion show for poodles.

TODAY, IT IS all but impossible to imagine that moment in 1959 when the Cuban Revolution was fresh, Fidel and Che were young and handsome, and Americans could view the uprising as an embodiment of their own finest ideals. As Sullivan observed, here was a people fighting for freedom against injustice and tyranny, a modern echo of the War of Independence, with Fidel as a sexier version of a Founding Father and his guerrillas the reincarnation of Ethan Allen's Green Mountain Boys, the irregular sharpshooters who helped defeat the redcoats.

In fact, *The Ed Sullivan Show* was only the start of the Fidel craze for Americans. A string of other gushing interviews would quickly follow, conducted by everyone from the revered CBS newsman Ed Murrow to the Hollywood actor Errol Flynn. A few months later, in April 1959, Fidel even traveled on a victory lap of the northeastern United States: he was mobbed by admirers as he ate hot dogs in New York City, spoke at Princeton, and made dutiful visits to hallowed shrines of democracy such as Mount Vernon and the Lincoln Memorial.

Meanwhile, American Cubaphiles flocked to Havana to see the revolution firsthand and were warmly welcomed. They immersed themselves in the Mardi Gras atmosphere, attending mass rallies and wacky radical street celebrations such as a mock funeral parade for a nationalized telephone company, complete with musicians dressed as mourners and fake coffins. Havana was a round-the-clock fiesta, with buskers on every corner singing patriotic songs to raise money for the new Cuban state in a delirious wave of optimism.

Beat poets wrote odes to Fidel. African-Americans were exhilarated by Cuba's overnight abolition of all segregation laws just as the American civil rights movement was gaining pace, and joined special group tours for black writers and artists. A Creek Indian chief traveled to meet Fidel wearing a full Native American feathered war bonnet. US feminists rejoiced in Cuba's promise that women's liberation would be "a revolution within the revolution." In fact, the entire world was fascinated by the apparent explosion of idealism: Fidel, Che, and Celia basked in goodwill, entertaining intellectuals like Jean-Paul Sartre and Simone de Beauvoir. There was a chance, many felt, that Cuba would become a paradise of political, racial, and gender equality.

The reason for our amnesia about how the revolution was received is, of course, political: the popular memory of the guerrilla campaign was an early casualty of the Cold War. When *los barbudos* first rolled into Havana in January 1959, they were showered with admiration for what seemed a black-and-white struggle for liberty. But Atomic Age milestones such as the CIA-backed Bay of Pigs invasion in April 1961 and the near-Armageddon of the Cuban missile crisis in October 1962, which pushed the human race the closest it has ever come to extinction in nuclear war, quickly overshadowed any romance for most in the Western world. It became widely accepted in the US that Fidel and his supporters had been covering up Communist sympathies that had lurked in their hearts from the start.

And yet, the story of how a few amateur subversives defeated one of Latin America's most loathsome regimes remains a defining saga of the twentieth century. In the words of historian Nancy Stout, Cuba's was "the perfect revolution" for the visual media age that kicked off in the 1950s: it was short; it was successful; it unfolded in neat stages— "like an operetta"—and yet with the narrative arc of a paperback thriller. It was also full of larger-than-life characters. Coinciding with the birth of network television and the golden age of magazines, it became history's most photogenic revolt. Images of the dashing guerrillas and attractive guerrilla women—almost all in their twenties or early thirties, some of them fresh-faced teenagers—jolted the world towards the 1960s.

Today, thanks to the veil of suspicion and ideology hanging over Cuba, few are aware of just how improvised the revolution was; its

leaders were largely forced to make up their own brand of jungle combat and urban resistance as they went along. Even fewer recall the
genuine bravery and self-sacrifice of those years, when ordinary Cubans risked torture and death every day at the hands of Batista's
henchmen, who were as sadistic as Gestapo agents. Under Batista,
thousands of young rebel sympathizers disappeared into police torture chambers, their mutilated bodies strung up in parks or dumped
in gutters the next morning. (Nobody knows the exact death toll
during the seven-year dictatorship, but the most accepted figure is
20,000.) Today, long decades after *el triumfo*, "the triumph," a few famous images of the main characters—Fidel with his Old Testament
beard, Che in his beret gazing mystically ahead—have become frozen
as Soviet-era clichés.

This book will attempt to turn back the clock to recapture the atmosphere of Cuba in the 1950s, when the actors were unknowns, history was unformed, and the fate of the revolution hung in the balance.
In the process, it will attempt to unravel how the optimism of the
uprising went so badly awry. Were Americans—and the many moderate Cubans who supported the revolution—duped by Fidel, as hard-
liners would later allege, tricked by a Machiavellian figure who had a
secret agenda from the start? Or could the story of modern Cuba,
which reshaped international politics so radically, have gone another way?

Part One

THE
CUBAN
"MADNESS"

CHAPTER 1

DIY Revolution

(25 months earlier: December 1956)

A T AROUND 9:00 a.m. on Sunday, December 2, 1956, a wiry campesino set off from his thatch-roofed hut into a coconut grove called Los Cayuelas on one of the remotest coastlines of eastern Cuba. The cool morning air carried a whiff of decay from nearby mangrove swamps, a primeval barrier of dark water and roots that kept this rural world in dreamy isolation, its shores as mysterious as when Christopher Columbus first drifted by, lost, in his caravel.

As the farmer strolled back from loading his charcoal kiln, he was surprised by a wild-eyed man lurching from behind a palm tree. The intruder was carrying an antique rifle and sporting ill-fitting military fatigues with a red-and-black armband that read "M-26-7." He was also soaked from head to toe with seawater and encrusted in rich brown mud. This strange apparition, part bandit, part castaway, led the apprehensive farmer into nearby bushes, where eight more armed men were in even worse condition. The sludge-covered figures were emaciated, with sunken eyes and lips raw from dehydration. Their faces and hands were scratched and bloody. Many of their uniforms were torn. Several were even missing boots.

A man who was evidently their leader stepped forward like an actor on the stage. He was tall and gangly, with horn-rimmed glasses, a wisp of a mustache, and a week's stubble on his cheeks.

"Have no fear!" he grandly declared. "My name is Fidel Castro and we have come to liberate the Cuban people!"

The farmer, Ángel Pérez Rosabal, evidently resisted any urge to burst out laughing. He was the lucky first Cuban to learn that members of the 26th of July Movement, known in shorthand as M-26-7, had landed in this forsaken corner of the Caribbean—halfway between a beach called Playa las Coloradas and the aptly named Purgatory Point—to start a guerrilla war.

The men were clearly in a sorry state, so the farmer led them to his *bohío*, a one-room, dirt-floored hut, where his wife offered them what little food was on hand: some chunks of pork, apples, and fried *plátanos*. (It was a generous gesture; Ángel's profession as "charcoal burner," the ancient art of creating charcoal from wood in a kiln, provided a bare subsistence living.) Bemused children were sent to chase a chicken for a meal, but when they were unsuccessful, Pérez decided to slaughter a piglet. There is no record of what the family thought of their half-starved "liberators"—a grand total of eighty-two men was staggering through the swamps, Fidel informed them—but it's a safe bet they didn't look like promising revolutionaries. The more energetic among them began hacking at coconuts with knives and furiously devouring the flesh; others prostrated themselves in numb exhaustion, as if they had just swum from Jamaica.

Despite the Marx Brothers air to the scene, the stakes could not have been higher that morning, nor the guerrillas' cause more high-minded. As Fidel explained to the Pérez family—he alone seemed unaffected by their travails and was garrulous to the point of mania—their aim was no less than the overthrow of the detested Batista, who had been brutalizing Cubans ever since he had seized power in a military coup nearly five years earlier. From the day he became dictator in 1952, Batista set new standards for criminality in the crowded field of Latin American despots, openly pillaging the national coffers, hobnobbing with *yanqui* Mafiosi, and lining his pockets with bribes while many Cubans lived in destitution. Any criticism of this carnival of corruption was silenced with casual savagery. Politicians, journalists, and student activists were being kidnapped, inventively tortured, and assassinated on a daily basis, turning the entire island into a cemetery.

Fidel and his followers had long ago concluded that Batista would never give up power by peaceful means, so they had fled to Mexico to train themselves as guerrilla warriors and then return to Cuba by boat. Unfortunately, their Job-like sufferings had begun from the moment they had left port a week earlier. The eighty-two men were packed "like tinned sardines" into a barely seaworthy pleasure cruiser called the *Granma*, purchased from an American expat dentist, and for the entire journey they were tormented by seasickness, hunger, and lack of sleep. Then, in the predawn darkness of December 2, Fidel mistakenly ordered the pilot to land at the worst possible spot on the Cuban coast. The vessel hit a sandbank and shuddered to a halt; the weakened band had then been forced to wade ashore and clamor for hours through the endless, dismal swamp.

"It was less an invasion than a shipwreck," complained the twenty-eight-year-old medic from Argentina, Ernesto "Che" Guevara, one of the four foreigners in the group. Having worked in the Amazon, he was one of the better prepared for the ordeal. Most of the other men were overeducated city slickers who had never seen such a hostile tropical wilderness before. Like doomed conquistadors, they sank waist-deep into mud and struggled over abrasive roots, jumping at the sight of scuttling crabs and squid that drifted nightmarishly between their legs. Many abandoned crucial equipment in their panic before finally crawling to dry land on hands and knees.

It was the vanguard of this abject "army," staggering zombie-like from the swamps, that the startled campesino Ángel Pérez had encountered at 9:00 a.m. Over the next two hours more rebels emerged, all looking just as shattered, including Fidel's baby-faced younger brother Raúl, aged twenty-five. The *Granma* expedition had been conceived by Fidel as a grand gesture of defiance against Batista, but it was also wildly optimistic. To any sane observer, the idea that this callow crew intended to take on the Cuban army—the dictator's 40,000 well-armed troops backed by a dozen battleships, battalions of Sherman tanks, and a US-supplied air force that could refuel in Guantánamo Bay—would have seemed the purest fantasy.

MUCH TO THE famished men's chagrin, there would be no time to rest, let alone savor suckling pig. At around 11:00 a.m. they heard explosions back in the mangroves. A coast guard gunship had spotted the abandoned *Granma*; now it was randomly shelling the shore. Army assault by land was now an imminent danger. Fidel asked the campesino if there were any trucks nearby that could be commandeered for a quick escape to their goal, the Sierra Maestra mountain range, whose foothills lay about thirty-five miles due east. There were not. The only option was for the guerrillas to make their way there as best they could on foot, even though their guns were still caked in mud and some of the men were ready to faint in the gathering heat. They shouldered their heavy backpacks and rushed into the scrappy lowland forests, marching in single file and dodging for cover whenever they heard a plane passing overhead.

It was a farcical start to the long-planned revolution, and Fidel was in a rage, filling the air with a barrage of creative curses. But farce would soon turn to tragedy. Within days, many of them would be dead.

THIS FAR-FLUNG CORNER of Cuba had been chosen for the landing in part because it was almost uninhabited; now, without a guide, the expeditionaries could find nobody to help them obtain food or water. By afternoon, almost every one of them was suffering from blisters from their new boots; some were developing fungal infections. They were "stumbling along like so many shadows or ghosts," Che later wrote, "marching in response to some obscure psychic impulse." Many were as skittish in the wild as Woody Allen characters today, startled by strange animal noises or the sight of large flying bugs.

After dark, the demoralized group tried to sleep while pinkish land crabs crashed through the underbrush around them like miniature tanks. One man woke the next morning to find that one of his bootlaces had been cut by the crustaceans in three places. Matters looked slightly more cheerful when they ran into some friendly peasants, who sold the famished revolutionaries their first breakfast in Cuba: cassava and bread dipped in honey. The latter was so delicious that some of them gorged, causing long-empty digestive tracts to suffer sudden bouts of diarrhea. It was the first of many gastrointestinal attacks that would plague them. From that moment on, the scribbled war diaries of the guerrillas would be filled with lurid accounts of bowel disorders.

The frequency of air patrols was increasing, so Fidel decided that they would rest during the day and march at night, even though scrambling in the dark over boulders and sharp stones nicknamed by Cubans "dog fangs" made progress agonizing. Over the next two evenings the rebels caught some lucky culinary breaks: in one empty peasant house they found a vat of rice and beans being cooked on a stove; they devoured it and left a five-peso note on the table as payment. The owner of a lonely bodega sold them his entire supply of crackers, tinned sausages, and sweet condensed milk, which the men savored like elixir of the gods. Most importantly, Fidel found a peasant guide who agreed to lead them towards the Sierra Maestra. The men were starting to regain their confidence and believe they might somehow escape detection.

None of them realized that the surrounding countryside was already seething with activity. Alerted by the coast guard, agents of the Cuban military intelligence service, the dreaded SIM (Servicio de Inteligencia Militar), were gathering reports about the landing from their network of rural informers. All over the Oriente ("the East," shorthand for the entire region, which also gave its name to the province at the time), troops had been mobilized; army trucks rumbled through the darkness. The commanding officer, a certain General Pedro Rodríguez, was so confident of his ability to wipe out the rebels that he had—bizarrely—made an announcement of victory as soon as the *Granma* was found. According to the press release, all "forty" expedition members had already been killed, "among them its chief, Fidel Castro, thirty years old." That report was an Orwellian fabrication, but it is easy to see why the general was so certain of the outcome. As the eighty-two unsuspecting guerrillas trudged towards the mountains, Batista's minions were tracking their every step—quite literally, since they foolishly left a trail of sugarcane pieces they chewed to stay hydrated—and the military noose was tightening.

ON THE MORNING of December 5, after walking all night, the expeditionaries stopped in a thinly wooded area next to a cane field and fell into a bone-tired sleep. In the three days since landing, they had advanced only fifteen miles. Their campsite, a field called Alegría del Pío—literally, "the rejoicing of the pious"—was dangerously exposed, but Fidel did not feel he could ask his weary men to march farther towards a thicker forest nearby. He then made the mistake of allowing the peasant guide to leave. The man went straight to a nearby military post and confirmed the guerrillas' exact location.

The attack, when it came, was a total surprise. The men had just woken up in the middle of the afternoon and were sharing their meager daily rations—two dry crackers, half a sausage, and a swig of condensed milk each—when a single shot rang out. This was followed, Che wrote, by a "symphony of lead." Total panic ensued. Some men were cut down in the crossfire. Others grabbed their rifles but abandoned their backpacks. Many had taken off their shoes and were forced to run barefoot as bullets whistled all around them. Survivors recalled absurd scenes. One man, paralyzed by fear, hid behind a single cane stalk as if it were a tree trunk. Someone kept yelling at the top of his lungs: "Silence!" Another wandered in shock, cradling a shattered hand.

An army officer shouted out for the rebels to surrender, but Camilo Cienfuegos, a happy-go-lucky former waiter from Havana, yelled back cockily, "Nobody surrenders here, you prick!" before diving for cover. Despite the cowboy bravado, the rebels had lost any pretense of discipline; it was every man for himself. The rout only became more frenzied when clouds of black smoke began to waft across the battlefield: the dry cane crop had been set aflame to smoke the rebels out and was now a blinding inferno.

In a cinematic moment, the soulful doctor Che was forced in his first experience of combat to choose between grabbing his knapsack full of medical supplies or a box of ammunition. He hesitated for an instant—poised "between my obligation as a doctor and my duty as a revolutionary," he would recall—and chose the latter. Immediately afterward he felt a bullet hit him in the neck. He declared to a friend, *"Estoy jodido"* ("I'm fucked"), and leaned against a tree to quietly expire. Che pondered, in his poetic if strangely detached Argentine way, the death scene in his favorite Jack London story, until an Afro-Cuban bricklayer named Juan Almeida shook him out of his reverie. Che quickly realized he had only suffered a flesh wound and sprinted to the safety of the dense forest nearby.

A man running alongside him, Ángel Albentosa, was less lucky. When he was hit in the chest, he shrieked, "They've killed me!" and began spinning, firing his rifle randomly in the air.

Fidel tried to organize an orderly retreat but it was hopeless. His second-in-command, a fellow lawyer named Juan Manuel Márquez, grabbed him and yelled, "Fidel! Everyone's already gone!" He would have to run for it or the army would take him alive. As Márquez dashed off in panic, Fidel plunged alone into the twelve-foot-high sugar cane, desperately clutching his cherished weapon, a Swiss hunting rifle with adjustable telescopic sights. He then covered himself with a pile of fallen leaves, as if he were playing a game of hide-and-seek in his rural childhood home. Soon army trucks were thundering past, only feet away from where he was lying.

Of the eighty-two rebels, only three were killed outright at Alegría del Pío. Seventeen were wounded and captured. But the disaster was total. The expedition was completely dispersed. Cuban historians have discerned that the sixty-two survivors were scattered into twenty-eight different groups, with thirteen men, including Fidel, finding themselves entirely alone. Many had run in completely the wrong direction. Without radios, none of these disparate groups knew if anyone else had escaped the ambush alive. As Che later recalled, with admirable understatement: "The situation was not good."

IF THE GUERRILLAS' fortunes seemed at a low ebb, the situation managed to grow even worse in the following days as the splintered forces wandered, lost and desperate, in the inhospitable coastal lowlands. Plotted on a map, their movements zigzag across the Oriente like a drunken salsa step.

The seventeen who were captured by the army at Alegría del Pío turned out to be the lucky ones. They were treated with surprising decency, given the murderous habits of Batista's army, and transferred to prison cells in Santiago de Cuba, the picturesque capital of Oriente Province. There they were given medical treatment and photographed by the press, along with their three dead *compañeros*. Here was apparent proof of General Rodríguez's assertion, several days earlier, that the expedition had been wiped out, although the cadaver of Fidel was conspicuously absent. Carlos Franqui, a pushy young journalist traveling from Havana, asked if he could talk directly to the prisoners. According to Franqui's account, the wardens were unaware that he was a member of M-26-7 and, in an obtuse moment of overconfidence, left him with the men in private. He was able to confirm that nobody had actually seen Fidel being killed or wounded, although his fate was unknown.

For the sixty-two rebels who had escaped the ambush, it was a different story. The army and SIM agents hunted them down like rabbits in the desolate countryside, where, far from the prying eyes of the press or civil authority, more ruthless justice would be meted out.

The gloomy fate of one group augured poorly for them all. On the night of the ambush, seven shell-shocked men had found one another by chance in the forest and accepted the leadership of a brawny twenty-four-year-old agronomy graduate named José Smith. With only one rifle and two pistols between them, they cautiously set off after dark towards what they hoped was east towards the sierra. They hit the Caribbean coast instead. With no sustenance other than putrid water caught in the hollows of rocks, the men were soon pushed to their limits. After three nights of aimless wandering, early on Saturday, December 8, they were relieved to spot a secluded farmhouse. Its idyllic setting would suit a boutique hotel today, nestled between the lapping turquoise waves, a shallow river, and a scrub-covered cliff—a juncture called Boca del Toro, "the Bull's Mouth."

A drama then unfolded like a medieval morality play. The owner of the farm, a middle-aged campesino known as Manolo Capitán, greeted the seven men with caution. He had heard the first rumors of a subversive landing the day before while coming home from a cockfight in a nearby village. The survivors who now materialized on his doorstep were clearly in atrocious physical shape, so Capitán offered to ride by horseback to the local army post, where he had friends who would broker their safe surrender. An argument ensued amongst the men. Most agreed it was hopeless to continue, but one dissenter, Jésus "Chucho" Reyes, loudly insisted that it was insanity to throw themselves at the mercy of Batista's butchers. They should keep going, no matter how agonizing things got. He set off alone.

When a contingent of marines arrived at the farm by jeep, local campesinos gathered on a hillside to watch; they obviously had a premonition that things would not go well. As was later pieced together from their testimony, the six rebels were filing towards the beach, when the marines opened fire without warning. One farmer who missed the point yelled, "Don't shoot, these men are trying to surrender!" Five of the revolutionaries went down in the first volley; those who were merely wounded were executed on the spot by the cold-blooded chief of naval intelligence, Lieutenant Julio Laurent. The sixth, a twenty-seven-year-old student activist named Cándido González, managed to hide in the underbrush for a few hours but was discovered and also summarily offed. Chucho had been wise to take his chances in the wilderness. Thanks to a string of lucky breaks, he managed to make his way half-dead to Havana, where he took refuge in friendly foreign embassies; he was then smuggled out to Miami to work as a fund-raiser for M-26-7, recounting for Cuban exile audiences the harrowing saga of his escape.

THAT SATURDAY, DECEMBER 8, qualifies as the nadir of the revolution. On the same night, by extraordinary bad luck, three more rebels knocked on the farmhouse door at Boca del Toro and met the amiable Manolo Capitán, who again arranged their surrender to Lieutenant Laurent and his marines. This time, the prisoners were led by torchlight to the beach where Laurent told them to put their hands behind their heads and look out to sea until a boat came to transport them. They were then machine-gunned in the back. At around the same time, not far from Alegría del Pío, six other exhausted insurgents were surprised by patrols and taken to an improvised army outpost for interrogation. After dark, they were loaded into a truck with their hands tied behind their backs. Their bullet-riddled corpses were found at the gates of Niquero cemetery the next morning.

In the end, almost twenty men from the *Granma* met their end that Saturday night. Fidel would only learn of their fate much later. At the time, more than three days after the ambush, he had emerged from beneath his pile of leaves but had not moved a foot from his hiding spot in the cane field by Alegría del Pío.

THE REST OF the world observed this hapless uprising with incredulity. Perhaps the bluntest critique came from the *New York Times*, which published an op-ed titled "The Violent Cubans" two days after *Granma* landed, following Batista's assertion that the expedition had been wiped out. The political extremism in Cuba "does not make sense to outsiders," the newspaper intoned. Fidel's whole idea of an amphibious invasion was little short of "pathetic." The most perplexing aspect of it all, the *Times* felt, was that he had made no real secret of his overall plan. Quite the opposite: Fidel had made a public declaration many months earlier that he intended to land a guerrilla force somewhere behind the lines in Cuba, which made the sacrifice of so many young men, mostly aged eighteen to thirty, both inevitable and futile.

"Could anything be madder?" the author wondered.

CHAPTER 2

The Curse of San Juan Hill

(Flashback to 1898)

IRRATIONAL AS THE *Granma* landing may have seemed to outsiders, it had plenty of precedent for Cubans: Fidel and his comrades knew that they were part of a glorious tradition of near-suicidal revolts. Even the choice of landing spot was rich with tragic meaning. While the official center of Cuba was the capital city Havana, famed for its rococo mansions, raunchy nightclubs, and Mob-run casinos, the cradle of rebellion had always been the Oriente, at the opposite end of the slender, 780-mile-long island, whose shape has often been compared to a crocodile at rest. As remote in spirit from Havana as the Appalachians are from New York City, the East had always been Cuba's wildest, poorest, and most racially diverse region. It was derided by rich *habaneros* as a provincial backwater, but it was here that the greatest dramas of Cuban history were played out. In the Oriente's inaccessible mountains and beaches, the last Taíno Indians had been nearly exterminated by the conquistadors. Its vast sugar plantations were where bloody slave uprisings erupted and armed revolts against the Spanish began—and failed. It was in the Oriente that illustrious Cuban heroes were martyred, and here that the greatest humiliations during the War of Independence—referred to as the "Spanish–American War" in the US—were acted out.

It's no accident that Fidel and his men had spent almost as much time in Mexico studying Cuban history as training for jungle warfare. Their "mad" landing was a frustrated response to problems that could be traced back over a century. A brisk history lesson also explains the bitterness Cubans often felt towards the United States. Only ninety miles from Havana across the Straits of Florida, the northern behemoth was for most of the nineteenth century an inspiration to Latin Americans as a beacon of freedom and democracy. But as the twentieth century approached, its actions became hypocritical at best, destructive at worst. Many Cubans could relate to a famous quote from another embattled neighbor: "Poor Mexico. So far from God, so close to the United States."

CUBA WAS ALWAYS exceptional; almost nothing about its history fit the patterns of Latin America. Its singular status dated all the way back to the first visit by Columbus in 1492, who declared the island "the loveliest land that human eyes have ever seen." With one foot still in the Middle Ages, the Spanish settlers who arrived soon after grappled to understand what they saw. They imagined the tracks of crocodiles were those of enchanted lions, and groups of distant cranes were monks in robes; the Taíno Indians carried mysterious "firebrands" of flaming leaves they inhaled and called *tabaco*. This magical island was soon the jewel in the Spanish crown. With its deep harbor and strategic location, Havana became the natural staging post for the conquest of the Americas: conquistadors sallied forth in search of El Dorado and the Fountain of Youth, and the wonders they did find proved more incredible than the fantasies. Soon galleons heavy with Aztec and Inca treasure gathered in Havana beneath a string of honey-stoned fortresses, built to protect against pirates like Sir Francis Drake, and twice a year, heavily guarded armadas would catch the Gulf Stream back to Seville on the "Indies route." (The same current brought the marlin that would lure fishermen like Ernest Hemingway to Cuba centuries later, the fish traveling "like cars along a highway," as he put it in *Esquire* magazine.)

In faraway Oriente, the port of Santiago, fringed by palm trees and nestled among verdant mountains, developed as Havana's alter ego. It was funded not by pillaged treasure but "white gold"—sugar—which was farmed by African slaves in an inhuman system of plantations. By the eighteenth century, the impoverished, forgotten East was producing the wealth that kept the cosmopolitan capital humming. But Cuba's dependence on the sugar economy meant that it ignored the calls for freedom that rippled through the rest of Latin America in the early 1800s. White planters presided over huge slave populations, and they lived in terror of the bloody race rebellion that had consumed neighboring Haiti after the French Revolution. By the 1820s an unbroken chain of liberated colonies ran the length of the New World; only the Caribbean islands of Cuba and nearby Puerto Rico were still tied to the apron strings of Spain.

On the surface, Cuba, "the Ever Faithful Isle" (as Spaniards fondly called it), continued to thrive. It became the most technologically advanced country in Latin America, the first to receive such marvels as railroads, electricity, and telephones. But its submissive role as a colony was humiliating to many Cubans, and two convulsive wars of independence eventually tore the island apart. The first spasm began in 1868, when machete-wielding armies surged around the island shouting *"¡Viva Cuba Libre! ¡Independencia o Muerte!"* ("Long live free Cuba! Independence or death!"). The revolt was crushed; but afterward the Spanish could only control the island by running it like a police state.

Towering over the crucial next bout for Cuba's independence was the figure of José Martí, a brilliant poet and political thinker who tried to put his theories into action on the battlefield. His revered status in Cuba—busts of Martí, frail, balding, and dressed like an office clerk, stand in every town square—borders on the religious. (He is even known as "the Apostle.") Fidel grew up regarding himself as the virtual reincarnation of Martí, who became the main inspiration for the guerrilla war. Even in comic books about the revolution given to Cuban school children today, the cover image of the 1956 *Granma* landing shows the disembodied visage of Martí looking down with approval from the heavens like the Great and Powerful Oz.

Martí's path to deification began in 1869, at the tender age of sixteen, when the secret police found an incriminating letter he had written urging a friend not to join the Spanish colonial army. For this mild youthful transgression Martí was forced into years of exile in Europe and Latin America. He eventually came to rest in New York City, which was then the center for Cuban refugees. Martí was at first intoxicated with his new home. "One can breathe freely," he raved of the US. "For here, freedom is the foundation, the shield, the essence of life." The enthusiasm was short-lived. Martí soon sensed that the "turbulent and brutal North" had designs on his beloved Cuba. "I have lived within the monster and I know its entrails," he warned.

Over his fourteen years living in Manhattan, the multitalented Martí plotted a Cuban uprising while cranking out reams of journalistic essays, scathing political tracts, and exquisite avant-garde love poetry. (His "Guantanamera" provided the lyrics for the most famous of all Cuban folk songs, with versions recorded by Celia Cruz, Pete Seeger, and the Gipsy Kings.) He hobnobbed with American bohemians, wrote the first major appreciation of Walt Whitman in Spanish, and made regular fund-raising trips to the Cuban cigar factories of Tampa, Florida, always in a heavy black suit and bow tie, his brush mustache tidily clipped. His conviction that no country could be truly free without economic, racial, and sexual equality added a potent—and, for its time, deeply radical—social element into the Cuban nationalist mix that Fidel and his generation would take to heart.

But Martí was never content to pontificate from the sidelines: He wanted to get his hands dirty in a revolution. In 1895, at the age of forty-two, he sent a message hidden in a cigar to Cuba to start the new rebellion. Martí landed on the coast of the Oriente one night with five companions, in a tiny boat that was nearly dashed to pieces by a storm, and was soon joined by thousands of supporters, many of them former slaves whose lives had hardly improved since the trade had been finally abolished seven years earlier. But military life was harsh for the waifish poet. Still clad in his heavy coat, Martí struggled to carry his pack and rifle, and he often slipped and fell on the rugged mountain trails. In the end he lasted only a few weeks. At noon on a fine spring day, he arrived at the front lines of combat while riding a white horse and carrying a picture of his daughter over his heart. When gunfire was heard in the distance, Martí eagerly galloped towards the fray. It was a trap. Spanish troops opened fire and caught Martí in the chest, killing him instantly.

Historians have argued that the day Martí fell was the turning point of Cuban history, a loss from which the island never recovered. Universally admired, he was the only one who might have guided fractious Cubans towards genuine independence—and avoided the devil's bargain with the Americans that was offered instead.

WITHOUT MARTÍ, THE war he fought in dragged on for three years as the ragged irregular rebel troops known as *mambises* harassed the larger and better-equipped Spanish army, to the surprise of other European colonial powers. (The young Winston Churchill even came to Cuba to study the conflict, traveling on the Spanish side for several months as a war correspondent. He was recommended for "valorous conduct" after coming under fire, celebrated his twenty-first birthday in a Havana hotel—an experience he reported as "awfully jolly"—and left with ideas that would help him understand the hit-and-run tactics of the Boer War.) The death toll escalated, although more Spanish soldiers fell from the "black vomit," as yellow fever was called, than bullets. The frustrated Spanish tried to weaken rebel support by herding rural civilians into prison camps. These *reconcentrados*, "reconcentrated ones," died in appalling numbers: an estimated 10 percent of the Cuban population succumbed to disease and starvation, most of them women and children.

This callous behavior led to a groundswell of support for Cuba in the United States. Postcards of emaciated infants went on sale in the streets, and indignant newspaper editors began to call for military intervention. But the US's motives were far from pure: as the world's new industrial superpower, Americans of the Gilded Age were in the mood for some empire building of their own. The resulting "Spanish-American War" has receded into distant memory within the US and is rarely even taught today in schools. (In photographs, the conflict seems oddly remote in time: All those men with walrus mustaches! All those dusty flannel shirts and tight leggings!) But it was a monumental event for Cuba, laying the broken foundation for the troubled century to come.

From his office in New York, the flamboyant upstart newspaper magnate William Randolph Hearst, model for the Orson Welles character in *Citizen Kane*, set out to whip up American support for an overseas adventure. At the same time Cuban politicians were losing faith in the hardscrabble *mambises*, who appeared unable to drive out the Spanish alone. They began to make overtures to Washington for assistance—inviting the Monster into the boudoir.

The warmongers' dream came true at 9:40 p.m. on the night of February 15, 1898, when a massive explosion lit up Havana Harbor. The visiting American warship USS *Maine* was engulfed in flames and sank within minutes, trapping over 260 sleeping sailors and officers belowdecks. An investigation proved that the explosion was almost certainly an accident, but the Hearst press blamed a Spanish mine and patriotic fervor surged across the US. The battle cry became: "Remember the *Maine*! To hell with Spain!" When war was finally declared on April 21, a million men jammed the US Army volunteering offices the next day. Among them was the thirty-nine-year-old Teddy Roosevelt, who helped form a cavalry regiment dubbed the Rough Riders (after Buffalo Bill's famous Western show) from a colorful mix of cowboys, ranch hands, and fellow gentlemen hunters from Yale and Harvard.

The reality of the campaign quickly dampened spirits, with a level of bumbling straight out of *Catch-22*. After months of pointless delays, the US Navy flotilla finally made it from Florida to the Oriente, where military bands played "There'll Be a Hot Time in the Old Town Tonight" while battleships randomly shelled the shore, even though the only troops to be seen were America's Cuban allies. It was a poor omen for future relations. The Americans were shocked to discover that local soldiers were barefoot, poorly armed, and—most disturbingly of all—largely black. They even had black officers commanding white men. Roosevelt dismissed the mixed-race Cuban soldiers as "utter tatterdemalions." Other US officers were harsher, especially those from the South. "Treacherous, lying, cowardly, thieving, worthless half-breed mongrels," said one; "degenerates," said another, "no more capable of self-government than the savages of Africa."

Thus began what one American diplomat called (from the safety of London) "a splendid little war." The result was never in doubt. On the steaming hot morning of July 1, Roosevelt rallied the Rough Riders and led the charge on San Juan Heights, his blue-and-white bandana trailing behind him. As the American Gatling guns raked the lines, Spanish resistance crumbled. It proved to be a bitter victory for the Cubans. When the Spanish formally surrendered in Santiago a few days later, the Americans did not invite local troops to the ceremony in case they ran amok. The Cuban commander, General Calixto García, made a dignified appeal to the Americans' sense of history. "We are a poor, ragged Army," he wrote to his US counterpart, "as ragged and poor as the Army of your forefathers in their noble War of Independence, and like the heroes of Saratoga and Yorktown, we believe in our cause too much to disgrace it." His request was refused.

It was a snub that set the tone for the high-handed treatment to come. On New Year's Day, 1899, the Americans hoisted the Stars and Stripes above the old conquistador fortress in Havana Harbor, starting a military occupation that would last for three years. Cubans discovered that they had traded one colonial master for another as American carpetbaggers descended on their island like ravening locusts. The US Army Corps of Engineers instituted public works projects that are still in use today, including highways, tunnels, and sewerage systems. But by the time the military finally packed up in 1902, a flood of *yanqui* investment had turned Cuba into a dependency, with power plants, railroads, sugar plantations, and telephone companies all in American hands. Congress even meddled in Cuba's new constitution, adding the so-called Platt Amendment to give the US the right to intervene in the island's politics, a power it exercised three times. For decades to come, Cuba would drift along in the feverish half-life of a stunted independence. The new pseudo-republic was a "monster," Jean-Paul Sartre wrote, like a force-fed goose that is slowly poisoned by its over-rich diet.

This is not to say that the Americans did not make contributions to Cuban culture. Baseball became an obsession, replacing bullfighting as the most popular spectator sport. And then there were the cocktails. According to a Bacardi executive, a barman in Havana decided to amuse his US soldier customers one night by mixing rum with the new *yanqui* soft drink Coca-Cola and adding a twist of lime. When the barman toasted them with the traditional independence cry of "*¡Cuba Libre!*" the soldiers latched on to the phrase as the drink's name. At around the same time in the Oriente, American mine workers near the town of Daiquirí began to mix rum with lime juice, raw sugar, and crushed ice, creating the second definitive Cuban tipple.

Alcohol helped make the US presence even more grating in the 1920s as Prohibition sent thousands of rich Americans on booze-addled tours of Cuba. Seaplanes called BlackTails would transport thirsty drinkers directly from New York's Hudson River to the Havana waterfront, where they flocked to bars that served Mary Pickfords and Highballs around the clock. "'Have one in Havana' seems to have become the winter slogan of the wealthy," chirped one travel writer, Basil Woon, author of the classic 1928 guidebook *When It's Cocktail Time in Cuba.* The climactic chapter is called "Naughty-Naughty Nights," a titillating guide to the pockets of vice flourishing around the city.

Cuban politics echoed the decadence. Presidents came and went, displaying ever more shameless levels of corruption. A sense of disillusion and helplessness settled over the island as every promise of change was betrayed. The extremes of this fractured political situation would eventually be distilled in two of the twentieth century's most extraordinary opponents, nicknamed, like prize fighters, "the pretty mulatto" and "the crazy one."

CHAPTER 3

Fulgencio Versus Fidel

(1901–1952)

T HE ARCHENEMIES FULGENCIO Batista and Fidel Castro were born only fifty-three miles from one another in the succulent sugar country of the Oriente, although their births were separated by twenty-five years and a yawning social chasm. Whereas Batista entered a world of grinding poverty, Fidel was born into a happy landscape of wealth and privilege. In fact, their life stories have the air of a Gilbert and Sullivan opera in which rich and poor babies are swapped at birth. Given their upbringings, Batista should have grown up to be a rabid firebrand and Fidel a complacent upper-class lawyer with no more serious ambition than playing tennis at the local social club. Instead, their destinies were transformed by the peculiar moments of Cuban history in which they came of age.

Batista's self-invention was at least as extreme as Fidel's. He is remembered today as the very caricature of a Latin American dictator, a thickset, middle-aged figure strutting about in Italian tailored suits, toadying to American gangsters, and fawning over the US politicians who supported him with weapons and cash. His remorseless criminality in the 1950s has become the stuff of legend, while the ferocity of his regime presaged the horrors of General Pinochet in Chile and the military junta of Argentina. It is difficult to even imagine that

Batista had a life before seizing power and ruling Cuba as his personal fiefdom. And yet he had the sort of rags-to-riches youth that Dickens might have invented.

Rubén Fulgencio Batista y Zaldívar was born in 1901 in a ramshackle eastern village, the eldest son of a hard-drinking plantation worker and a doting fifteen-year-old mother. Wealthy white Cubans would always look down on him for his mixed racial background, with possible Indian, African, and Chinese ancestry. Fulgencio was only eight when he quit school to help his father in the cane fields of the American-owned United Fruit Company. He later recalled how he and his bedraggled childhood friends would watch with envy as the pampered *yanqui* children rode into town on well-groomed ponies, then retreated to their gated community, an enclave of tidy cottages, manicured gardens, and shiny Model Ts that might have been shipped intact from suburban Florida. Dreaming of a future beyond the Oriente, he attended a Quaker missionary night school, where his prize possession became a biography of Abraham Lincoln, whose own impoverished childhood he would always cite as an inspiration. By all accounts, he was a good-looking, quick-witted, and charming child. His mother's sudden death when he was age fifteen inspired Fulgencio to leave home without a centavo to his name, hitching rides on ox carts to the western provinces in search of a new life. For the next five years he drifted from one dusty town to the next, sleeping in railroad stations and amassing an impressive resumé of menial jobs: water boy, timekeeper, tailor's assistant, carpenter's apprentice, barbershop sweeper. After nearly losing a leg as a train brakeman, the army seemed a safer bet, and he began washing bridles for cavalry soldiers, who dubbed him El Mulatto Lindo, "the pretty mulatto," a nickname that stuck for the rest of his career. Batista was finally sponsored to enter the military himself at age twenty. Because he had remained an obsessive reader, he trained to be an army court stenographer in Havana, a move that turned out to be a career breakthrough.

Batista spent the 1920s rising through the ranks and witnessing the fragmentation of Cuban society firsthand. Politics in the capital had descended into pointless cycles of violence, with riots and assassinations commonplace. Clever and articulate, Batista came to national prominence when he gave a funeral oration for three murdered soldiers. The *New York Times* correspondent praised Batista's mind, which, he wrote, "moves like lightning. He smiles readily and often" and was "plausible in the superlative degree."

He was already being groomed for the role he would play. But around the time he turned twenty-five, Batista's future nemesis was letting out his first howl.

LITTLE MORE THAN an hour's drive from Batista's birthplace in the Oriente, the Castro family mansion still stands in the verdant outskirts of a village called Birán. A force of nature straight out of a Gothic novel, Fidel's father, Ángel, was a crusty, irascible Galician who became one of Cuba's great self-made men. Riding the sugar boom known as the Dance of the Millions, he carved an empire of 25,000 acres from the rain forest by sheer force of will, turning his plantation into a miniature township with its own post office, train station, and general stores. Although most of the structures have vanished today, the original wooden cockfighting pit remains, as do the last traces of the Camino Real, "the Royal Road," which brought travelers to stay in Ángel's hotels, keep their horses in his stables, and drink at his bars. The family's rambling Caribbean-style plantation house was built on stilts to allow pigs and chickens to sleep underneath, their noises and barnyard scents wafting up through the wooden floor. Downstairs, Fidel's baby crib is today preserved like the holy manger, while his sunny bedroom has several neatly pressed baseball uniforms he wore as a teen.

As Fidel himself often admitted, his affluent birth made him one of the world's least likely revolutionaries. But despite his father's wealth, his childhood was less than aristocratic. The Castros were regarded by their more established neighbors as an unruly, half-feral bunch, and the parents' union a local scandal. Fidel's mother, Lina Ruz, was a devout Catholic girl who arrived as a cook and maid in the Castro household but soon took the place of Ángel's first wife and bore him seven children. For her third offspring, a baby boy delivered on August 13, 1926, she chose a resonant name that would one day become a powerful political gift—*fidel*, "faithful." As far as sketchy rural records show, he was born out of wedlock and legalized only at age sixteen. Amateur psychiatrists have suggested that Fidel's obsessive desire to excel at every possible contest comes from a chip on his shoulder about his illegitimacy.

By his own account, Fidel enjoyed an idyllic, Huck Finn–like childhood, running loose in the forests, swimming, horseback riding, hunting with slingshots and rifles. But he also grew up keenly aware of his family's status. He was the only child to wear shoes in the small elementary school that still sits on the property. He would later assert that his passionate sense of social justice was first established there, since all his boyhood friends were so obviously living in squalor. What's more, Birán lay in the heart of American sugar country, which had refined its virtual apartheid system with locals. The company towns had grown even more sumptuous since the young Batista had stared at them in envy a quarter century earlier. They now had glittering swimming pools, shops as full of luxury goods as Bloomingdale's, and private beach resorts with names like El Country Club. At the same time Cuban laborers—his schoolmates' fathers—were paid a pittance to work the *zafra*, "sugar harvest," and were then abandoned to near starvation during the so-called dead time.

The stories of Fidel's childhood often sound as if they are half-embedded in myth, but they have been verified by family members and school friends and provide insights into Fidel's unique character. He displayed an early penchant for rebellion, throwing violent tantrums if he did not get his way, as well as a level of stubbornness that bordered on the pathological. Once, when his parents told him that they were taking him out of school for bad behavior, he threatened to burn down the family house. In exasperation, they dispatched him to the prestigious Jesuit-run Colegio de Dolores, a boys' boarding school in Santiago, where he quickly made an impression. Fidel promised a crowd of schoolmates that he would ride his bicycle into a wall on a five-peso dare. He charged the wall at full pelt, knocking himself out and ending up in the school infirmary—just to prove that he could do something that nobody else ever would. His nickname became El Loco, "the crazy one."

His reputation grew at age twelve when he wrote a letter to US President Franklin Roosevelt asking him for ten dollars. ("My good Roosvelt [sic]," he began, "I don't know very English, but I know as much as write to you . . . I have not seen a ten dollars bill green american and I would like to have one of them.") The polite US government letter of refusal was then posted on his school notice board. Many years later Fidel's original missive was discovered in the US State Department archives; foreign policy mavens have joked that FDR might have saved America a lot of trouble if he had sent the schoolboy a ten-spot at this impressionable age.

The Jesuits found the teenage Fidel to be a promising student with a virtually photographic memory, as well as an excellent athlete with a particular talent for basketball and baseball. (Sadly, the story that he was offered a contract as a pitcher for either the New York Yankees or Washington Senators is a myth.) But they also remarked on his total lack of discipline. "He succeeded in everything," Fidel's younger brother Raúl summed up of those adolescent years. "In sport, in study. And every day he fought . . . He defied the most powerful and the strongest and when he was beaten he began again the next day. He never gave up." Fidel also overcame a fear of public speaking by spending hours in front of the mirror, practicing the speeches of Cicero and Demosthenes, and soon excelled at debating. He was fascinated by great historical figures such as Julius Caesar and Alexander the Great, and was deeply impressed to learn that he had been born only twenty-five miles from where the great José Martí was killed by the Spanish in 1895, sensing an almost spiritual connection.

Despite his solidly middle-class schooling, Fidel continued to be outraged by the inequality he saw on holidays back home in Birán. At age thirteen he even tried to organize his father's workers to strike for higher wages. He denounced Ángel as a capitalist exploiter, sparking passionate arguments with the rabidly conservative patriarch. Even so, the precocious teen remained only dimly aware of the volatile national politics in Havana, where every new government was more blatantly self-serving and venal than the last.

In the rogue's gallery of Cuban presidents, a once-admired independence hero named Gerardo Machado gained a place of honor during the Great Depression for his gleeful love of graft and the cruelty of his henchmen, only leaving the country after riots in Havana led to the massacre of around one thousand of his supporters. The growing sense of malaise provided the perfect opportunity for the rising star of the military, Fulgencio Batista. In 1933, Batista led the so-called Sergeants' Revolt, an alliance of lower-ranked and enlisted soldiers, who were often of color, to oust the white officer corps and take control of the country. It was a meteoric ascent for the penniless farm boy; he would tower over Cuban politics for the next quarter century.

After this first coup, Batista was not the cartoonish rightwing tyrant he would later become. To the joy of Cuban nationalists, he pushed to have the despised Platt Amendment repealed by US Congress and supported such liberal reforms as eight-hour workdays and the minimum wage. By 1940, the ever-smiling Batista (now a colonel) was popular enough to win the presidency himself in new elections. But despite the civilized veneer, he was always proactive with his critics, sending a strapping former New York cabdriver known as "Captain Hernández" on house calls to rough up recalcitrant journalists and force castor oil down their throats.

Batista stepped down in 1944 a fabulously wealthy man, having acquired at least $20 million in bribes and insider real estate deals. But although he pandered to Havana's ruling classes, he was never accepted into their ranks, thanks to his dark complexion and fondness for Afro-Cuban bodyguards. Cuban high society was still dominated by *blanco* descendants of the Spanish, who sneered at Batista as "the brown dictator" or simply El Negro, "the black one." Social snubs abounded. On one occasion, when Batista, his wife, and his military entourage arrived at the star-studded Sans Souci nightclub in Havana, the wealthy white guests simply got up from their seats in silence and walked out en masse, leaving Batista to impotently fume. On another occasion, his application for membership in a top Havana social club was blackballed in a secret vote.

After leaving the presidency in 1944, Batista went into a sulky, self-imposed exile in the United States. There was less chance of assassination, he explained, in Daytona Beach or New York's Waldorf Astoria Hotel than in Havana. But he was far from finished with Cuba.

IN LATE SUMMER of '45, a few days after the atom bomb was dropped on Hiroshima to end the Second World War, the nineteen-year-old Fidel was driving across Cuba in a beige Chevrolet given to him as a present by his father. He had agreed to study law at the University of Havana by default, in part because his teachers could see he never stopped talking. Fidel later described himself as a "political illiterate" when he first climbed La Escalera, the broad paved stairway that led into the leafy campus, whose stately classical buildings had been modeled on those of Columbia University in Manhattan. But that political ignorance was about to change in short order.

The university at the time resembled less the Upper West Side than a war zone. Under the 1940 constitution, the police and army could not venture onto the grounds. As a result, a kaleidoscope of radical student groups all kept stockpiles of knives, pistols, and machine guns around the campus, making beatings and murders as regular as college dances. With his penchant for self-dramatization, Fidel was drawn into this political cauldron, ignoring his law studies for the theater of the streets. A fiery orator and reckless physical force in brawls, he quickly became a fixture in the turbulent rallies that punctuated student life. He was particularly vocal when some American sailors climbed onto a statue of "the Apostle" Martí in Old Havana and emptied their bladders on it—a symbol, students felt, of how the US regarded the island in general.

Fidel was easily recognized: along with his penetrating brown eyes, Hellenic profile, and pencil mustache, he deliberately set himself apart from his classmates by wearing a dark striped woolen suit and tie, no matter what the weather, while other male students wore guayaberas, the loose and casual short-sleeve shirts suited to Havana's heat. But even today his role in the more vicious aspects of student life is hazy. There were rumors that he was involved in gunfights and even assassinations, although no charges were ever proven. More certain is that he joined a secret Cuban militia training to overthrow a right-wing dictator in the Dominican Republic. (The group was shut down and Fidel allegedly swam through shark-infested waters to escape arrest.) Trouble seemed to follow him around. His first overseas trip, as a student representative to Bogotá, Colombia, in 1948, coincided with an eruption of antigovernment rioting in which thousands were killed. Fidel got hold of a pistol and—at the very least—joined the peripheries of the strife.

Still, these radical antics might have fallen by the wayside as the youthful follies of a "champagne socialist," for Fidel the student agitator also led a parallel life of august respectability. In 1949, at age twenty-three, he completed his law degree and married a girl from a well-connected family. The lavishly named Mirta Francisca de la Caridad Díaz-Balart y Gutiérrez was a philosophy student and daughter of a conservative politician—a "lovely green-eyed girl with . . . dark blond hair and [a] wistful smile," writes Georgie Anne Geyer, who later conducted interviews with Mirta. The pair were introduced in the college cafeteria, where Fidel immediately declared to a friend, "This is the girl I am going to marry." Mirta quickly fell for this "vigorous young 'god' with his curly brown hair, his broad shoulders, and his aquiline Gallego nose" (as Geyer describes him). The romance blossomed during beach holidays together, always suitably chaperoned. They were soon married in an opulent church ceremony, although Fidel boasted that he carried a pistol to the altar in case of a surprise attack.

Through his new in-laws, Fidel was suddenly close to Batista, the éminence grise of Cuba. Although the two men did not meet, they often dabbled in the same social circles, connected but not touching, like a double helix: Mirta claimed Batista even gave them $1,000 as a wedding gift.

Their honeymoon destination was, of all places, the Monster of the North. The newlyweds flew to Miami and took the train to New York, where they stayed for nearly three months in an apartment arranged for them by one of Mirta's brothers, a pastor on the Lower East Side. It was the beginning of Fidel's love affair with La Gran Manzana. He visited the sites where his hero José Martí had once lived and worked, and became fascinated by New York's daily life—the oversized hamburgers, the soaring skyscrapers, and the cacophonous subway. He was intrigued to find that despite America's virulent anticommunism he could buy *Das Capital* in any bookstore. With his typical tenacity, he decided to improve his English by obtaining a dictionary and memorizing two hundred words a day.

Like other politically aware young Cubans, Fidel was developing a contradictory attitude to the US. He admired its inspiring role since 1776 as "the land of the free" and happily quoted the words of Washington, Jefferson, and Lincoln on democracy. The American people, on an individual level, he regarded as warm and sympathetic. But he was also repelled by the dire reality of US behavior—its economic stranglehold on Cuba, the hateful racial politics of segregation in the South, and its government's increasingly cavalier foreign policy towards Latin America as the twentieth century progressed.

%

RETURNING TO HAVANA, the couple had a child the following year, a boy they named Fidel Ángel—"Fidelito." But Fidel the elder was winning no Father of the Year awards. Moving his family into a cheap hotel room, he threw himself back into politics, spending night after night with his student *compañeros*. He turned down offers to join top law firms, preferring to work pro bono for the poor.

Yet another new president had taken office—Carlos Prío, who hypnotized Cubans with his debonair looks and promises of change— and was an immediate disappointment. Revealing a grasp of the media that would one day prove invaluable, Fidel disguised himself as a gardener and snuck with a hidden camera into Prío's graft-funded rural estate. Like a spy in a cheap thriller, he roamed about taking snapshots while the president and his sidekicks sipped cocktails next to an artificial waterfall and enjoyed manicures in a private barbershop. The images caused a sensation when they were published, propelling Fidel further into the public eye.

Running for office was Fidel's logical next step. A reformist group called Los Ortodoxos ("the Orthodox Party") had been founded to challenge the old order, and he agreed to run as a candidate for them in the 1952 elections. He was supported in these first political endeavors by his youngest brother, Raúl, with whom he had become close. Five years Fidel's junior, shorter, quieter, less athletic, and with a pouting lip, Raúl had been rescued from virtual juvenile delinquency by his older brother, who guided him into Havana University and its radical underbelly. The election campaign began with great promise. The Orthodox Party was gaining support even though its charismatic founder, Eduardo Chibás, had killed himself in a protest that seems misguided even by Cuban standards. On his weekly radio show, Chibás denounced the state of the nation then shot himself in the stomach with a .38 pistol. Unfortunately, the dramatic effect was lost: he had miscalculated the broadcast times and the blast occurred during a coffee ad.

Instead of his heartfelt farewell ("Forward! People of Cuba, good-bye! This is my last call!"), listeners heard a cheesy jingle: "Café Pilón! The coffee that is tasty to the last drop!" Even so, Chibás's funeral turned into a mass rally for reform, and as the elections drew near, Cubans felt an unfamiliar optimism: the half century of paralysis since the island had gained its tainted independence was surely about to end. Fidel seemed a shoo-in to become a congressman, and from there, his career trajectory looked rosy. In another four years he could run for the Senate, and four years after that—1960—the presidency.

BUT LOS ORTODOXOS didn't factor in competition from a familiar face. Ensconced in his art-filled Florida mansion, Batista had watched Cuba slide into its political morass and decided to heed calls to save it. With great fanfare the fifty-one-year-old strongman, now stouter but still with his matinee-idol good looks, returned from self-exile to contest the election. Batista had the faithful support of the army, but he had miscalculated the national mood. Change was in the air; the prospect of an embarrassing defeat for "the pretty mulatto" loomed. If he was going to regain power, it would have to happen through other means.

Before dawn on March 10, a friend burst into Fidel's apartment with the news that Batista had staged a coup. Fidel and Raúl both leapt out of their beds, threw on some clothes, and fled to their half sister Lidia's flat five blocks away. It was a prudent decision: by mid-morning, Batista's officers came looking for the brothers, terrifying Mirta and two-year-old Fidelito. For the next week Fidel kept moving nightly between hotel rooms and friends' houses.

Cuba was entering a new and more explosive era, which historians have compared to a collective nervous breakdown.

CHAPTER 4

The Misfire Heard Around the World

(The Moncada—July 26, 1953)

For me there is only one date: July 26, and two eras: before the Moncada and after the Moncada.   —HAYDÉE SANTAMARÍA

F ROM A DISTANCE, it might have looked like they were headed for a weekend auto show. In the velvet darkness before dawn on July 26, 1953, a convoy of sixteen classic American sedans lumbered along an unpaved highway in the tropical countryside near Santiago, the headlights of bubblegum-colored Buicks, Chevrolets, and Dodges lighting up clouds of dust and flashing tailfins ahead of them. On either side, the walls of sugarcane created virtual tunnels as they lumbered ahead.

Eight men were crammed into each car, all of them dressed in light brown military uniforms, all with sergeants' stripes. Most of the outfits were makeshift, sewn from cheap fabric. A few men cradled decent weapons—Belgian shotguns or Luger pistols from army surplus stores, a submachine gun dating from the Spanish Civil War—but the majority were carrying cheap, low-caliber sport rifles. Many were wearing civilian street shoes, including two-tone spats.

Even before sunrise, the summer air was oppressively humid inside the vehicles, and nobody spoke. Almost none of the 160 or so men and two women had slept the night before. Fidel, who was driving the second car (and wearing a uniform several sizes too small for his frame, giving him a slightly comical appearance), had not rested for nearly four days. A few tensely puffed on cigarettes or hummed the national anthem to themselves. Having only learned their target a few hours earlier, most believed they would not survive the morning.

The troop's plan of attack was reckless. They intended to storm a string of military sites, chief among them a thousand-man barracks in the heart of Santiago called the Moncada. It was the last night of Carnival and the soldiers, ideally, would be taken by surprise in their underwear as they slept off hangovers in their bunks. Even though they were outnumbered roughly ten to one, the rebels intended to take the whole lot prisoner, seize their weapons, and use the radio to issue a call to arms interspersed with bursts of rousing music including Beethoven's *Eroica* Symphony. This audacious act would shake Cubans from their lethargy, provoking them to rise up en masse against Batista and demand the restoration of democracy.

What could possibly go wrong?

Three and a half years before the *Granma* landing, Fidel's first stab at an armed uprising has elements of both Shakespearean tragedy and a Three Stooges skit. It was born from the mix of desperation and naïveté that suffused politics after the 1952 coup, when Cubans realized that all peaceful options for protest had been closed to them. Had things gone differently, El Moncada (as the attack is simply referred to in Cuba) might have caused barely a ripple in world history, of no more interest today than a skirmish between two forgotten medieval principalities. But, thanks to some extraordinary strokes of fate, it became the foundation stone for the entire revolution, joining the roll call of military fiascos that are celebrated by the losers—Cuba's answer to the Alamo, Gallipoli, Dunkirk, and the Battle of Little Bighorn. The date of July 26 is engraved on every Cuban's mental calendar. Without it, nothing that followed could have occurred.

※

A VIOLENT CONFRONTATION like the Moncada was all but inevitable from the moment Batista had seized power fifteen months earlier. At first the putsch had gone off quietly. After midnight on the night of March 9, 1952, wearing a brown leather jacket and packing a pistol, Batista had driven into the Camp Columbia barracks in Havana, "the Pentagon of Cuba," and mobilized the troops. Power was transferred almost without bloodshed. At 1:00 p.m. the next day, Radio Havana simply announced that a new government was ruling Cuba, and few shed any tears as the disgraced President Prío was bundled onto a plane to Miami. The upcoming elections were canceled and Washington rushed to recognize the new military regime. At a black-tie dinner soon after, the US ambassador offered to sell Batista state-of-the-art weapons at discount rates and even train counterinsurgency forces.

The coup ended any illusion that Cuba was heading for democratic reform. Batista might have had some redeeming qualities during his first rule, but in his fifties he had become cynical and smug. "The people and I are the dictators," he boasted. Although the economy was one of the healthiest in Latin America, his second presidency was soon marked by a contempt for law that shocked even the most jaded observers. Batista openly offered sweetheart casino deals to celebrity American mobsters such as Meyer Lansky, Albert Anastasia, and Lucky Luciano—they deposited suitcases full of cash at his office every Monday—while the savagery of his enforcers escalated. The military intelligence service, SIM, was given free rein to kidnap opponents of the regime, whose mangled bodies would be found in the city morgue or strung half-naked from telegraph poles.

As his death squads roamed the night, Batista would retreat to his estate on the rural outskirts of Havana, behind walls garlanded with barbed wire and patrolled by armed guards. He entertained ambassadors in a sumptuous library filled with the marble busts of his heroes, including Benjamin Franklin, Gandhi, and Joan of Arc, and unwound by playing endless rounds of canasta with acquaintances or watching horror movies in his screening room. (He was particularly fond of Bela Lugosi's *Dracula* and anything starring Boris Karloff.)

Within a year of the coup, frustration had begun to bubble up all over Cuba, although opposition to Batista was divided, to say the least. A budding agitator could choose from a smorgasbord of clandestine groups whose welter of acronyms have a certain Monty Python ring: there was the DEU (University Student Directorate), the DR (Revolutionary Directorate), the FCR (Civic Revolutionary Front), the MNR (National Revolutionary Movement), the FON (National Workers Front), and the FONU (United National Workers Front). One might join the AAA (Friends of Aureliano Arango, a leftist college professor) and, for those who could not make up their minds, the ABC—which, charmingly, stood for nothing. With his hopes as a political candidate dashed, Fidel had gone back to work as a lawyer for the poor while fostering his underground contacts. He offered his legal services in exchange for food—much to the exasperation of Mirta, who was now raising Fidelito almost alone in a shabby apartment, trying to make ends meet with an allowance provided by Fidel's father. The city regularly cut off their gas and electricity. On one occasion Fidel returned home to find that debt collectors had repossessed all their furniture, leaving Mirta on the floor with the baby. Only once did it seem that Fidel might have a limit for this bare-bones life, when he left a nighttime meeting to find that his treasured Chevrolet had been repossessed, a fate no less dismal in 1950s Havana than in modern Los Angeles. He went to his favorite café, but the owner wouldn't give him more coffee or cigars on credit. A newsstand owner shooed him away because he was trying to read a magazine without buying it. Fidel had no choice but to walk the three miles to his apartment, where he sank into bed with tears of black despair. It's possible he considered tossing in the whole revolutionary enterprise and joining a decent law firm, perhaps even becoming a family man and one day living off his inheritance. But when he awoke, the gloom had vanished and he threw

himself back into his two careers, as the public lawyer and furtive agitator.

Mirta watched her husband's behavior with confusion. Fidel felt
obliged to keep her in the dark about the true nature of his activities,
since her brother had joined Batista's government as a minor minister. In fact, unbeknownst to his wife, Fidel had decided that armed
insurrection was the only option left to save Cuba and almost as
quickly chose the Moncada barracks in Santiago as the best target. He
began to gather a circle of supporters, although like Fidel himself they
hardly fit the stereotype of down-trodden revolutionaries. Fidel's
partner, Abel Santamaría, was a dapper twenty-four-year-old Walter
Mitty type whose day job was as an accountant at the local Pontiac
car dealership. He had met Fidel at a secret meeting in the Havana
necropolis and the two had seen eye to eye immediately. Photos show
Abel as a grinning, skinny figure in thick sunglasses and a white
short-sleeved shirt, looking like Buddy Holly on vacation. He was a
voracious reader and known amongst his friends for his sunny dispo-
sition; he exuded an air that nothing bad could ever happen to him.

Abel slept on the couch in the one-bedroom apartment belonging
to his older sister Haydée, who became Fidel's next key recruit. "Yeyé,"
as she was nicknamed, had been forced to drop out of elementary
school but educated herself to become a nurse and teacher. Her shy
manner and dowdy appearance hid a crackling intelligence. As an urban operative, she soon discovered a talent for disguise, making herself look like a different person entirely just by changing her hairstyle.
But Haydée also suffered from depression, which could be so severe
that she would spend days in bed. To cheer herself up, she filled her
modest apartment, a sixth-floor walk-up, with dozens of daisies.

Melba Hernández was the final member of the "general staff" of
the group Fidel simply called "the Movement," a name that evoked a
religious cult. One of Cuba's first women lawyers, the thirty-one-year-
old Hernández was mesmerized by Fidel the moment they met.
"When I gave my hand to this young man, I felt very secure," she later

recalled. "I felt I had found the way. When this young man began to talk, all I could do was to listen to him." Many others would report falling under Fidel's spell in exactly the same way.

IN RETROSPECT, THERE is a poignant disconnect between the youthful high spirits of the Moncada's planning stage and the violence of its aftermath. Memories of this early phase—revolution on a shoestring— would be suffused by a golden hue of innocence, with a lighthearted atmosphere closer to a *Friends* episode than the grim cells of Dostoyevsky novels. "We all fitted in together, we all ate together, we all lived together and we were all happy together," Yeyé recalled of her daisy-filled apartment. "Never did we share anything the way we shared that little place. Never did we taste meals that were tastier than those we cooked then." The only office equipment needed for the Moncada plot was Fidel's Art Deco desk, a mimeographing machine to print their newsletter the *Accuser,* and an ashtray in every corner. Nights were spent feverishly discussing strategy in the bare, neon-lit teahouses of Havana's Chinatown, sharing plates of oily Cuban-Chinese noodles. Supporters often ended up sleeping on Haydée's floor, which (she insisted) "was the springiest, most comfortable mattress in the world."

The final budget for the Moncada attack was a paltry 40,000 pesos (which at the time was pegged one to one with the US dollar), half of it donated by Movement members themselves. New recruits were asked to cut back on cigarettes and coffee to buy bullets, which Fidel would then count out and record one by one. The subversive protocol was just as threadbare, as if cobbled together from stories of the French Resistance or the Hollywood film noirs that were all the rage. Haydée and Melba smuggled rifles in florist's boxes, pistols in their handbags, secret messages in their beehive hairdos. Military training (such as it was) was provided by Pedro Miret, an engineering student who had some experience with ballistics. It's a sign of how liberated

Havana college life was that they often did their shooting practice on the university grounds, using weapons that were as casually available as soft drugs on a campus in California today.

By spring, some three hundred men and women had drifted into the Movement. Most of them were in their early twenties and drawn from a broad cross section of Cuban society, including laborers, factory workers, students, and professionals. There was a poet, a cook, a dentist, a doctor, a male nurse, and an oyster vendor. The Movement even boasted members of Havana aristocracy. Fidel's man-of-action aura had drawn the attention of a glamorous socialite, twenty-six-year-old Natalia Revuelta. Educated in France and the US, exquisitely groomed and poised, "Naty" was married to one of Cuba's top heart surgeons but had become bored by the high-society circuit of card games and cocktail parties. She was also a stunning beauty with large jade-colored eyes and gleaming blond hair—the Grace Kelly of the revolution. She first met Fidel at an anti-Batista rally and immediately offered her sumptuous apartment for meetings when her husband was out of town. Naty soon became one of the Movement's crucial supporters. She pawned her jewelry and donated her 6,000-peso savings to the cause. She helped Haydée and Melba sew uniforms. She chose the music that would be played after the victory (including *Eroica* and Chopin's Polonaise in A major). Naty was also trusted with the genuinely risky task of delivering the so-called "Moncada Manifesto" to politicians and journalists in Havana on the morning of the attack. Written by Fidel and a delicate young poet named Raúl Gómez, it explained that Batista should be expelled for "the crimes of blood, dishonor, unlimited greed, and looting of the national treasury."

Although Fidel was later accused of already harboring communist sympathies, at this early stage there was no sign of it. He and his supporters joined together under the banner of José Martí, with broad calls for social justice and democratic elections. Like any respectable student, Fidel had read his Marx and even carried a dog-eared copy of Lenin's writings with him during the Moncada attack, but his political language was purely nationalist. Only two members of the Movement were card-carrying Communists, one of them his younger brother Raúl, who had turned bolshie during his college days. Meanwhile, the Party itself showed no interest at all in Fidel's eccentric little splinter group. (In fact, Cuban politics rivaled that of postwar Italy in its unlikely alliances, with the Communists at one stage joining forces with Batista.) One student friend, Alfredo Guevara, later reported that he tried to convert Fidel to communism in the early 1950s, but Fidel had joked: "I'd be a Communist if I were Stalin!" He wanted power above all else; ideology came a distant second.

In fact, nobody in the Movement was plotting a socialist utopia. In 1953, Cuba without Batista was dream enough.

As summer approached, Haydée and Melba relocated to the Oriente, renting a quaint, well-hidden farmhouse seven miles outside of Santiago as a base of operations. Called Granjita Siboney, it would have made a pleasant writer's retreat in happier times. Instead, the two women spent their days preparing for the arrival of *los chicos*, "the guys," as they fondly called their underground army—adding the finishing touches to one hundred and sixty uniforms on a hand-operated Singer machine, sleeping in an airy room painted white with red trim, and hiding rifles in wells in the garden. As the July 26 deadline neared, they were joined by Haydée's brother Abel and the girls' activist fiancés—Haydée's love, Boris Luis Santa Coloma, and Melba's Jesús Montané, a gourmand who cooked up delicious meals like chicken with tomatoes and peppers. For several weeks, the men scoped out the Moncada, whose oppressive yellow walls rose above a parade ground in Santiago, and timed its patrols.

Haydée continued to surprise her fellow conspirators with her inner calm and was often given the most dangerous smuggling missions. On one train trip from Havana, she had such difficulty lugging a valise full of guns on board that a young soldier felt obliged to help her. (She told him it was full of college books; he spent the entire overnight trip by her side.) And yet, with her tendency to melancholy, Haydée also had dark intimations about the future. When her brother went to Santiago with some friends to attend Carnival one night, she was happy for them, but caught herself thinking: *Perhaps it will be the last Carnival they will ever see.*

Two DAYS BEFORE the planned attack, 160-odd handpicked Movement members in Havana were given instructions to leave for the Oriente by car, bus, or train. Obeying "clandestine protocol," only the six leaders knew the real reason for their trip; the others were simply told to bring a comfortable change of clothes.

The twenty-six-year-old Afro-Cuban bricklayer Juan Almeida—one of the early recruits who would stay with Fidel for years—was at work on a contruction site when a friend arrived and told him they had to go east for "target practice." It was the farthest from Havana he had ventured in his life, but he jumped without question into a waiting car. Even during the grueling two-day drive across 540 miles of sunbaked sugar country, Almeida was kept in the dark. ("I thought we were going to Santiago for Carnival as a reward for my doing well in training exercises," he later joked.) Only when they arrived at Siboney farmhouse, where the girls were handing out uniforms and weapons, did he realize what was happening. Almeida eagerly lined up for his rifle but was bitterly disappointed to be given a .22-caliber—more suitable for shooting pigeons, he felt, than any military target.

Raúl was woken up in Havana with a blinding hangover after a wild party and told to get himself to the train station. The easygoing twenty-two-year-old, who still looked like a teenager, had only recently returned from an extended tour of Europe, where he had visited socialist youth conferences with the festive spirit of a modern backpacker at Oktoberfest. He had promptly been arrested for carrying anti-Batista propaganda, and Melba had only barely managed to spring him from jail in time for the attack. Although he would later become Fidel's "relief pitcher," Raúl was not trusted with the target at this stage. Even so, when he groggily boarded the train and a friend gave him his ticket to Santiago, he shrewdly guessed: "El Moncada?"

Fidel himself was the last to leave Havana. He shaved off his mustache, gave his wife and son a good-bye kiss (but didn't tell Mirta about the plan), donned a white guayabera, and went to a hire car office with his driver. He told the clerk that he was going on a beach holiday and roared off in a blue Buick. By the time he arrived at the farmhouse, Fidel hadn't slept for three days and was running on adrenaline. Still, there were signs the pressure was wearing on him: he had to stop halfway in the city of Santa Clara to buy a new pair of spectacles, since he had somehow forgotten his in Havana. (Today, the optometrist's store bears a proud plaque.)

Fidel arrived at the farmhouse on the night of Saturday, July 25, and outlined to the 165 recruits his plan to attack the Moncada barracks. He himself would lead the main assault with 123 men. There would be two supporting strikes in Santiago, and a third, with twenty-seven men, on a garrison in the provincial town of Bayamo, ninety miles away. It was a daunting prospect. Few of the men had even been to the Oriente before; now they were going straight into battle against one of the largest military bases in all of Cuba.

Haydée recalls that the evening passed in a sort of romantic delirium. It was "the most joyful of nights," she later said. "We went out to the patio, and the moon was bigger and more brilliant; the stars were bigger and brighter; the palms taller and greener . . . Everything was more beautiful, larger, lovelier, finer; we felt ourselves to be better, kinder." Not all the invitees were so enraptured. Four college students who had previously bragged of their bravery decided Fidel's plan was absurd and refused to take part. They were locked in the bathroom, along with a radio expert who got cold feet. The others waited out the night, savoring a sense of destiny. Come what may, everyone knew that Cuba would never be the same again.

※

As THE MOTORCADE navigated Santiago before dawn on Sunday the 26th, signs of Carnival's debauched final night were evident. A few die-hard revelers still stumbled along the sidewalks; some were passed out in doorways or embracing in alleys. The humid air was heavy with the scents of sweat and rum, and drifting from distant windows came the last strains of salsa.

Events at the Moncada would become so confused that almost every participant had a different memory; even Fidel would contradict himself. But there is no doubt that his intricate battle plan went awry from the start. One car got a flat tire as soon as it left the farmhouse. Many of the *habanero* drivers became confused in Santiago's maze of dark streets. Several took wrong turns and arrived at their destinations late.

Still, there was a brief moment of hope at 5:20 a.m., when the first car of the convoy ground to a halt at the Moncada's gates and the driver shouted to the sentries as planned, "Clear the way, the general is coming!" The passengers then showed the guards their sergeant stripes and relieved them of their weapons. But the second car, driven by Fidel, unexpectedly ran into two patrolmen carrying submachine guns. Later, Fidel realized that he should have ignored them; the pair might have just gaped uncertainly as the motorcade passed. Instead, he stepped on the gas and rammed the car against a curb to cut them off. When Fidel produced his pistol, the other rebels in the vehicle panicked and started to fire wildly.

The shriek of an alarm bell tore through the Moncada. The element of surprise was lost, and within seconds soldiers were everywhere. The street became a firestorm. A machine gun on an observation tower raked the shiny flanks of the American cars, shattering windshields and perforating radiators. Five men from the first vehicle actually made it inside the barracks, but quickly retreated. They ran into the bizarre sight of Fidel yelling, "*¡Adelante, muchachos!*" at the gate, while everyone else was shouting at him, "Fidel! Get out of there! Get out!" The attack was a debacle. The soldiers spread the word to shoot at anyone wearing civilian shoes. Fidel managed to escape the scene unharmed by diving into the last working car as it roared off. Others, including Raúl, fled on foot into the back alleys.

Abel Santamaría and the twenty-odd rebels under his command were not so lucky. They had seized a nearby hospital to tend the rebel wounded; Haydée and Melba had come along to assist as nurses. Now, unaware that Fidel's attack had failed, they kept shooting from windows as the army encircled them. Some sympathetic nurses disguised the men in hospital gowns and tucked them into spare beds. A bandage was wrapped around Abel's head and one eye to make it look like he was an ophthalmology patient. Then they waited.

Unfortunately, as soon as the soldiers burst in, a pro-Batista patient betrayed the disguised rebels. Abel was dragged to the floor, his head beaten mercilessly with rifle butts. The twenty-one men and both women were then marched to the Moncada, where the doctor, a timid bespectacled man named Mario Muñoz, was thrashed to a pulp in the courtyard then shot in the back. Around 3:00 in the afternoon, word arrived from Havana that the soldiers were free to deal with the other captives as they wished. Haydée and Melba sat in a cell listening to the screams. Melba could recognize one viciously beaten man only when they saw his handwriting on a note he tried to pass them for his mother. It was the delicate poet Raúl Gómez, who had joined the mission as a noncombatant so he could read his Moncada Manifesto over the radio. He was then taken out and shot.

The horrors piled up. When the girls overheard a guard laughing grimly about torturing a rebel wearing black-and-white spats, Haydée realized it was her fiancé Boris. The next parts of her story have become part of Cuban revolutionary lore. First, the story goes, Yeyé was presented with the gouged-out eye of her brother Abel, and told that they would cut out the other if she didn't reveal the rebels' hideout. Then she was shown Boris's severed testicle, with the promise that the other would soon also be removed. According to legend, she stoutly replied: "If you did that to them and they didn't talk, much less will I." The reality appears to have been marginally less grotesque. The forensic report, conducted later by civilian doctors, is today sealed in the archives of the Office of Historical Affairs in Havana; Cuban historians who have seen it privately confirm that the medics found that Abel and Boris had been savagely beaten before their murders but not maimed. It appears that the army torturers threatened to show Haydée her brother's eye and fiancé's testicle to intimidate her. Later, the story so perfectly captured the barbarity of Batista's soldiers that it was passed on as fact.

The hellish scene at the barracks that night hardly needed embellishment. "Abel was dead, Boris was dead, and I did not even cry," Haydée recalled years later. "I was feeling nothing." She was permanently scarred. "There are those moments during which nothing can shock you," she wrote. "Neither the bursts of machine gun fire, nor the smoke, nor the smell of burned, bloodied and dirty flesh, nor the smell of warm blood, nor the smell of cold blood, nor blood on one's hands . . . nor the silence in the eyes of the dead. Nor their semi-parted lips, which seem about to speak a word that would freeze your soul."

ONLY EIGHT REBELS were killed outright in the shoot-out at the Moncada, but of the thirty or so who surrendered there, only five survived. The rest were executed and their corpses scattered around the barracks in a halfhearted attempt to make it look as if they had died in battle. Three of the five survivors owed their lives to a heroic army doctor who protected them, at one point waving a pistol to keep soldiers at bay. Ninety miles away, the diversionary attack in Bayamo had also been a disaster. All but one of the twenty-seven men were put to death; three of them were dragged behind jeeps for several miles before being shot.

The first confused news of the assault electrified Cubans. Demonstrators took to the streets of Santiago demanding information about the captives; when police began arresting protesters, butchers ran out of the market with cleavers and forced them to be released. Luis Cambara, a seventeen-year-old activist in the provincial town of Maffo, recalls the first report being brought by a taxi driver at noon. Within an hour the whole population was in the plaza. "The idea that someone would attack an army barracks, such an established place!" he marveled years later. "It was incredible." In the following days, excitement turned to outrage as reports of atrocities at the Moncada leaked out, along with grisly photographs. When the army began tracking rebels who had escaped into the countryside and finishing them off, civic and Church leaders tried to intervene. The silver-haired archbishop of Santiago, Enrique Pérez Serantes, who was a friend of the Castro family, drove himself around the rural back roads in a jeep, calling out with a megaphone for any men in hiding to surrender. (The feisty cleric was quite a sight in his full medieval regalia of black cassock and white cross, but surprisingly effective. At one stage he spotted five rebels who had been cornered by the Rural Guard in tall grass. Like a character in an Italian screwball comedy, he lifted up his cassock and vaulted a barbed wire fence to throw himself in front of the captives. The soldiers at first wanted to dispatch Pérez then and there, one merrily chanting: "I'm gonna kill me a priest! I'm gonna kill me a priest!" But they all returned to Santiago safely.)

Fidel himself was discovered by the army—alive—at dawn on August 1, sleeping in a campesino's hut with thirteen companions. Rural Guards awoke the haggard group, who had been wandering for five nights, by raking the walls with machine-gun fire. In the first of countless lucky breaks in Fidel's career, the detachment was led by a chivalrous older officer, Lieutenant Pedro Manuel Sarría, who managed to control his trigger-happy men. Still, it was a tense moment. When one soldier spat that Fidel was "nothing more than an assassin," he replied theatrically: "It is you who are assassins. It is you who kill unarmed prisoners."

"Lieutenent, let's kill them," muttered a corporal.

"No!" Sarría ordered, then quoted the Argentine intellectual Domingo Sarmiento: "You cannot kill ideas."

Handcuffed in the back of an army truck, Fidel asked Sarría sotto voce why he hadn't just shot him; his execution would surely merit a healthy promotion. Sarría, a fifty-three-year-old Afro-Cuban, replied simply: "I am not that sort of man, *muchacho.*"

In Santiago prison, Fidel was greeted with cheers by his surviving followers, including Raúl, who had been arrested trying to hike to the Castro family home in Birán. He celebrated his twenty-seventh birthday a few days later with hopes that the Moncada disaster might be turned into a triumph. The army's behavior had sickened most Cubans and turned public opinion against Batista—particularly among the middle classes and professionals, who began to see Fidel and the "Moncadistas" (as they were now known) as heroes.

Fidel was placed in solitary confinement for seventy-five days, a time he used to prepare a legal defense. It was Cuba's trial of the century: 122 handcuffed prisoners (fifty-one of them Moncada veterans, the rest Movement supporters), were led into the packed courtroom by rifle-toting soldiers, followed by twenty-two lawyers and a legion of expert witnesses. The proceedings were filled with coups de théâtre, starting from the very first minute, when Fidel brazenly held up his handcuffed hands: "You cannot judge people who are manacled!" (They were removed). But the result was a foregone conclusion. The judges doled out thirteen-year sentences to most of the rebels. Melba and Haydée received seven months in a women's prison.

Fidel himself was tried separately and in secret. The judges gathered in a tiny nurse's office in the bullet-scarred hospital that Abel had captured on July 26, whose only decor was a human skeleton hanging in a glass display case and a portrait of Florence Nightingale. The prosecutor spoke for only two minutes. Fidel, dressed in a blue winter suit, spoke for two hours straight. His epic speech would become the sacred text of the Cuban Revolution. Looming above a desk with a few notes, Fidel held forth on Cuban history, politics, and international law. He condemned the army's brutality in baroque terms—"Moncada barracks was turned into a workshop of torture and death. Some shameful individuals turned their uniforms into butcher's aprons. The walls were splattered with blood . . ."—and quoted Thomas Paine, Jean-Jacques Rousseau, and Balzac to argue that Cubans had a duty to resist the tyrant Batista. Throwing in references to republican Rome and ancient China, he then worked methodically through the English, French, and American Revolutions, with the Declaration of Independence receiving special mention for its "beautiful" introduction.

It was a rhetorical tour de force now known to all Cubans by its resounding last line, *La historia me absolverá.* "Condemn me," Fidel thundered. "It does not matter. History will absolve me." A stunned silence fell over the temporary courtroom when Fidel stopped speaking, but once again the decision was in no doubt. After only a minute's consultation, the judges sentenced him to fifteen years.

Fidel emerged to the applause of supporters gathered in the street. The rules of Cuban politics had shifted irrevocably. He had become the public face of opposition to Batista, transformed from an erratic ruffian into an admired, idealistic figure. The Moncada attack had also made news around the world. It was Fidel's splashy debut on the front page of the *New York Times*. This global attention didn't escape Batista himself. Fidel and his companions had become too well-known for him to simply murder.

As he was shipped off to prison, Fidel began to let his mustache grow again.

CHAPTER 5

Island of Lost Souls

(The Model Prison, 1953–55)

On October 17, 1953, a propeller plane banked over the Isle of Pines, a fertile, comma-shaped island surrounded by reefs and sapphire waters, and landed at its only township, the sleepy hamlet of Nueva Gerona. There, Prisoner 3859 was ushered directly under armed guard to the Presidio Modelo, the most dreaded jail in Cuba.

Its sheer scale was bewildering: some 5,000 convicts were housed in four enormous circular cellblocks, which rose like sinister yellow missile silos above a sprawling mess hall. These were surrounded by a string of workshops, medical clinics, and guard barracks that formed their own miniature village. Opened in 1931, the so-called Model Prison was also a rare example of the panopticon devised by the eighteenth-century English philosopher Jeremy Bentham. At the heart of each round cellblock stood a tower that allowed a single guard to monitor more than 1,200 inmates at once, as if he were at the center of a tropical Colosseum.

The nation's most notorious political prisoner had been sent here to join twenty-five of his *compañeros* from the Moncada to serve their long sentences on what was, in theory, Cuba's answer to Devil's Island. Once a favored refuge for English pirates and a model for Robert Louis Stevenson's *Treasure Island*, the enormous Isle of Pines—today called the Isle of Youth—had become a neglected appendage of the republic. Nobody had ever escaped across the sixty miles of open water back to the main island's southern coast. It was also not uncommon for inmates to simply disappear, the victim of the guards' abuse or the convict gangs who ruled the prison's underbelly with murderous weapons crafted from iron spikes and nails.

Despite the Presidio's ominous reputation, Fidel's arrival was a festive moment. In an inexplicable move, the Moncadistas, as they were now known, were not locked in the cramped two-man cells of the main prison blocks but placed together in a single ward of the hospital wing, their twenty-six beds lined up in two neat rows. When Fidel entered, it was to cheers, hugs, and backslapping as comrades such as Juan Almeida, Pedro Miret, and Raúl crowded around. Over the coming months the group would treat the prison as a revolutionary boot camp. They devised their own daily schedule for exercise and self-improvement. They started their own library of five hundred books, and a "college" they named after Abel Santamaría to honor their murdered coleader. For five hours a day they gathered before a blackboard on the airy hospital patio, where Fidel and others conducted lessons in philosophy, history, public speaking, and Spanish grammar. The men were also permitted to cook their own meals to supplement the prison gruel, while fresh fruit and coffee were carried in by visitors to keep their spirits up. ("Bring me some grapefruit to refresh me," Fidel wrote to his half sister, Lidia, before one visit.) They were even allowed to start lawsuits from prison, on one occasion suing Batista himself.

History is filled with jail sentences that achieved the opposite of what was intended: the Marquis de Sade writing his pornographic novels in the Bastille, Martin Luther King Jr. penning his *Letter from Birmingham Jail* in Alabama, Nelson Mandela becoming a symbol of resistance in South Africa. The story of the Moncadistas is a textbook case. Their jail term transformed the undisciplined "Movement" into a coherent organization with a definite plan of action. To Batista's intense annoyance, Fidel became more of a political force behind bars than he had ever been as a free activist, as the enforced leisure concentrated his mind. "What a fantastic school this is!" he rejoiced in one prison letter. "From here I'm able to finish forging my vision of the world."

He read voraciously, giving himself virtual PhDs in Western literature and political science, and became more radical in his opinions. Nothing short of true revolution would change Cuba, he concluded, a total upending of its social and economic base. The chances of him becoming personally involved seemed negligible to outsiders, given his fifteen-year sentence—but not, apparently, to himself. Every day pressure for an amnesty increased, and he was convinced that his early release was inevitable.

Prison was, biographer Tad Szulc sums up, "the great turning point in the history of the revolution."

THIS IS NOT to say that incarceration did not have its ups and downs. After four months of relative freedom, the idyll was interrupted on February 12, 1954, when Batista himself made an official visit to the jail. He was inaugurating a power plant less than two hundred feet from the Moncadistas' cell, and Fidel could not resist the opportunity to taunt his despised adversary. As the dictator rose to speak, the men gathered under a window to loudly sing the new theme song of the Movement, "The 26th of July March." This rousing hymn had been penned by one of their number, a young Afro-Cuban named Augustín Díaz Cartaya, who now led the singing himself.

To begin with, Batista thought the wafting hymn was some sort of obscure homage from the yardbirds. Then he began to make out the lyrics:

We're soldiers united, fighting so our country may be free,
Our weapons destroying the evil that has plagued our troubled
    land

Of errant, unwanted rulers and of cruel insatiable tyrants
Who have dragged us down into the mire.

The dictator's face turned purple and he stormed out of the Presidio; guards rushed in to break up the choir. Fidel was thrown into solitary confinement. Díaz was more harshly punished. "So you're the author of this piece of shit," bellowed a warden known as Cebolla, "Onion," a former inmate who ran the hospital ward. "Well, now you are going to sing it for us." A trio of guards flayed Díaz with bullwhips, then beat him senseless.

Fidel's new cell measured only twelve by fifteen feet and faced the morgue; it was dark and grim, but he had his own toilet, a cold-water shower, and a hot plate for cooking. He was given a decent mosquito net and allowed to bring his culinary treats and personal library. (One visitor described his cot as "an island, surrounded by books" which ranged from Tolstoy to Oscar Wilde and Thomas More's *Utopia*). He was even permitted the occasional conjugal visit from his wife, Mirta. The cell did have drawbacks, including a tendency to flood when it rained, but he was clearly still being treated with kid gloves.

Their leader's sudden isolation forced the Moncadistas to come up with inventive means of communication. Secret messages were passed back and forth written in lemon juice and smuggled in cigars or mashed potatoes; held over a candle, the invisible ink would become legible. (Prison officials never seemed to grow suspicious at the Moncadistas' sudden passion for citrus fruits). During exercise time, men would "accidentally" kick a football onto a roof near Fidel's cell; while retrieving it, they would toss letters wrapped in rags to him through the window, returning with messages he had dropped there in cans. Raúl and the engineering student–cum–ballistics expert Pedro Miret taught themselves sign language from a book they found in the prison library so they could coordinate these ploys under the noses of the wardens.

Using these painstaking means, Fidel was able to keep in touch with his network in Havana and Santiago and keep the Movement alive. Even more remarkably, the entire text of his defense speech, *History Will Absolve Me*, was smuggled from his solitary cell to the printing press. In one of the lesser-known triumphs in the history of publishing, Fidel reconstructed the entire two-hour harangue from memory and scrawled it on paper scraps in microscopic handwriting. Over a period of three months, the shreds were smuggled by visitors to Havana, where Haydée and Melba were living after their release from women's prison. The pair painstakingly deciphered Fidel's crabbed script and secretly had 27,500 copies of the incendiary text published. Over time, *History Will Absolve Me* became an underground phenomenon. (Fidel's biographer Tad Szulc declared it a "masterful piece of oratory—it is really much more than a speech—and his superb command and love of the Spanish language transformed it into a work of literature as well.") Frayed copies were passed back and forth by taxi drivers, teachers, and factory workers, making it Cuba's answer to Mao's Little Red Book. It remains in print today in dozens of translations. At the time, the backstory of the opus only added to its cachet. It was not lost on Cubans that the Isle of Pines was where José Martí had spent several months as a political prisoner at age seventeen in 1870 before going into exile, or that 1953, the year of the Moncada attack, was the centennial of Martí's birth. These were parallels with the great martyr that Fidel could relish in his confinement.

WHILE IN PRISON, Fidel received a steady stream of flirtatious letters from the alluring socialite Naty Revuelta, the details of which she revealed to historians only after she had turned eighty. Naty sent him a copy of W. Somerset Maugham's *Cakes and Ale*, the novel about a misunderstood artistic woman, with a beguiling photograph of herself pasted inside. She sent him her favorite poem, Rudyard Kipling's

"If," an ode to British stiff-upper-lip stoicism in the face of adversity. She sent a concert program from Havana signed by the conductor. She even sent him an envelope filled with sand, to remind him of the beauty of Cuban beaches. Fidel was captivated. "I am on fire," he wrote back to her. "Write to me, for I cannot be without your letters." In another missive he begged her to use her own handwriting rather than a typewriter, so he could revel in her penmanship—"so delicate, feminine, unmistakable."

Clearly, the long-simmering attraction between the two was reaching a higher pitch, even though they knew their words would be read by the prison censor. Then came disaster. Someone swapped one of Fidel's love letters to Naty with one to his long-suffering wife, Mirta. The switch may have been arranged by the prison governor to cause mischief. Or the culprit may have been Mirta's brother, Rafael Díaz-Balart, now Batista's deputy minister of the interior, to sabotage a rocky marriage that he found a career embarrassment.

The final blow came in mid-July, when Fidel heard on a radio news broadcast that Mirta had been receiving a secret salary from her brother's office. At first Fidel assumed this was a fabrication to undermine him—it implied that he knew about the payoffs, compromising his reputation—and he sent a string of virulent letters to his supporters insisting that they sue Díaz-Balart for libel. ("I am ready to challenge my own brother-in-law to a duel at any time," he railed in one.) But his half sister, Lidia, soon wrote to confirm that the charge was in fact true and, what was more, Mirta wanted a divorce. Trying to raise Fidelito alone had proven too difficult, so she had gone on the Batista payroll. For Fidel, it was an unforgivable betrayal, and he responded to his sister tersely: "Do not be concerned with me, for I have a steel heart and I shall be steadfast till the last day of my life." When Fidel learned that Mirta also planned to move to New York with their son, he flew into paroxysms of impotent rage. He demanded full custody of Fidelito rather than allow him to fall into the clutches of her family, "those miserable Judases." His lawyers politely informed him that a radical political prisoner serving a fifteen-year jail sentence would have little leverage in a custody trial.

Before the year's end, Mirta had her divorce. Fidel's only consolation was that the judge ordered that his son should be schooled in Havana rather than the US. Fidel and Mirta would never see each other again—although he would continue to have contact with Fidelito through the explosive years to come.

IN AUGUST, FIDEL'S isolation was eased when he was allowed to join Raúl in a brighter and more spacious cell. After being trapped in silence for so long, Fidel began to talk nonstop to his beleaguered sibling, who almost crumpled under the deluge of words. ("I have heard enough of Fidel for a lifetime," Raúl later joked.) Raúl's sign language now came in handy to send messages from Fidel straight to Pedro Miret.

Depressing news from the outside world filtered in via radio. The men were stunned to hear in June 1954 that the democratically elected president of Guatemala had been overthrown in a military coup backed by the CIA and funded by the United Fruit Company. Although little remembered today, the takeover sent shock waves around Latin America, signaling that Washington was willing to intervene aggressively to support dictators, no matter how unsavory, so long as they protected US economic interests. The second bleak piece of news came in November when Batista won an uncontested—and openly rigged—presidential election and was now, in his own words, "constitutional." The prospect of a fair vote being held in Cuba seemed more distant than ever.

Cubans were also becoming increasingly despondent at the offhand depravity of Batista's regime. A malevolent enforcer named Rolando Masferrer now led a private paramilitary army, Los Tigres, "the Tigers," to do the dictator's dirtiest work. Although he was a senator in Batista's government, Masferrer was borderline psychotic and took a hands-on interest in the torture and murder of opposition activists. He became a familiar sight, cruising the streets of Havana in a white Cadillac with two machine-gun toting guards—"like a pirate king," the historian Hugh Thomas puts it. The flourishes of cruelty were even more extreme in the Oriente, where revulsion towards Batista was fueled by its long tradition of intransigence. Today the daily horrors of the mid-1950s are captured in Santiago cemetery. A moving memorial to "Those Fallen in the Insurgency" is a simple wall with dozens of bronze plaques, each one adorned with a fresh red rose every morning, naming the Movement supporters who were gunned down or tortured to death by the security forces. The most disturbing thing is the victims' ages: some were as young as fourteen and fifteen. On one occasion the mothers of Santiago staged a protest march carrying a placard that said: *Stop the Murder of Our Sons.*

In the end, it was Cuban women who secured the Moncadistas' freedom. In 1955 the prisoners' mothers banded together in an action group calling for amnesty. Batista, in a magnanimous mood, was keen to repair Cuba's image as an economic dynamo and carefree tourist destination. He sent emissaries to offer Fidel a pardon if he would renounce armed rebellion. Fidel flatly refused. His freedom would have to be unconditional. Finally, on May 6, Batista succumbed and signed an amnesty bill "in honor of Mothers' Day." Fidel and his men had been in prison for only nineteen months; Pedro Miret, who had been teaching the inmates world history, jokingly complained that his lessons had only reached the Middle Ages.

NO SOONER WERE the Moncadistas released than their defiance resumed. As Fidel stepped out of the prison doors in his blue woolen coat and open-necked white shirt, he raised his arm in a sign of victory to a waiting crowd of admirers and journalists, an image that was splashed across the front pages of Cuban newspapers. The indefatigable Haydée and Melba had traveled from Havana for their first reunion since the Moncada trial. The horrific memories flooded back: Yeyé rested her head on Fidel's shoulder and burst into tears.

In the town of Nueva Gerona, well-wishers stopped the celebrity ex-cons in the street to shake their hands and ask for autographs. On El Pinero, the overnight ferry to the Cuban mainland, nobody tried to sleep. Fidel and his men spent the night coming up with a catchier name for their group. Typically, Fidel overruled other suggestions and settled on his own favorite, "the 26th of July Revolutionary Movement"—M-26-7 for short.

When the train rolled into Havana's central station the next morning, the waiting crowd was so large that Fidel could not get out the carriage door. Fans pulled him out through the window and carried him on their shoulders; a group of mothers then wrapped him in the Cuban flag. Two patrol cars followed Fidel back to the small bachelor apartment his half sister, Lidia, had arranged for him. When the cavalcade arrived, one of the police officers offered his hand in a gesture of goodwill. Fidel coldly refused it.

FIDEL LASTED IN Havana for only six weeks. He began to suspect that he had only been released from prison to be more easily eliminated. Rumors spread that the police kept a bullet-riddled car on standby so that they could gun Fidel down, then say that he had started a shoot-out. "They want my head!" he declared. When the government threatened to ban newspapers from printing Fidel's pronouncements, M-26-7 members realized it was time to hatch their plans elsewhere. Mexico was the obvious choice.

First Raúl slipped off. Then a six-month tourist visa was quietly obtained for Fidel. On July 7, sporting his now threadbare blue suit, he kissed his two sisters and Fidelito good-bye at Havana airport then boarded a flight to the port of Veracruz on the Gulf coast. (Lidia had sold her refrigerator to fund the trip, but Fidel still didn't have enough cash to fly the whole distance to Mexico City and would have to take the bus.) Absent from the send-off party was the jade-eyed Naty Revuelta. During Fidel's brief sojourn in Havana, the epistolary romance had ignited into a full-blown affair. At their last tryst, Naty neglected to tell him that she was pregnant with his child. A little girl, Alina, was born the next March and successfully passed off as her husband's. Naty continued to correspond with Fidel, but she resisted his entreaties to join her ever more notorious paramour in his precarious exile. He would find out that the child was his only several years later.

CHAPTER 6

Fellow Travelers

(July 1955–November 1956)

MEXICO CITY IN 1955 was a far more serene and approachable place than the traffic-clogged megalopolis it is today. Cars sidled in leisurely fashion down broad, tree-lined avenues modeled on the boulevards of Paris, and the surrounding ring of mountains was always visible under pollution-free skies. The city was Latin America's most welcoming home for political exiles, playing the role that neutral Zurich had for Europeans during the First World War, when the likes of Vladimir Lenin, James Joyce, and Tristan Tzara congregated there.

For the Movement members who arrived one by one, Mexico City was also an inspiration: here was a Latin American city with its own confident and independent culture, and they explored it first as wide-eyed tourists. They rushed to the Zócalo, the vast plaza where Spanish cathedrals rose on the ruins of Aztec pyramids and peasant women in brilliantly colored dresses sold fiercely spiced tacos. They admired the frescos of Diego Rivera, depicting scenes of world revolution with cameo appearances by Lenin and Pancho Villa, Mexico's own sombrero-wearing hero. And they went to the bullfights that had been banned in Cuba. Raúl was particularly impressed, and in high spirits would pretend to hold a cape in front of passing cars in the avenues.

But stimulating as it was, Fidel and his penniless followers wrestled with the logistics of expat life. They found cheap shared apartments and accepted any work they could. Calixto García took a job as a masseuse for a Mexican baseball team despite the fact that he had no experience at all. Most were forced to rely on the charity of Cuban exiles and sympathetic natives to survive. Although he was a near vagrant, Fidel lost no time in seeking out new recruits in the capital, often bewildering them with his zeal. Alberto Bayo, a Cuban veteran of the Spanish Civil War who had lost an eye in combat, recalled Fidel's outrage that he would not commit to training a guerrilla force in Mexico that had almost no soldiers, weapons, or funds. "You are Cuban, you have an absolute obligation to help us!" Fidel roared at him. To the old soldier, Fidel's latest plan—to return to the Oriente in a secret amphibious landing—was even more harebrained than the botched Moncada attack. He dismissed it out of hand as "child's play."

The Castro brothers were still receiving a small allowance from their father—$80 a month for Fidel, Raúl half that—but they might have been pushed to the edge of starvation in Mexico City were it not for María Antonia González, a well-off Cuban woman married to a local wrestler. María Antonia became the guardian angel for the wastrels of M-26-7, offering her spacious apartment in the colonial quarter as their unofficial headquarters, a safe house where they could find a bed and a meal when they were down-and-out.

It was here, at a dinner party on a chilly winter's night, that Fidel met a quiet twenty-seven-year-old Argentine with the eyes of a poet named Ernesto Guevara de la Serna.

THANKS TO THE posthumous publication of his journal as *The Motorcycle Diaries* and subsequent film starring Gael García Bernal,

Che's adventurous youth wandering South America has become a part of popular culture. Like Fidel, two years his elder, he was raised in privilege—although, in Che's case, as the eldest son of a faded aristocratic family in provincial Argentina with ties to the left-wing intelligentsia. Ernesto grew up much closer to his free-spirited, doting mother than his melancholy father. As a medical student in Buenos Aires, he was regarded as a handsome oddball who excelled at sports despite his debilitating asthma and who displayed such dubious hygiene that he was nicknamed El Chancho, "the Pig." He was always a restless soul. After graduation he set off on his formative road trip in 1952 along the spine of the Andes with his friend Alberto Granado. That journey included a stint in a leper colony in the Peruvian Amazon, an experience that awoke him to the social injustices plaguing Latin America. Absorbing Marxist texts, he made a second trip the next year that led him to Guatemala, where he worked as a doctor for the poor. There he fell in love with a Peruvian leftist with the profile of an Inca carving, Hilda Gadea, but they were both forced to flee the country after the 1954 coup.

By the time he arrived in Mexico City, Guevara had the brooding good looks of the young Marlon Brando and a steely willpower honed by his endless struggle with asthma. He worked as a doctor in a hospital for the poor and freelance photojournalist for Argentine news agencies, and spent his spare time writing poetry with a political edge.

Raúl was his first friend among the Cuban exiles, who took him to Soviet films and bullfights. It was also Raúl who invited Ernesto and Hilda to the fateful dinner at María Antonia's house, where Fidel was in attendance—as usual, holding forth at length as if he were at a political rally. It was the beginning, as they say, of a beautiful friendship. The introverted Ernesto observed Fidel with fascination from the sidelines until after the meal, when he took him aside to a window. The pair then launched into an intense conversation that continued for ten hours when they retired to a nearby café.

It was an attraction of opposites. Fidel was a natural exhibitionist with the strapping physique of his basketball champion days, a stark contrast to the introverted Argentine betrayed by his lungs. But they shared a belief in Latin America's common problems, and the need for an armed uprising to snap the region from its historic chains. Fidel grilled Ernesto about his travels. Ernesto, for his part, was mesmerized by Fidel's confidence and intellect. He was not uncritical of Fidel's fuzzy political ideas, but at the time he simply noted in his diary that "we agreed completely." Neither had quite shed their affluent backgrounds. Che still looked like a student doctor from the cover of a dime novel—clean-shaven, with short, neat hair—while according to Hilda, Fidel could have passed "for a well-turned-out bourgeois tourist." But when he spoke, she added, Fidel's eyes "lit up with passion." His hypnotic charm, she believed, stemmed from a "truly admirable naturalness and simplicity."

Later that day, Ernesto asked his fiancée what she made of Fidel's plan to "invade" Cuba. Hilda recalls saying: "There's no doubt that it's madness, but we must be with it." He hugged her and declared that he had already decided to go with the group as medic.

The other Cubans were at first wary of a foreigner in their midst, but most soon warmed to Ernesto and dubbed him affectionately "Che," the Argentine slang equivalent of "buddy." The veteran M-26-7 lawyer Melba Hernández was less impressed. When they met, Che looked her up and down and pompously declared that "a true revolutionary" would not dress with such elegant clothes and jewelry. *True* revolutionaries were decorated on the inside, not the outside, he opined. Melba was livid. Having experienced the Moncada and spent months in prison, she began cursing at Che as a callow middle-class playactor, and had to be pulled away by her fiancé.

THE BROAD OUTLINES of Fidel's amphibious landing had been plotted out in prison. In Mexico City the blueprint had to be turned into reality.

Step one was to pick a landing spot in the Oriente. To this end, Fidel dispatched Pedro Miret to meet with clandestine M-26-7 agents there. Step two was to raise cash. Fidel cobbled together enough to make a seven-week fund-raising trip to the United States, where he could emulate José Martí once again by tapping the ample wallets of Cuban exiles. Fidel was given a US tourist visa without question, and in late October 1955 he bounded from the *Silver Meteor* train into New York's Penn Station. The Moncada attack had galvanized Cuban-Americans, so Fidel's return to the Monster of the North was triumphant. After his climactic speech in the ballroom of the Hotel Palm Gardens in midtown Manhattan, eight hundred Cuban patriots lined up to deposit money into a deep straw cowboy hat of the style once favored by *mambí* independence fighters.

It was in the Palm Gardens that Fidel also made a promise that seized new headlines across Cuba (and astonished the *New York Times*): "In 1956, we will be free men or we will be martyrs." He swore to return to the island with an army within little over a year; only the precise date and location of his landing were secret. The sheer boldness of it all captured the imaginations of students back in Cuba, who began to paint *M-26-7* in the streets. In New York, Fidel also spent a day with the Cuban photographer Osvaldo Salas taking promotional portraits in Central Park and other places José Martí had frequented in exile. Salas's teenage son Roberto went one better when he and some friends climbed the Statue of Liberty and hung an M-26-7 flag from its crown. The enterprising Roberto then took photos of the striking scene and sold them to US newspapers and *Life* magazine.

Back in Mexico City, a financial infusion came in from an unexpected American source. From his exile in Miami Beach, Cuba's last elected president, the suave and vain Carlos Prío, decided to funnel his considerable wealth into anti-Batista plots, including Fidel's. Overcoming his disdain for his former enemy, Fidel accepted the millionaire's largesse. According to one CIA agent, he even traveled to the US-Mexico border and illegally swam across the Rio Grande after dark to collect $50,000 from Prío in a motel room in Texas.

Now M-26-7 HAD enough funds to rent a dozen apartments in Mexico City and give each recruit a living allowance—a regal eighty cents a day. These safe houses were run like radical youth hostels. No outsiders were admitted. Nobody could go into the city alone. No alcohol or telephone calls were permitted, and there was a midnight curfew. The volunteers were also bound to total secrecy, and forbidden to even discuss their personal backgrounds. It hardly needed saying that no dating was allowed outside the small pool of female Movement supporters. In their spare time the men mostly played chess; Che proved to be the only one who could beat Fidel.

By the spring of 1956, Fidel had sixty men, whose training took advantage of Mexico City's natural setting. Like an urban fitness camp, they went on long walks up and down the tree-lined avenues and the Bosque de Chapultepec park. Afternoons were devoted to classes on "military theory" and "revolutionary education." In an attempt to gain genuine outdoor experience, some men took to hiking nearby mountains with backpacks filled with stones. Che pushed himself to climb the 17,930-foot volcano Popocatépetl, battling asthma to the ice-covered summit. He also made the ultimate sacrifice for an Argentine, giving up steak for breakfast for a sparse guerrilla diet.

Of course, this was all a far cry from the reality of combat in the jungles of Cuba; it was like a modern mountaineer training for an Everest assault by working out on the treadmill at the gym. The one-eyed veteran Alberto Bayo, surprised that Fidel was managing to enact his wild dreams, now agreed to oversee military drills in a ranch he rented called Santa Rosa twenty-five miles outside the city. Training was now a little closer to guerrilla life, with 5:00 a.m. wake-up calls and overnight marches. Soon Bayo leased another, wilder ranch

650 miles north of the capital, where tents were erected in desolate country slithering with rattlesnakes.

Despite the ascetic regime, Mexico City wasn't all revolution and no play, although for unmarried recruits the romantic options remained limited, to say the least. The men were not permitted to go on single dates, even with trusted *compañeras*—it was too much of a security risk—although double dates were permitted within the fold. Even Fidel was occasionally lured out on the town. Nightclubs were dicey: as a student, Fidel had become notorious as perhaps the only male in Cuba who couldn't dance. (Che was also notoriously lead footed.) Even so, in a fit of optimism Raúl invited his brother to go out with two attractive young Mexican supporters of the Movement, along with Melba and her fiancé. The only condition, Raúl insisted, was that his older brother would for once refrain from gabbling about politics. As soon as the musicians struck up, everyone left the table for the dance floor except Fidel and his date. Upon their return, the others were exasperated to find Fidel holding forth like an orator on the podium to his glazed-eyed companion. Raúl kicked his brother under the table and he hurriedly changed subjects. But after a few minutes he returned to politics to the resigned sighs of all.

Only one woman was able to distract Fidel from his monomania. According to a Cuban expat supporter, the novelist Teresa Casuso, Fidel fell in love with one of her houseguests, a highly educated eighteen-year-old Cuban girl identified only as "Lilia." Fidel met her on one of his regular visits to hide weapons in Casuso's villa, and he was immediately captivated by Lilia's fresh beauty, erudition, and unusual frankness in conversation. The pair secretly became engaged— at which point, the prudish Fidel insisted that his sweetheart trade in her swimsuit, a daring French bikini, for a one-piece. Sadly, Fidel became too absorbed in planning his invasion to spend much time with his young lover. She broke off the engagement and went back to her ex-fiancé. Fidel took the blow on the chin. He proudly told Lilia that she should go ahead and marry her old suitor. He did not mind, he said, because he already had his own "beautiful fiancée": the impending revolution.

DESPITE ALL OF their precautions, the M-26-7 men were only one step ahead of the law. On June 20, after a cache of weapons was seized, Mexican police surrounded Fidel in the street and twenty-five rebels were arrested, Che among them. With clear evidence that the group was fomenting insurrection in Cuba, the Batista government pressed for extradition. It looked like Fidel's mad enterprise was about to collapse.

Remarkably, Raúl was able to hire left-wing Mexican lawyers to have all charges dropped within a month. But a sense of urgency was now growing, with the chances of another police sweep more likely every day. Fidel still insisted that he would return to Cuba before the end of 1956 as he had promised in New York, although he still had no means of transport and had lost many weapons. Even the head organizer for M-26-7 in eastern Cuba, a twenty-two-year-old student teacher named Frank País, thought the timeline was crazy and traveled to Mexico City to beg for a delay. Fidel refused to listen. He had given his solemn oath. He passed his thirtieth birthday on August 13 without celebration and soon afterward received news of his father's death. Outwardly, Fidel showed no emotion; he could not pause the revolution for personal indulgences such as mourning.

Fidel now had around 120 men at his disposal, mostly well-educated young professionals in their twenties and thirties, but there were still no leads on a invasion craft. Fidel scoured the arms catalogs that floated around the Mexican underground as readily as furniture brochures, spotting a US Navy surplus PT (patrol torpedo) boat for sale from a private owner in Delaware for $20,000. The fast, agile vessel had acquitted itself brilliantly in the Pacific War—the young JFK had commanded one—and it seemed perfect for the Caribbean. A sympathetic Mexican arms dealer named Antonio del Conde, known as El Cuate, "the Friend," was dispatched to the United States to put down a 50 percent deposit, but the deal went awry when the State Department grew suspicious. (To Fidel's fury, the owner kept the deposit.) Plan B was to buy a Catalina flying boat to whisk the rebel army to the Oriente, but Fidel scuttled the idea when he learned that it could only carry twenty-seven men.

The final choice was suitably spontaneous. After a shooting practice trip near the Gulf of Mexico, El Cuate took Fidel to inspect an old pleasure craft he wanted to buy for himself in the river port of Tuxpan. Sitting in dry dock above the muddy shore was a decaying sixty-three-foot tub called the *Granma*. Castro took one look and declared: "I'm taking this boat to Cuba." At first the Mexican thought Fidel was joking: the cabin cruiser had been built to carry only two dozen passengers safely and was in dire need of basic repairs. It had sunk during a hurricane three years before and was still badly waterlogged. But Fidel's mind was made up. ("You just can't say no to Fidel," El Cuate shrugged years later.) The owner, a retired American dentist who lived in Mexico City, agreed to sell the *Granma*—which he had named, funnily enough, for his grandmother—for $20,000.

Repairs began immediately. But by mid-November, the *Granma* was still barely seaworthy, when events span out of control. First, Mexican police arrested Pedro Miret and confiscated another arms cache. Then, on November 21, Fidel learned that two recruits had disappeared and were potentially turning informers. There was no time to lose. The departure date was pushed forward to the night of November 25. Coded telegrams were sent to Cuba alerting M-26-7 in Oriente. Frank País's local operatives would have to scurry to prepare their diversionary attacks to coincide with the *Granma*'s arrival, which, using nautical charts, Fidel had calculated would occur exactly five days later. For better or worse, the grand adventure was about to begin.

ON SUNDAY, NOVEMBER 24, Che kissed his newborn child, a little girl named Hildita, nicknamed "Little Mao" for her resemblance to the cherub-cheeked Chinese ruler, and bid good-bye to Hilda as if he were heading off on his usual weekend training trip. She had no idea that he was about to vanish to Cuba. Che did write a more explicit postcard to his mother, with whom he was still very close: "To avoid pre-mortem pathos, this card will only arrive when the potatoes are really burning, and then you will know that your son, in some sun-drenched land of the Americas, will be kicking himself for not having studied enough surgery to help a wounded man."

Fidel, meanwhile, composed his will while sitting in a car in Tux-pan. He declared that, in the event of his death, his son Fidelito should be removed from the corrosive influence of Mirta's pro-Batista family. Somehow Fidel had convinced his wife to let the seven-year-old visit him in Mexico City in the company of his sisters. Unsurprisingly, he refused to allow Fidelito to go home. (The well-connected Mirta had other plans; not long afterward three armed men stopped the sisters' car in broad daylight, kidnapped Fidelito, and spirited him back to Havana. We can only speculate how these Wild West custody arrangements affected the boy's psyche.)

Rain was pelting down after dark as volunteers arrived in the port. The river was deserted: a storm warning was in effect and the Mexican coast guard had closed down ocean traffic. Sodden groups of twos and threes made their way in silence through muddy back streets, then took rowboats to the meeting point. By late evening some 130 men, still in their civilian clothes, had gathered in the slippery weeds near where the *Granma* was docked. Old friends who had not seen one another for months embraced wordlessly. Many were taken aback by the modest size of the boat. Melba, who was assisting with logistics, took one look and told Fidel that he wouldn't get more than a dozen men on board. One of Fidel's bodyguards, Universo Sánchez, assumed the *Granma* was merely a transport to a larger vessel anchored elsewhere. "When do we get to the real ship?" he asked.

Dressed like an eighteenth-century Spanish nobleman in a full-length black rain cape, Fidel supervised the final loading of weapons and supplies, including Hershey's chocolate bars, fresh fruit, and sides of ham. When he gave the go-ahead to board just after midnight, there was a sudden rush, like musical chairs. Only eighty-two men could be squeezed on in a tangle of limbs, leaving around fifty men standing forlornly on the riverbank.

The rain was pounding even harder at 2:00 a.m. when the overloaded *Granma* eased sluggishly from the dock. Everyone on board was hushed, the lights were off, and only one of its two engines was used at low throttle to avoid detection. The men left behind watched the *Granma* disappear into the darkness. Fidel and his *compañeros* were now out of contact, with 1,235 miles of raging seas ahead of them.

CHAPTER 7

Waiting for Fidel

(Late November–December 5, 1956)

FIVE DAYS LATER, on Friday, November 30, two M-26-7 operatives sat in an abandoned ice-packing plant above Playa las Coloradas in far eastern Cuba, scanning the moonlit horizon with increasing anxiety. Lalo Vásquez and Manuel Fajardo were expecting *Granma* to land on the beach well before dawn, when Fidel and his eighty-one men would be bundled into five waiting trucks and spirited thirty miles away into the labyrinths of the Sierra Maestra. With almost Swiss precision, diversionary attacks had been planned to start at 7:00 a.m. that same morning on military sites around the Oriente, using the few men and weapons that could be mustered. But the hours crept on with no sign of Fidel. Darkness slowly gave way to the lavish blues of the winter sky and shimmering Caribbean, exposing any arriving vessel to detection by air and sea patrols. There was still nothing to see but gentle waves lapping rhythmically on the white sands of the *playa* and a few small fishing boats chugging home with their evening catch.

Communications technology in 1950s Cuba was closer to the nineteenth century's than to today's. There were few telephones in the countryside (and those were easily tapped); postal services were erratic; many local messages were still carried by hand. The fastest international correspondence was by telegram or, for businesses and journalists, dedicated Telex machines. The last word from Fidel had been the coded telegram sent from Mexico City to Frank País in Santiago—OBRA PEDIDA AGOTADA, "The book you ordered is out of print," signed "Editorial Divulgacio"—which announced the *Granma*'s imminent departure on November 25. Another message arrived at a Havana hotel switchboard to alert supporters: MAKE RESERVA-TION. (The receptionist delivered it to an M-26-7 agent who was being tailed by the secret police; they chased him, but, like Maxwell Smart, he ate the telegram before capture and was released.) All over the palm-fringed coastline, a thin network of farmers allied to the Movement was expecting some sort of arrival, although details were kept vague. Peasants in the mountains were ready to open their barns to hide a troop, or let them camp in their coffee fields.

Nobody was in more turmoil than Celia Sánchez, the coordinator of the rural reception parties, who paced back and forth in a farmhouse above the coast, chain-smoking and knocking back cups of sweet coffee. A diminutive thirty-six-year-old with black hair tied back in a severe ponytail, Celia had never met Fidel but had worked almost nonstop for months to help usher him in secret from the beachhead. She knew this empty shore intimately and had even offered to fly to Mexico and sail on the *Granma* as guide. The idea was rejected in part because she would have been the only woman on board. Seven a.m. passed—the point of no return, Celia knew, when the attacks were starting across the Oriente. The plan had its own momentum; she could not contact anyone to halt it. But if the *Granma* was delayed, the diversions would backfire. The army would be put on high alert, placing everyone involved in danger.

Celia was not used to being so powerless. All she could do was pace the farmhouse back and forth impatiently and light another cigarette.

OUTSIDE CUBA, FIDEL and Che are the poster boys of the guerrilla war, but on the island Celia Sánchez is a celebrity of equal importance, the revered third figure of a revolutionary Trinity. A blur of nicotine-fueled energy, she was a masterful planner whose lifetime of experience in the Oriente infused the rebellion and at many key moments kept it alive. She was backed up on the ground by two other outsized characters, the urbane charmer Frank País and a grizzled peasant patriarch, Crescencio Pérez, both of whom might have been plucked from the pages of a García Márquez novel. Without them, Fidel's entire project would have been stillborn.

Celia's subversive credentials were a unique product of the 1950s, where much of the Cuban countryside drifted at a genteel Old World pace. She was the third of six daughters of a progressive doctor who had forsaken a lucrative practice in Havana to live among sugar workers in the sunbaked port of Pilón. She and her father became intensely close after her mother's early death; by her teenage years, Celia was arranging every detail of his life, scheduling appointments in the clinic, timing his siestas, and arranging the details of his vacations. At the same time, she was dismissed by many of her teachers as an uncontrollable tomboy who preferred fishing, hunting, and finding orchids in the forest to study. Despite her obvious intelligence, Celia refused to finish high school or attend university, preferring to stay in Pilón and help her father. Indeed, Celia's paternal devotion was described by one friend as a "passion," according to her biographer Nancy Stout, whose intensity would one day be transferred to Fidel.

For years her talents were channeled into good works: arranging church dinners, dances, and her annual New Year's Eve party, where a raffle raised cash to buy toys for poor country kids. Celia would also pay nursing visits to remote villages and arrange free medicine from her uncles' pharmacies. All this meant that she had personally met most families in the Oriente; they, in turn, referred to her with affection as "the doctor's daughter." Soon these intimate bonds—and Celia's furious, pent-up energy—would be harnessed for a higher cause.

LIKE MANY OF her compatriots, Celia was drawn into politics by Batista's 1952 coup, when she was a spinster (in the eyes of rural residents) of thirty-two. Not long after, she joined her father in an oblique act of protest when local intellectuals lugged a stone bust of José Martí to the top of Cuba's tallest mountain, Pico Turquino, in the Sierra Maestra. The military was baffled by this odd gesture of dissent, which resembled performance art.

After the Moncada attack, Celia offered her services to the Movement. By then the whole of the Oriente, and the city of Santiago in particular, was seething with homespun resistance, and women became involved at every level. They began making Molotov cocktails from old soda bottles in their homes, which could then be transported in wooden Coca-Cola racks. They smuggled ammunition in baby strollers and underneath their dresses—the voluminous 1950s petticoats could hide a dozen grenades—and couriered secret correspondence in their brassieres. But even in the radical underground, Celia always took care with her appearance, never venturing out without fashionable clothes and plucked eyebrows, lipstick and makeup carefully applied.

In the summer of 1956, when Pedro Miret, Fidel's confidant from Mexico, and Frank País needed to choose a landing spot for Fidel's secret invasion, they went to Celia for guidance. As they motored along the coast in a small fishing boat, the group could have been taken for holidaymakers on a jaunt, pausing to admire empty beaches and cliffs down which rain forest cascaded. Celia recommended a site at the base of the Sierra Maestra where the guerrillas could be trucked directly to safety. She was overruled. País and Miret opted for Playa las Coloradas, which was easier to reach from Mexico; the drawback was that some thirty-five miles of exposed countryside would have to be somehow traversed. Since it was obvious that Celia knew the Oriente "from palm tree to palm tree," as the Cuban saying goes, they assigned her the crucial job of arranging Fidel's ground support.

Over the next eleven months Celia, now codenamed "Norma," threw herself into the task. Using a *yipi* (slang for jeep) and motorboat provided by M-26-7, she called in twenty years' worth of favors and used her regular social events—picnics by local swimming holes, overnight fishing trips, baseball games in village paddocks—to recruit a rural network. Celia found many willing supporters among the impoverished farmers, who regarded the Cuban army as an enemy occupation force. She made a particular point of visiting women who had been raped by Batista's soldiers to arrange medical assistance at her father's clinic. Celia's status as "the doctor's daughter" provided a perfect cover. Nobody in the Oriente's insular high society guessed that their eccentric, manicured friend was a closet revolutionary. But as 1956 progressed, the military intelligence service, SIM, became increasingly suspicious. Like other well-to-do Movement members, Celia purchased an open-date air ticket out of the country, ready for the moment when the secret police might come knocking.

CELIA'S CHIEF, FRANK País, was about to celebrate his twenty-second birthday when he received the coded telegram from Fidel in Mexico City; today, he is still remembered for his movie star looks, spiffily dressed in a white linen jacket and pencil tie, and flashing a pearly smile like Cuba's answer to Frank Sinatra. He made a deep impression on everyone he met, and was often described as a "superior human being" with an otherworldly air. Even historians have developed crushes on Frank, noting, for example, that he had "a beautifully shaped mouth, wide, full and sensuous." One of Celia's cousins summed him up in a single word: "divine."

Frank was the boy wonder of the revolution. He became a student activist while studying at the teachers college in Santiago and proved so capable that by age twenty he was put in command of all M-26-7 operations in the Oriente, placing him on a par with Fidel in the Movement's hierarchy. But he still lived with his mother and two brothers in a humble Santiago neighborhood, and would often meet agents in his bedroom, where he liked to play the piano or jazz records so conversations would not be overheard by nosy neighbors as they hung their washing over the backyard fence. His was the most dangerous position in the Oriente, and he had to shuffle between safe houses for days after street protests. But he also liked to hide in plain sight: he used M-26-7 funds to buy a lipstick-red Dodge his friends nicknamed the "Red Menace," speeding around town like a playboy.

Although he appeared carefree, Frank could be ruthless. It is almost certain that he was personally involved in the assassination of stool pigeons as well as two recruits who deserted and sold their weapons. In April 1956, when a group of army officers drove by a student demonstration and started shooting randomly, killing two, País helped some friends steal cars and drive around looking for revenge. They shot dead three soldiers.

As 1956 wound down, Fidel's promise that he would return to Cuba before the end of the year was provoking wild rumors all over the island, and SIM was working overtime to find out whether he would make good on his oath. In Santiago, Frank had managed to muster twenty-eight men for diversionary attacks and sabotage, far fewer than Fidel wanted. Still, when the coded telegram arrived announcing that the *Granma* would arrive on November 25, he excitedly contacted Celia. Now, at last, the months of planning were over.

ON THE NIGHT of November 24, Celia staged a loud dinner party in the country with an array of M-26-7 supporters posing as guests. Then, after midnight, she slipped in secret to the house of the Movement's third key organizer, Crescencio Pérez, the godfather of the Sierra Maestra. The bearlike sixty-one-year-old with a frayed white beard, Coke-bottle glasses, and piercing blue eyes, was her most controversial recruit. A throwback to a feudal era, he claimed to have fathered over eighty children, all of whom he financially supported. Despite an unsavory reputation as an enforcer for sugar companies, his stature in mountain society was unrivaled. He had legions of loyal friends and relatives and bitterly loathed Batista's henchmen, the Rural Guard. Celia recruited him to alert her backwoods supporters—none of whom had telephones—of the *Granma*'s imminent arrival.

When Crescencio opened the door, Celia said simply, "Fidel is coming." He quickly changed into what seemed an outlandish costume: wearing a fancy white guayabera and a broad felt hat, with a lariat around his neck and a revolver slung on his hip, he looked like a bandit in an old Zorro movie. "Where do you think you're going dressed up like that?" Celia asked, incredulous. Crescencio patiently explained that he could tell policemen he was traveling the sierra to invite family members to a wedding. He then set out on horseback to spread the word of Fidel's imminent arrival, a tour of duty that historians have compared to Paul Revere's ride.

That same day, Frank had been driving around Santiago in the Red Menace, its trunk loaded with weapons. At one point a recruit riding with him was horrified to see that the trunk had popped open. Frank stopped the car and coolly got out to close it, flashing a winning smile at the pedestrians who raised their eyebrows at the arsenal.

Before dawn on November 30, he gathered his twenty-eight-man task force in an abandoned house in Santiago to dress in fatigues and red-and-black M-26-7 armbands. Assuming that Fidel had landed, they set off to strike at 7:00 a.m. Given their modest numbers, the cadres did surprisingly well. One team sprayed a customhouse with machine-gun fire and tossed firebombs through the windows. Another seized a police station and freed the prisoners. Electricity and telephone lines were cut. Over the course of the day, eight police officers were killed; the rebels lost three men. But when Frank and Celia finally got messages through to one another that afternoon, they were shocked to learn that neither had received any word of the *Granma's* arrival. By then the military retribution had begun. Nine Movement members were executed in Santiago. Hundreds of opposition figures around Cuba were arrested. Batista suspended the constitution.

By the next morning, December 1, there was still no sign of Fidel. Celia now had to make an agonizing decision. With army patrols scouring the Oriente, her supporters could not wait with their trucks by Playa las Coloradas forever. She reluctantly gave the order for everyone to return to their homes. If the *Granma* did ever make it to shore, Fidel and his men would have to fend for themselves.

CHAPTER 8

The Cruise of the *Granma*

(November 25–December 5, 1956)

UNBEKNOWNST TO THE cadres of M-26-7 in Cuba, the *Granma* was still chugging doggedly across the Caribbean Sea that morning of December 1, many miles from its destination, with its eighty-two passengers in wretched physical condition. Thanks to a mixture of inexperience and bad luck, Fidel's expedition had descended into operatic misery from the moment it left Mexico six nights before.

Spirits were high when the vessel first eased from the dock into the dark river at Tuxpan, the men crouched on top of one another in silence while listening to the hammering rain on the deck above. When the harbor was left behind an hour later, they spontaneously broke into the Cuban national anthem. But the euphoria evaporated as soon as they hit open ocean. The tropical gale tearing across the Gulf of Mexico sent huge waves across the bow, making the overloaded cruiser rock violently from side to side. Nausea soon surged through the cabin. Che, as medic, desperately tried to find the seasickness tablets, but somehow they hadn't been packed.

In Steven Soderbergh's epic 2008 biopic *Che*, Guevara and his companions are shown gazing stoically from the *Granma*'s calm decks. Nothing could be further from the truth. "The entire ship soon assumed a ridiculously tragic aspect," Che later wrote. "Men . . . held their stomachs, while their faces reflected their anguish. Some buried their heads in buckets while others were lying about, motionless, their clothes covered with vomit." Few of the men had ever been to sea before. Only Che; Fidel; Faustino Pérez, a thirty-six-year-old doctor-turned-revolutionary; and the three experienced sailors were unaffected by the hideous motion.

Even more disastrously, the *Granma* began to ship water. The seasick men tried to work the bilge pumps, but the water only began rising faster, covering the cabin floor planks. Fidel, still in his black cape, pitched in to pass a bucket back and forth in the pelting rain. In the pandemonium, some men panicked that the cruiser might sink and began tossing random objects overboard. A few suggested that they should abandon ship and swim back to shore—an absurd proposition, given the churning waves. Luckily, at the last minute, someone realized that the bilge pumps were set on reverse, so they were actually pumping water into the boat instead of out. It didn't help that there was also an open faucet in the lavatory. Soon the cabin floor planks were visible again.

The more superstitious credited an intervention from on high: "The *Granma* was invincible," Faustino recalled piously. "Forces other than purely physical ones . . . were driving the ship to her destination."

Unfortunately, the divine hand didn't concern itself with Fidel's schedule. The rough seas were slowing the *Granma*'s progress and fuel was being guzzled at an alarming rate. The storm continued to lash them for two days, turning the journey from hapless to hellish. Belowdecks, the men were made even more queasy by the reek of petrol. Potable water was low. They discovered that in the initial panic much of the canned food had been tossed to the bottom of the gulf. A few of the more adventurous tried drinking condensed milk or eating Hershey bars, with regrettable results. Some sampled the newfangled vitamin pills Fidel had purchased as an experimental dietary supplement, which were advertised in Mexico as having "the nutritional value of chicken or beef."

By the third day the swell was calming and morale began to improve. On the next, they neared the coast of western Cuba, but remained 170 miles from the shoreline to avoid naval patrols. Every time a ship or airplane was spotted on the horizon, the men scrambled below to hide. The expeditionaries were right to be paranoid. Several days earlier the Mexican secret police had alerted their Cuban counterparts of the *Granma*'s departure; military bulletins had been sent out to look for a sixty-three-foot yacht, painted white, name unknown.

ONE OF THE many odd last-minute packing decisions on the *Granma* was to leave Mexico without a radio transmitter. When Fidel had calculated his travel time, he did not factor in the storm or the overloaded vessel's sluggish speed. Now, as the rendezvous date approached, Fidel had no way to communicate their delay to M-26-7 operatives on shore. On November 30 he and his men could only listen helplessly to Cuban news bulletins on his transistor radio as Frank's wave of sabotage and shoot-outs went ahead in Santiago as planned.

"I wish I could fly!" Fidel yelled out in anguish.

The last of their fresh water was gone, along with the food; dehydration and hunger were now the main torments. To distract themselves, some of the men tossed empty cans into the waves to shoot for target practice.

At last on December 1, Fidel gathered his hollow-eyed *compañeros* on deck and announced that they would be landing the next morning. Until then, following the usual protocol, only the top officers had been told their precise destination, Playa las Coloradas. The men were given their uniforms, knapsacks, and equipment—including brand-new leather boots, even though hiking in footwear that had not been broken in was an error any Boy Scout would have known to avoid. They then threw their bile-encrusted civvies into the ocean, along with anything "unnecessary for guerrilla life." Razors and toothbrushes had already been left behind in Mexico.

Fuel was running low when, sometime after midnight, the flashing beacon of the Cabo Cruz lighthouse was glimpsed on the horizon. The landing site was close. But the run of bad luck continued. Like a scene from a Laurel and Hardy movie, one of the seasoned sailors, an ex-navy officer named Roberto Roque, was trying to make out the coast when he lost his balance and fell overboard. Chaos ensued. Fidel ordered the captain to circle back and forth in the darkness. The searchlight was turned on for the first time on the voyage. Men scoured the inky waters. On this starless, drizzly night, the chances of Roque surviving were all but nil.

Just when they were about to give up, a crewman heard a faint cry of "Here!" The half-frozen Roque was plucked from the waves to delirious cheers. (It was an early sign that Fidel would obsessively ensure that individual men were safe, even at the risk of a greater cataclysm; this, in turn, inspired near-fanatical loyalty. As Che noted, Fidel's personal bond with each of his men made the Movement "an indivisible block.") It was a miracle, but they had also lost precious time—a full hour—and were now nearly out of fuel. Around 4:00 a.m. on Sunday, December 2, the pilot told Fidel that they might only have a few minutes of cruising time left. They had to land somewhere—anywhere—before dawn. "That's definitely the mainland?" Fidel asked the pilot as they peered at the coast. "You're absolutely sure that it's not Jamaica or some cay?" Once reassured, Fidel told him to open the motors to maximum throttle and head straight to shore, arriving "wherever we arrive."

A ripple of anticipation ran through the boat. After the tortuous voyage, the moment of destiny was nigh. Then came the sickening lurch. The *Granma* stopped dead on a sandbank, sixty yards from the coast. There was no choice but to load up with gear and prepare to wade ashore. But as the sky began to pale at 5:40 a.m., the men were appalled to discover that this coast was not one of the golden-sand beaches for which Cuba is renowned but a wall of mangroves, their roots knitted together to create a dense green brocade. Hoping for the best, the first rebels lowered themselves over the side at 6:30, holding their rifles above their heads as they worked their way forward. The water, writes Cuban historian Heberto Norman Acosta, was "a dense broth, warm and pestilential." The muddy floor sucked off boots like glue. But the real challenge was getting through the swamp itself—a "tangled net" of roots, Norman says, that could only be traversed by "an act of acrobatics."

The men's knees and palms were slashed as they tripped on sunken logs. Clouds of mosquitoes and sand flies descended. Fidel fretted that they might have landed on an offshore cay after all—Cuba has some 4,000 of them—where they would be picked off by the navy. After an hour of agonizing progress, he ordered an agile country boy named Luis Crespo to climb a small tree and see what lay ahead. Crespo was discouraged to report that he could see nothing but more mangroves stretching to the horizon in an endless verdant wasteland.

It was a huge relief when, after about a mile, the vegetation began to change. Soon a distant line of coconut trees was spotted—a sure sign of terra firma—and the murk beneath the rebels' feet became more solid. After two and a half hours of punishing exertion, men fell to their knees when they hit dry land, shakily thanking God. Eight had gone off on a complete tangent and would only catch up with the rest of the group the next afternoon.

Little wonder that the campesino Ángel Pérez Rosabal was startled when he encountered the battered army in the coconut grove of Los Cayuelas at 9:00 a.m. Over the next two hours, rebels continued to stagger into his family hut, where Fidel took stock of the dire situation. They had crash-landed in the middle of nowhere, with no way of letting Frank or Celia know they had arrived. As Faustino recalled with admirable honesty, "All of our plans had failed completely." Fidel was apoplectic, but politely kept his cursing out of earshot of the peasant family. And then, around 11:00 a.m., they heard the sound of shelling back in the mangroves.

※

At around the same time, unaware that SIM had put out word that she should be brought in dead or alive, Celia was leaving Crescencio's house in the Sierra Maestra. She was still wearing the same chocolate-brown skirt she had worn at the dinner party three days earlier, and had decided it was time to head home herself. A friend gave her a lift as far as the tiny sugar port of Campechuela, where her life was turned on its head.

As reconstructed by biographer Nancy Stout, Celia entered a bodega, where a twenty-year-old bartender named Enrique de la Rosa was one of her contacts. He modeled himself on American greasers, wearing jeans with the cuffs rolled up, a white T-shirt with a packet of cigarettes folded into the shoulder, and a lick of blond hair brilliantined in place. As Celia later recalled, morning light flooded through the bar's batwing doors onto the few lonely liquor bottles to create a hypnotic kaleidoscope on the walls. Seconds after she arrived, patrol cars screeched up. Two SIM agents burst into the bar and put Celia under arrest. She sat down in shock: this was the moment all *clandestinos* ("urban operatives") dreaded, when she would vanish into a prison cell.

Instead of bundling Celia into a patrol car, the agents stayed sitting with her in the bar, evidently using her as bait for other M-26-7 agents who might pass by. She realized she knew one of the SIM agents personally as one of her father's longtime patients. He was named Hatuey after a famous Taíno Indian chief, but was better known as "the Machete King" for his habit of beating victims with the flat of a machete blade. He looked the very cliché of a fiendish police enforcer, his face pockmarked from acne and florid scars from a knife fight. But he was obviously uneasy with his role and avoided her gaze. She forced herself to remain calm and think of a plan. First she took out a cigarette and asked Hatuey if she could buy matches. After smoking as calmly as she could, she then asked if she could also buy a packet of Chiclets.

The officers shrugged. She walked over to a glass display case near the door, took a deep breath, and made a dash for it. The officers gave chase, firing their pistols wildly as Celia wove nimbly between families and vendors. ("I ran like a rabbit," she later recalled, and boasted that she could dash through a sugarcane field without rustling a single blade.) Turning a street corner, she sped to an empty lot and crawled into a patch of thorny scrub called *marabú*. The police had lost her.

For nearly ten hours, Celia hid among the spines. In mid-afternoon, she heard army trucks rumble towards the coast and planes roar overhead. This could only mean that Fidel had arrived—more than two days late.

Although there is no proof, it seems likely that Hatuey let Celia escape. Instead of ordering a methodical sweep of the town, he drove to meet her father and warn him to get his daughter out of Cuba. It was the first the septuagenarian Dr. Sánchez had heard that his devoted daughter was mixed up in revolution.

The hipster bartender, Enrique, received no such consideration. Police went to his house, dragged him into the street, and pumped his body with forty-two bullets.

SLIPPING FROM HER hideout at dusk, Celia hitched and walked to a safe farmhouse. It was there that she heard the news over the radio: a group of guerrillas had landed by boat but were intercepted by the army. All were dead, including "the leader, Fidel Castro, thirty years old." His corpse was so pulverized, the announcer said, it could only be identified by documents in the pockets. The next day the headlines in Cuba screamed: FIDEL CASTRO MUERTO. It was Fidel's second death—an echo of the fake Moncada announcement three years earlier. Despite the lack of evidence, the report was accepted by the United Press bureau chief in Havana and made its way to the front pages of world newspapers, including the *New York Times*.

Celia, for one, was convinced the report was false. But three days later, on December 5, came more bad news: the rebels had been ambushed at a remote field called Alegría del Pío. This time there was no doubt that something had gone terribly wrong. Prisoners began to arrive at Santiago jail. Army dragnets were closing in on the survivors. Every day, more savaged bodies of guerrillas were found dumped at the gates of Niquero cemetery, and a rumor spread that the Castro family had been invited to identify Fidel's corpse.

CHAPTER 9

"Now We've Won the War"

(December 5–18, 1956)

FOR HOURS AFTER the December 5 ambush Fidel had remained alone in his cane field near Alegría del Pío, hiding under a pile of leaves, half-choked with smoke and listening to soldiers stomp past on nearby trails. Only as the sun began to set did he risk a glance around. Two other guerrillas were cowering in the same field, and Fidel whistled quietly to get their attention. When they crawled over to join him, they turned out to be Faustino, the former physician, and Universo Sánchez, one of his burly young bodyguards. Their prospects were not promising. Fidel still had his rifle with its telescopic sights, but in the anarchy of the retreat Faustino had dropped his weapon and Universo lost his boots. None of them had saved any food or drinking water.

After shivering through the night, Fidel declared that they would dash to the forest and start hiking to the Sierra Maestra. He got into a whispered argument with the other two, who felt there was still far too much military activity to risk moving. "Damn it, Fidel," Universo finally hissed. "Democratically, it's two against one, so we stay!" It was one of the very few times that Fidel allowed himself to be talked out of anything.

In the end the trio stayed put for five excruciating days. The afternoon heat was asphyxiating; by night they froze in the damp winter air. For sustenance they gnawed on sugarcane and licked morning dew. Fidel muttered incessantly about how the guerrillas would recover from their defeat and regroup in the mountains. Faustino and Universo did not have the heart to contradict him. "Victory will be ours," Fidel kept repeating like a mantra. "We are winning!" Universo recalled thinking, "*Mierda*, he's gone crazy!"

Fidel later joked that in the cane field he was commander in chief of an army of three. Despite his bluster, he slept with his rifle pointed under his chin so that he could shoot himself if they were discovered, ignoring his companions' objection that the gun was far more likely to go off by accident. For his part, Universo was convinced it was only a matter of time before they were discovered by the army, and spent his time carving his name on his rifle butt with a bayonet. He wanted his family to be able to recognize his corpse.

Their patience paid off. On December 10, their fifth day in hiding, they noticed a marked drop in army movement. The trio decided to leave that same night, so the bootless Universo lined his socks with strips of sugarcane husk to protect his feet. (He was so traumatized by the experience that when he was finally given decent boots, he refused to take them off even to sleep.) They crept along slowly, making as little noise as possible, and covered only three miles before dawn. After two more nights of hiking, the bedraggled group spotted the moonlit silhouette of the Sierra Maestra on the horizon. Feeling a little safer, they decided to knock on a farmhouse door. Fidel's luck held. The family had never heard of M-26-7 but were sympathetic: they offered them a delectable meal of roast pork, root vegetables, and the first fresh water they had drunk in a week.

Two nights later, December 14, their prospects improved further when the three made contact with a stocky, powerfully built twenty-seven-year-old campesino named Guillermo García. He had been one of Celia's first rural recruits and volunteered to guide the trio across a highly patrolled road into the sierra proper. They spent nearly twenty-four hours in a culvert near a village, observing guards move back and forth, until García felt the noise of a jukebox and Saturday night partying in a nearby bodega would cover any noise they might make. They then crawled through the drainage pipe over rotting vegetables and mud to the other side.

At last, on the morning of December 16—exactly two weeks after the *Granma* landing, and after marching for eleven hours straight under a gleaming full moon—they saw an idyllic *bohío*, a thatch-roofed shack, nestled among palm trees and coffee terraces. They had reached Cinco Palmas, the home of Ramón "Mongo" Pérez Montano, the baby brother of the patriarch Crescencio Pérez, which Celia had designated as the regrouping point should the guerrillas become separated. Fidel and his men had finally made their way into the bosom of the rural resistance. The twenty-four-year-old Mongo immediately recognized Fidel from photographs and brought the emaciated trio reviving cups of sugary coffee. Before dozing off in a coconut grove, they took off their shoes and socks. Mongo was shocked to see their feet as encrusted with blood as if they'd dipped them in a trough.

To FIDEL'S DISTRESS, Mongo had no news to offer about the fate of the other guerrillas. As far as anyone knew, he and his two friends were the only ones who had escaped the ambush. Then, two nights later, the three were wolfing down pork and fried plantains at Mongo's table when a farmer burst in with the revolution's first concrete piece of good news. Raúl was alive with four companions, and he was only a mile away.

"*¡Concho!*" Fidel exclaimed. "My brother! Where is he? Is he armed?"

The farmer was carrying a letter from Raúl with his Mexican driver's license as proof of his identity. Still, Fidel was wary of an army trap. He sent the campesino back to ask Raúl to write down the names of all the foreigners who had sailed on the *Granma*. A letter soon returned identifying Che Guevara and three others.

Fidel was ecstatic. His rebel army had more than doubled in number, from three men to eight. At midnight Raúl was finally permitted to visit Mongo's house. According to the eyewitnesses, no sooner had the Castro brothers embraced than Fidel wanted to know how many guns Raúl had saved.

"Five," Raúl said.

"Well, we have two!" Fidel exulted. "That makes seven." Then he declared: "Now we've won the war."

The others shot sidelong glances at one another. Despite the litany of disasters, Fidel's Olympian self-confidence had not been dented.

THAT NIGHT, THE new arrivals recounted their own extraordinary survival story, the details of which can be reconstructed from Raúl's meticulous pocket diary from the time. On the night of the ambush, he and his four *compañeros* had stumbled into one another in the forest near the battle site, unaware that Fidel was hiding only a few hundred yards away. They also spent five grueling days in hiding before deeming it safe to leave, with the added aggravation of mosquito plagues. These were Raúl's particular bane: they loved biting his nose, leaving it as swollen, he complained, as Cyrano de Bergerac's. He lay awake at nights, tormented by the thought that his brother had been killed and listening to the land crabs that crashed ghoulishly through the thickets. One morning Raúl was disconcerted to find that the alien creatures had torn to shreds the sleeve of a shirt he had left out.

The five men left their hideout on the same day as Fidel's group and unknowingly followed a parallel route to the Sierra Maestra. At first, Raúl found the mountain range a "magnificent spectacle" in the starlight. He became less enthusiastic when his group became trapped in a dead-end ravine and had to make a tortuous climb out over steep ridges. But soon they were welcomed by friendly peasants who offered food and *café con leche*, often at 3:00 in the morning. Raúl had no money, so he left IOUs to be paid after *la victoria*. ("If we die, [the bearer] can take this document to any official body of the future Revolutionary Government" for cash reimbursement, he wrote.)

On December 18, they knocked on the hut of the farmer Hermes Cardero, who opened the door with a revolver in hand, convinced the group were Rural Guards in disguise. "I really am Raúl Castro, the brother of Fidel!" Raúl kept insisting. When Cardero told him that there were three unidentified guerrillas staying at the nearby Cinco Palmas farm, Raúl excitedly whipped off his letter and added his driver's license to make contact.

THREE DAYS LATER, Mongo's wife opened her door to find eight scarecrow figures dressed in torn peasant clothes. The most abject of all was in virtual rags, she later recalled, missing a shoe and doubled over from a severe asthma attack. It was Che.

This third guerrilla group had also survived by a mix of sheer luck and obsessive caution. After the ambush, the lightly wounded Che hid in a cave with Juan Almeida and three other men. Instead of staying put, they decided it was safer to head east for the Sierra Maestra that same night, using what Che thought was the North Star as guidance. Only when they hit the southern coast two days later did they realize he was completely wrong. On a more encouraging note, they ran into three other lost *Granma* members, including the dashing Camilo Cienfuegos.

The group, now eight, bickered about whether to ask farmers for food. Camilo, a self-confessed hedonist, was "as hungry as a piranha," as the saying went, and argued it was worth taking the chance. The more austere Che lobbied for caution. He turned out to be right. On one occasion they all crept up to a hut and heard music inside. It was an army platoon drinking to the victory at Alegría del Pío. Another night, they spotted a farmhouse nestled by a lovely river mouth. When Che went to investigate, he almost ran into a soldier with a carbine. They had found themselves in Boca del Toro, where the treacherous Manolo Capitán had delivered ten rebels up for execution only a few days earlier. Skirting the site, the eight climbed down to a desolate beach where Camilo chased crabs and devoured their flesh raw.

Their group's luck improved dramatically on December 12 when the family of a Seventh-day Adventist pastor took the famished rebels in and provided them "an uninterrupted festival of food," as Che put it, although with predictably dire digestive results. ("In a flash, eight unappreciative intestines gave evidence of the blackest ingratitude.") As word spread of their presence, curious campesinos came from all around to meet the exotic rebels. One woman brought candy and cigars as welcome offerings to the "saviors of Cuba" she had expected for so long, but when she set eyes on the men, they looked so pathetic that she burst into tears. The embarrassed Che accepted the gifts and boiled her a cup of coffee, "since she was so moved to see us."

The group now decided to change into peasant clothes and bury their few guns so they could travel incognito; only the leaders, Che and Almeida, kept pistols. As they meandered on, Che began to be racked by asthma and the others had to help him walk. It would take another nine days before they reached Mongo's refuge. But Fidel's initial delight at seeing them quickly turned to fury when he learned that they had left their guns behind. He dressed down Che in front of the other men, even though the Argentine was still barely able to breathe—"To leave your weapons behind was criminal and stupid!"— and angrily gave Che's pistol to Mongo as punishment. His fall from grace was short-lived, but Che would never forget the humiliation of losing favor with his idol.

Slowly the rump of the rebel army was regathering: now they were a force of sixteen men with seven rifles against Batista's cohorts.

As THESE DISPARATE groups were zigzagging the sierra, Celia Sánchez was also still a fugitive. After her escape from the police, she had
managed to dodge roadblocks and walk to her hometown Manzanillo, at one point hiding with friendly prostitutes in a dance hall. She
was still scratched and bloody from her *maribú* hideout; soon a family friend found a doctor to remove thirteen thorns from her scalp.
("Like Jesus Christ's Crown of Thorns," Celia joked.) For the next two
weeks, news about the *Granma* landing was confused and contradictory, but the steady flow of murdered guerrillas did nothing to dent
Celia's conviction that Fidel was still alive. Despite all their bragging,
the army had not produced his body. Hoping for information, she
traveled to Santiago in disguise to meet with Frank, cutting her hair
short and crafting a fake belly from chicken wire to pretend to be
pregnant. Although wanted posters for her were all over the Oriente,
she and her companion Eugenia "Geña" Verdecia joined their bus
driver for coffee with soldiers at a military checkpoint. But Frank had
no news.

It was not until the night of December 18 that Mongo Pérez breath-
lessly appeared at Celia's door with news that Fidel was alive. Celia
turned to her host, Angela Llópiz, and hugged her. "See, Angela, I told
you so," she laughed, and immediately set about finding treats for
Mongo to take back with him to the mountains.

The rebellion was hanging by the barest of threads but somehow
held fast.

Part Two

THE AMATEUR GUERRILLAS

CHAPTER 10

The Kindness of Strangers

(December 1956)

CAMPING IN THE shadowy forests behind Mongo's coffee plantation, Fidel and his fifteen tattered *compañeros* were forced to
take stock of their new reality. It had been a wildly incompetent
start to the grand uprising, and some radical adjustments to their expectations were necessary. None of their training in Mexico had prepared them for the ordeals they had already been through in the
Sierra Maestra: the hunger, the freezing nights, the bursts of torrential rain, the noises in the darkness, the hostile wilderness of slippery
rocks, roots, and mud. In this outdoor endurance test, their learning
curve had already been extreme. Now they had to figure out by trial
and error how to become a functioning fighting force. Over the coming weeks they would embark on a crash course in covert warfare, in
effect creating their own guerrilla rulebook as they went along. These
soft urban intellectuals had to accept that they were dependent on
Celia's rural support network, which she dubbed the "Farmers' Militia," for every aspect of their survival. They relied on the campesinos
to show them the tortuous mountain trails, find them the safest hideouts, and alert them to the movements of Batista's soldiers. Before
long, village girls would volunteer as couriers, carrying rebel missives
folded into tiny squares and hidden, as Celia mischievously explained,

"in a place where nobody can find them." Undercover teams of mules were organized to carry supplies. In the first days a young farmhand even saved Che's life by hiking into town to find asthma medication. Left to their own devices, the rump of the rebel army would have lasted only a few days.

Assisting Fidel's forces involved considerable bravery, since the Rural Guard savagely beat, raped, or executed peasants suspected of rebel sympathies. No sooner had the guerrillas arrived in the Sierra Maestra than soldiers randomly arrested eleven young men near Cinco Palmas and shot them as an example for the whole district. On another typical occasion, soldiers burned down the grocery store of a man known to have supplied food to Fidel with his two young sons trapped inside.

For their part, the guerrillas grappled with their new environment. The mountains would become their "natural habitat," Fidel later boasted. "We identified with the forest as much as the wild animals that live there." But at the time the transition was far from smooth. That first winter, the rebellion was on the verge of being snuffed out daily.

FOR THE FIRST week in hiding, the sixteen malnourished and barely mobile rebels licked their wounds. Food was donated from all quarters. A pig was slaughtered for a fricassee. Universo, a beekeeper by profession, found wild honey. Two of Mongo's relatives, Severo Pérez and his son Omar, brought cooked meals to the camp, including three buckets full of rice, root vegetables, and meat. Raúl could not believe his eyes: "When the revolution triumphs, we are going to make a monument of you carrying those three buckets of food!"

Fidel was not one to dwell on past mistakes; his eyes were firmly fixed on the future. Most of his trusted officers from Mexico had been killed or captured; even his second in command, the lawyer Juan

Manuel Márquez, who had helped save Fidel's life during the ambush, ended up in a shallow grave. Now, in a grandiose flourish, Fidel elevated seven of his fifteen ragtag campmates to officer's rank in what he proudly called the "Re-unified Revolutionary Army," while he himself carried on as if he were already president of Cuba. The survivors, most of whom had been minor figures in Mexico, now by default became key players.

The first order of business was to obtain a deeper sense of the geography around them, since none of the guerrillas had ever seen the Sierra Maestra before, let alone explored it. One thing was soon obvious: Fidel had made a string of mistakes in planning his invasion, but his choice of this theater of operations could not have been better. The same elemental difficulties the rebels faced daily also made these mountains an ideal refuge. The guerrillas had slipped into a self-contained and primitive world with almost no roads, hospitals, or schools. Even today it is an empty and rarely visited place. The 150-mile-long Sierra Maestra range rises steeply from the Caribbean in jagged folds like a tropical Big Sur. The most spectacular and isolated stretches are around Pico Turquino, which at 6,469 feet is Cuba's highest mountain; the surrounding valleys are home to nearly impenetrable swathes of rain forest whose canopies teem with fantastical wildlife—frogs the size of thumbnails and snails as big as basketballs, darting lime-green lizards, and huge dragonflies with transparent wings.

The Sierra Maestra also offered a built-in reservoir of potential support. For generations its denizens had lived as refugees within their own country. Many had been evicted from their homes in the lowlands by the Rural Guards and escaped into this lawless hinterland where they could squat on small plots and subsist on coffee and marijuana crops or raise a few cattle and pigs. Their settlements were thinly spread—only 60,000 lived in the vast area, in hamlets connected only by mule tracks—but news could travel across the mountains with miraculous speed, transmitted by word of mouth along a grapevine nicknamed "Radio Bemba." The farmers were known as *guajiros*, the Cuban version of hillbillies, and were the butt of jokes among the sophisticates of Havana for their backward ways and slurred, incomprehensible dialect. This contempt, shared by many of Batista's army officers, would prove to be a gross underestimation.

Sleepy Manzanillo, where Celia was headquartered, was the easiest town to reach from the sierra and would become the guerrillas' main supply point. After delivering the news there that Fidel was alive, Mongo returned in his old jeep with a care package from Celia, including new uniforms, boots, and tinned food for Christmas. There was also much-needed cash and ammunition: Mongo brought along a female passenger, the adventurous young Geña Verdecia who had accompanied Celia on her nail-biting bus trip into Santiago; she now smuggled three hundred bullets and nine sticks of dynamite under her voluminous skirt. (Geña would help look after the crumpled rebels with such affection that the men nicknamed her "the Angel.")

Che was now forgiven for failing to keep his weapons and given one of the prized new rifles with telescopic sights—"a jewel," he swooned in his diary. Also included in this first revolutionary shipment from Celia were books: the guerrillas never neglected intellectual nourishment. One of the men, Calixto Morales, had been a teacher in his former life, so he led reading and writing classes for illiterate campesinos in his spare time, while the "multifaceted" Che tried his hand at algebra and began teaching French to Raúl. The Argentine also took up the habit of smoking cigars to keep the mosquitoes at bay, despite his ongoing asthma attacks.

Essential though local farmers were, the guerrillas had to be wary of informers. They knew they had been betrayed by their guide at Alegría del Pío, and many of their comrades had without doubt been sold out to the army after the landing. Their presence at Mongo's farm was kept a closely guarded secret; the few who knew were told that *chivatos*, "stool pigeons," would face "revolutionary justice" and be executed.

Still, the men began to feel vulnerable. Some nights they could hear drunken soldiers shooting in the distance. On December 21 officers drove nearby in a jeep and two rebels hid just in time. Fidel moved the camp to a more private coffee field, where he concocted some nerve-wracking training drills. One morning he rushed among the hammocks shouting: "We're surrounded! Take your positions to fight!" The men started firing wildly at the bushes, but no attack came. Fidel explained that it was just a test to keep them on their toes. He soon decided that even this new camp was too close to civilization. They would have to hide in the deep sierra.

The group spent a festive Christmas Eve dining on roast piglet and wine, aware that it would be the last decent meal they might enjoy for months. When they broke camp next morning, Fidel neatly handwrote a document for Mongo expressing the guerrillas' gratitude for saving their lives: "We don't know how many of us will fall in the fight, but below are the signatures of all, as proof of our infinite thanks." Carefully signed by each of the men, it became as cherished a founding document in Cuba as the American Declaration of Independence.

RAÚL'S PERSONAL WAR journal gives the most lyrical account of this first foray into the wild. He took time out to admire the lavish beauty of the sierra, marveling one morning at an enveloping fog—"I never believed that I would see such a dense cloud in Cuba"—or pausing to note a delicate pink flower called *el búcare*. But nature was more often an enemy. On their first afternoon—Christmas Day—the mule tracks petered out and the guerrillas were forced to hack their way cross-country with machetes. Every step became a battle. A downpour hit as they climbed a steep hillside, making them slide back in the mud almost as far as they advanced. It took four hours to cover four hundred yards, the hiss of whispered curses drowned out by the thundering rain. New Year's Day, 1957, was even more dispiriting. Caught in another freezing ninety-minute storm, the men had only enough ny-lon to keep their rifles and knapsacks dry as they huddled in the for-est. "Truly, these are the saddest moments so far in guerrilla life," mourned Raúl, "to be soaked without any protection at all." At dusk the drenched rebels ("chilled to the bone") discovered an abandoned farmhouse, where they laid out sacks of maize as rudimentary mat-tresses and spent the night kept awake by howling winds and pesky rodents.

Life *en plein air* involved endless annoyances. Men tripped and broke their spectacles. One chipped his knee and was forced to drag himself along in agony. Others suffered ankle twists or cramps or came down with fevers. Raúl caught a bad cold, which he tried to treat with herbal tea from a local plant, *cañasante*. Although he attended to the men's maladies as medic, Che himself seemed like a colossal liability. When he wasn't suffering from asthma, he was hit with malaria at-tacks. The other men would have to carry his pack or drag him along with encouraging cries of "Come on, you Argentine son-of-a-bitch! Walk, or I'll give you the butt of my rifle." Meanwhile, Fidel's boots fell to pieces. He painstakingly sewed the soles and leather uppers back together with metal wire so they looked "like open-mouthed croco-diles."

On the positive side, they were joined by three more stragglers from the *Granma*, each of whom had dodged bloodcurdling close calls. That made eighteen veterans in the Sierra Maestra, plus Fidel; eventually, two more would stagger to safety. Thanks to the to-and-fro of the initial group, the precise count has been surprisingly vague, but a detailed study by the Cuban historian Heberto Norman Acosta reveals that of the eighty-two men who landed, twenty-one made it to the mountains; twenty-one were killed by the army; twenty-one were imprisoned; and fourteen managed to escape entirely and rejoin M-26-7 elsewhere. Five are unaccounted for, probably murdered. However, in a rich piece of propaganda, the journalist Carlos Franqui would one day write a book about the survivors in the sierra called *The Twelve*, choosing a number to evoke the Apostles.

Food remained an obsession, and all the guerrillas' diaries document their diets as closely as any gourmand's memoir. Raúl went into paroxysms of delight when a campesino brewed up fresh coffee for breakfast, usually with a plate of bland peeled taro. (Many years later, Felipe Guerra Matos was asked to sum up the war. "*Mucha malanga*," he laughed. "Lots of taro.") Che recalled that the unexpected discovery of a can of four sausages led to "one of the greatest banquets I have ever attended." There were attempts at culinary creativity. One night, Efigenio Ameijeiras boiled beans and banana with wild garlic and cilantro for flavor. Raúl came up with a delicacy he called *chorizo à la guerrilla*, "sausage guerrilla-style," sautéing a single diced wurst in three tablespoons of honey, a squeeze of lemon, and a dash of Bacardi rum. Other experiments were less successful. After purchasing a scrawny cow, Che tried to prepare an Argentine-style *asado*, or barbecue. He stretched out the carcass on sticks like a crucifix as was done back home in Buenos Aires but couldn't find enough dry wood for a decent fire; some of the meat ended up raw, other parts charred. The next day the remains were maggoty, but the guerrillas ate it anyway. ("Only one man vomited," Raúl noted.)

If they were lucky, a marksman might shoot a wild pig, although it, too, had to be prepared carefully. On one occasion, an undercooked pork dinner provoked food poisoning, thanks to parasites. Nausea and diarrhea struck the men in unison the next day. They dubbed the site La Loma de la Cagalera, "the Shitting Knoll."

ON JANUARY 5, after twelve straight days of hiking, the guerrillas hacked through some vines to see Pico Caracas rising on the horizon. It was an awe-inspiring sight. The second-highest mountain in Cuba rose 4,186 feet above deep emerald-green ridges, which rippled before them like waves in the ocean. Fidel was elated: "If we make it there, nobody will be able to defeat us," he declared. "Not Batista, nor anyone else!"

Once again, the other men shot sidelong glances. They were getting used to Fidel's delusional declarations, but this was more egregious than usual. So far the revolution had offered nothing but cold, hunger, and pain.

The young Fidel was an excellent athlete in high school; the American sports of basketball and baseball were his favorites. COURTESY OF OFICINA DE ASUNTOS HISTÓRICOS, HAVANA

Fidel the budding lawyer making a rhetorical point at the dinner table, circa 1952. From the moment he went to university in Havana, he lived and breathed politics.
COURTESY OF OFICINA DE ASUNTOS HISTÓRICOS, HAVANA

The first known photograph of Fidel together with the wandering Argentine medic, Ernesto "Che" Guevara, sharing a Mexico City jail cell in 1956.

Frank País, the student teacher who became the top revolutionary organizer in Santiago; he was the first heartthrob of M-26-7, and one of its first martyrs. His murder would haunt those who knew him all their lives.

Granma, the leaky pleasure cruiser Fidel purchased from
a retired American dentist in Mexico City for his amphibious
landing in Cuba. For the eighty-two men squeezed on
board, the week-long voyage was an agonizing ordeal.
COURTESY OF OFICINA DE ASUNTOS HISTÓRICOS, HAVANA

The only known photograph of *Granma's* arrival in
eastern Cuba on December 2, 1959. According to
Che, it was "less an invasion than a shipwreck."
COURTESY OF OFICINA DE ASUNTOS HISTÓRICOS, HAVANA

Codenamed "Norma," the doctor's daughter Celia Sánchez was the key organizer behind Fidel's rebellion; a copy of her meticulous accounts from the uncertain first days after Fidel's landing.

COURTESY NANCY STOUT

The most influential photograph of the Cuban revolution: in February 1957 *New York Times* reporter Herbert Matthews hiked into the Sierra Maestra to prove that Fidel was alive and well, contrary to the dictator Batista's claims.

HERBERT L. MATTHEWS PAPERS,
RARE BOOK AND MANUSCRIPT
LIBRARY, COLUMBIA UNIVERSITY

When Fidel met Celia: the guerrilla leader shows off his beloved Swiss rifle with telescopic sites to Celia Sánchez (center), beginning one of history's great revolutionary partnerships. Haydée Santamaría stands on the left.

COURTESY OF OFICINA DE
ASUNTOS HISTÓRICOS, HAVANA

While the guerrilla war was brewing in Cuba's remote eastern province, Oriente, the capital Havana continued as one of the great "sin cities" of the Western hemisphere, rivaling Paris in the 1920s and Shanghai in the 1930s.
AUTHOR'S COLLECTION

Fidel's prime-time debut: NBC cameraman Wendell Hoffman prepares to film on Mount Turquino; journalist Robert Taber is out of the shot.
COURTESY OF OFICINA DE ASUNTOS
HISTÓRICOS, HAVANA

Fidel and Che in the early "nomadic" days of
the guerrilla war, when the harried handful
of men were forced to change camp every night.

Juan Almeida, the
poetry-loving former
bricklayer from Havana
who rose from the ranks
to be one of Fidel's top
commanders; his journal
reveals the loneliness
and tensions of guerrilla
life in its early days.

Camilo Cienfuegos (in helmet) and Fidel say good-bye to two of
the teenage American runaways from Guantánamo Bay naval base
who joined the guerrillas. The third, Chuck Ryan (in middle),
stayed on for several months to fight alongside the Cubans.

Che had a sentimental side,
and could be obsessively
fond of animals. When he
was forced one day to
order a whining pet puppy
be strangled to avoid
detection by an army
patrol, he was devastated.

Death of a *chivato*—an informer. The US photographer
Andrew St. George traveled with Fidel on several occasions
during the guerrilla war to capture such intimate scenes,
including the trial of turncoats and bandits, and this execution.

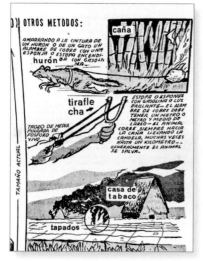

Arson 101: Leaflets distributed by
M-26-7 agents in late 1957 offered
practical tips on how to torch
agricultural fields using homemade
fire bombs, slingshots and (bizarrely)
phosphorous balls tied
to the tails of rodents.

Guerrillas took unexploded, US-made
bombs dropped by Batista's air force and
converted them into lethal land mines.
American permission for Cuban planes
to refuel at the naval base in Guantánamo
Bay before bombing civilians would long
be a sore point with Cubans.

New Year's Day, 1958: Che's whimsy. Thirteen months into the guerrilla war, he posed for the holiday with his men at El Hombrito camp. At this stage, he and Fidel believed the fight would continue for years.

Celia Sánchez and Vilma Espín in *Paris Match* magazine. The high society beauty Vilma, on right, was "burned" in early 1958—in other words, exposed as the top M-26-7 agent in Santiago. The daughter of the top lawyer for the Bacardi rum company, she escaped to join Raúl Castro in the Sierra Cristal, and eventually marry him.

Unidentified female guerrilla with sewing machine. Women who joined the macho guerrilla force were often frustrated to be relegated to domestic tasks such as repairing uniforms, cooking, or assisting in the hospital.

Unidentified female guerrilla with pistol. In mid-1958, Fidel created the Mariana Grajales Women's Platoon, a radical breakthrough for feminism in the Western hemisphere.

Party time in the Sierra. The support of local campesinos was crucial for the rebels' survival. While Batista's army raped and murdered its way across the mountains, Fidel's amiable guerrillas were assisted by farmers at every step.

A moment of relaxation: Che shares a joke with Camilo Cienfuegos, a charismatic former waiter and fashion store clerk from Havana who was once described as looking more like a rumba dancer than a guerrilla.

Che in his famous black beret, which he began to wear after his moth-eaten patrol cap, rescued from a dead *compañero*, was lost in the Escambray Mountains. He often traveled by mule thanks to his debilitating asthma attacks.

Aleida March, an M-26-7 operative from Santa Clara who joined Che in the Escambray Mountains. She soon became his aide-de-camp, and later his lover and wife.

The American war photographer Dickey Chapelle spent weeks with the guerrillas in December 1958. Here she captures Fidel in repose, dictating one of his endless letters to Celia. COURTESY WISCONSIN HISTORICAL SOCIETY

Che during the battle of Santa Clara, scene of his greatest victory. His arm was injured when he tripped over a fence during a bombing raid; Aleida (seen at left) gave him her scarf as a sling.
COURTESY OF OFICINA DE ASUNTOS HISTÓRICOS, HAVANA

New Year's Day 1959, as captured by Dickey Chapelle. As word filtered through
Havana that the dictator Batista had fled during the night, M-26-7 agents emerged
with weapons to help secure the capital. COURTESY WISCONSIN HISTORICAL SOCIETY

When Batista fled, American TV host Ed Sullivan rushed to Cuba to interview
Fidel on the eve of his triumphant entry into Havana; tens of millions watched as
Sullivan introduced the guerrillas as "a wonderful group of revolutionary
youngsters" on his hit variety show. PHOTO BY CBS PHOTO ARCHIVES/GETTY IMAGES

Camilo Cienfuegos in high spirits; when he arrived in Havana with three hundred motley *barbudos*, "bearded ones," to accept the surrender of 5,000 soldiers at the Camp Columbia barracks, it was "enough to make you burst out laughing," one observer noted.

Fidel and Che bask in their victory in Havana; their friendship was one of history's great revolutionary partnerships.

Party time: Guerrillas relax at a swank embassy reception in Havana in 1959; the young man with the Afro was one of Che's many teenage sidekicks.

Fidel finally met Cuba's most famous American expat, Ernest Hemingway, at a fishing tournament in 1959 (which the sporty Fidel naturally won). Fidel later confided that he studied Ernesto's Spanish Civil War novel *For Whom the Bell Tolls* for tips on irregular combat.

Guerrillas in New York City. Juan Almeida flirts with waitresses in a Harlem diner in 1960. The revolutionaries, who had abolished all segregation laws in Cuba, were immensely popular with African-Americans as the civil rights movement gained momentum.

Of the many radical Americans who came to visit
Fidel when he decamped to a Harlem hotel in 1960
was Malcolm X; for days, Nation of Islam militants
demonstrated in the streets in support of the Cubans.

The "Heroic Guerrilla." Cuban photographer Albert Korda took a
snapshot of Che during a rally in Havana in 1960. Seven years later, a
print was taken by a leftwing Italian businessman, cropped and
reproduced to become one of the modern era's most ubiquitous images.

CHAPTER 11

First Blood

(January 1957)

IDEL WAS GIVEN a harsh dose of reality a few days later when he met a likable *guajiro* named Eutimio Guerra. The thirty-seven-year-old, who lived as a semi-bandit on the fringes of sierra society, had just returned from a journey to the lowland towns, and Fidel quizzed him for the word on the street.

"What do they say about me?"

"Well," Eutimio shrugged. "They say you are dead."

Fidel was mortified. After six weeks of silence, Cubans were starting to believe Batista's claim that the *Granma* expedition had been wiped out. It was clearly time for the guerrillas to fire their first shots in anger. Going on the offensive would also lift the men's shaky morale, Fidel reasoned. But he had to choose his first target carefully. If an attack failed, they would use up all their ammunition and be defenseless in the wild.

The army maintained a string of isolated garrisons where the Sierra Maestra hit the Caribbean coast, and the most vulnerable was near the village of La Plata, where only ten soldiers were posted with a sergeant. It also happened to be in a corner of the Oriente where military abuses were rampant. A few weeks earlier, six young men suspected of sympathizing with Fidel were tied up, bundled into a

coast guard boat, and dumped several miles out to sea. Only one survived, swimming back to shore after fourteen hours; the others were
never seen again. If nothing else, the guerrillas could expect a well-
spring of sympathy in the scarred community.

SMALL-SCALE THOUGH IT was, the rebels' first skirmish tested
many of the tactics they would follow during the rest of the war. They
slipped into La Plata after dark on January 15 and spent a full day
staking out the army barracks, which was set in another picturesque
tropical setting on a triangular spit of land between the white-sand
beach and a shady river. Questioning some local farmers, they learned
that the soldiers intended to have a party that night with some local
Batista supporters, and that one guest, Chicho Osario, the most murderous and loathed farm foreman of the area, was about to pass by on
the trail.

When the fifty-year-old Osario appeared, he was hardly a menac-
ing sight. The man was blind drunk, waving a brandy bottle, and riding a mule with a barefoot black child. The guerrillas decided to
impersonate Rural Guards to milk Osario for information, and barked
for him to halt.

"Mosquito!" Osario slurred, giving the military password, before
putting in his false teeth.

Fidel relieved him of his pistol and explained that he was on a "special mission" to hunt insurgents in the area. The inebriated overseer
cheerfully rattled off the names of peasants he suspected of rebel
sympathies. When asked what he would do if he ever captured the
rebel leader Fidel Castro, Osario announced that he would "cut his
balls off," adding: "Do you see that .45 you took away from me? I'd kill
him with that same gun." Oblivious to the fact that he was signing his
own death warrant, Osario then showed his captors a promissory
note for twenty-five pesos from Batista's agents, then lifted a leg to
reveal Mexican-made boots. "I got these from one of the *hijos de puta*

we killed," he said, referring to one of the lost men from the *Granma*. Fidel left Osario with two guerrillas, who had orders to execute him once they heard the attack begin.

As the opening salvo of the war, the "Battle of La Plata" might not be confused with a Green Beret assault, but it went off more smoothly than expected. At 2:30 a.m., the rebels crept forward under a full moon to surround the barracks, which was little more than a brick box with a zinc roof. Two bursts from Fidel's machine gun were the signal for the others to open fire. The soldiers inside were completely surprised. When the first barrage stopped, the rebels shouted for the soldiers to surrender. (*All we want is your armaments! Don't be stupid! While Batista and his cronies are robbing without the slightest risk, you are going to die without glory in the Sierra Maestra!*) The offer was answered with gunfire. The rebels lobbed two hand grenades, but they were virtual museum pieces, obtained from Brazilian army surplus, and they failed to go off. A stick of dynamite fizzled as well. Finally, Che and Luis Crespo crept forward to torch a connected hut. It was a storeroom for coconuts and went up like a bonfire, forcing the choking soldiers to spill out with their arms in the air.

The combat had lasted forty minutes; two of the ten soldiers were dead; three more would expire from their wounds. The rebels had not suffered a scratch.

In his diary, Raúl recorded the conversation with the captives—many of whom were even younger than the guerrillas—and although it has a sanctimonious air, it is probably close to the truth.

"Why didn't you surrender earlier?" one rebel asked in exasperation.

"We thought you would shoot us if we did."

"That's what the government wants!" Raúl interrupted. "To foment hatred between us. But at the end of the day we're brothers, and we regret the death of your companions, who are young Cubans just like us. You're fighting for one man, we're fighting for an ideal." Fidel then gave the perplexed captives a formal speech: "I congratulate you. You behaved like men. You are now free. Look after your wounded, and leave whenever you want." The guerrillas had already donated their handkerchiefs and belts to the injured soldiers as tourniquets. To Che's annoyance, Fidel also left them precious medicine, a precedent that would continue throughout the war.

THE REBELS WERE elated by their first taste of victory. There was now a glimmer of hope that Fidel's deranged sense of confidence might actually have some basis. Without a single casualty, they had seized a valuable cache of weapons, bullets, and tinned food—"even rum," Che gloated. For the first time since Alegría del Pío, every man now carried some sort of weapon. This established another guerrilla tenet: wherever possible, they should resupply themselves with munitions seized from the enemy rather than rely on outside support.

But the propaganda effect of La Plata was far greater than its military value. Word of the assault filtered throughout Cuba, providing proof that at least some of the *Granma* expeditionaries were alive and carrying out their promises. Within the Sierra Maestra, the execution of the drunken "exploiter of the people," Chicho Osario, also sent a message to the *guajiros* that generations of cruel mistreatment by landowners would now be avenged.

As they dissolved back into the mountains, the rebels celebrated by washing. Few rivers they had found so far were big enough for bathing, and the perfume of stale sweat permeated their camps. Che was particularly rank, and regained his childhood nickname, El Chancho, "the Pig." He was notorious for an almost total indifference to worldly cares, never brushing his teeth and devouring whatever food was available, even rotten meat. Raúl was more fastidious. When they found a broad, idyllic river surrounded by ferns and waterfalls on January 21, he rejoiced like a schoolboy: "¡*Caray!*" ("Wow!") After a swim, he slept for twelve hours straight.

※

MEANWHILE, IN MANZANILLO, readers of the local gossip columns were enjoying the delicious news that Celia Sánchez, former beauty queen and leading charity organizer, had been arrested as a revolutionary—and, even juicier, she had made a daring escape. Some of the town's most respectable women let it be known that Celia could take refuge in their homes. An old friend of the family named Hector Llópiz (Angela's husband) also volunteered to be Celia's minder, shuffling her from one comfortable abode to the next during siesta hours and giving her a private code name, "the Dove." Much to his annoyance, his charge refused to dress down while in hiding and would even wear loud striped dresses and cat eye sunglasses during "secret" moves.

In this way, Celia was able to operate under the noses of the police. Her account books from this embryonic period of the uprising survive, with itemized purchases for the guerrillas neatly printed out by date. In total, the expenses for December 1956 were $1,956.70 and, for January 1957, $2,094.60. We also have the list for February (boots for Fidel and Raúl, $19; ham, tinned milk, and chocolate, $89.90), coming to a modest $1,756.55. The average monthly cost of the revolution in its first three months was thus roughly $65 a day.

Celia also organized a network of young women who were not full-fledged members of M-26-7 but were inspired by her bravery, her commitment, and her fashion sense. These well-groomed operatives became excellent couriers by manipulating the Cuban macho culture: they would travel with businessmen sympathetic to the Movement, aware that soldiers at checkpoints would never dare to search a lady in the company of a wealthy older gent; to do so would be a sign of disrespect. The women also sewed uniforms, wrote letters of support to the guerrillas, and solicited donations. Perhaps most crucial, female recruits were telephone operators, who could tap into the lines.

On one occasion, Celia was tipped off that police were about to storm her safe house, giving her time to escape using a bed sheet hung from a high rear window.

THE GUERRILLAS' LEARNING curve was far from linear. Despite the modest victory at La Plata, the rebel force had a long way to go before it might be taken for a serious threat to the ruling order. "Our column lacked cohesion," Che complained later; it had no esprit de corps or (worse in his eyes) "ideological awareness." They were also still embarrassingly green. Che's own glorious career nearly ended prematurely when a jittery Camilo Cienfuegos spotted him in the distance wearing an army helmet taken as a spoil of war from La Plata. Mistaking Che for the vanguard of an enemy patrol, Camilo took a potshot at him. Luckily he missed, his rifle jammed, and Che managed to identify himself. Instead of snapping into action, the sound of gunfire prompted everyone else to dive into the bushes.

Their newly found sense of confidence was repeatedly challenged. Early on January 30 the guerrillas were cooking breakfast in a high forest clearing when they heard the drone of airplanes overhead. Bombs whistled down from American-supplied B-26s; the entire landscape was suddenly erupting around them. Their stove was split in two, and the panicked rebels scattered into the jungle. It took them several days to regroup in a cave they had marked for rendezvous, enduring agonizing spells of thirst and hunger that harkened back to the dark days after the *Granma* landing. On the positive side, shell-shocked though they were, the men all managed to hold on to their weapons and meet up safely. Raúl and Che had assumed command of two of the three wandering groups; they were now acknowledged as the most capable leaders under Fidel.

The accuracy of the bombing was suspicious; it was as if the pilot knew their precise whereabouts. As Che noted dryly, it was a "unique display of marksmanship, never again equaled throughout the war."

Finding new recruits was another problem. The first few volunteers from the cities were invariably shocked by just how grueling life in the Sierra Maestra really was. Of nine men who hiked up from Manzanillo to join them in early February, five gave up after only a couple of nights bivouacking in the forest; one man gave the excuse that he had come down with tuberculosis. The handful of campesino volunteers showed more mettle, but midnight desertions plagued the rebel army. Che began to recognize a possible absconder when he saw "the look of a trapped animal" in his eyes. One new recruit cracked up entirely. He began to shout at the top of his voice that "he was being chased by planes and there was no place to hide, no food and no water" and had to be sent home.

To keep new men in line, Fidel made a speech declaring that the death penalty would be meted out for "desertion, insubordination and defeatism." But fleeing into the sierra carried its own dangers: one luckless teenage recruit, Sergio Acuña, ran away only to be captured by the army. He was tortured, shot four times, and hung. When the boy's corpse was discovered, Che coolly noted that "it was a great lesson for our troops."

DESPITE ALL THIS dogged activity in the Sierra, Cubans still had no hard evidence that Fidel himself was alive. The *comandante* decided to take matters into his own hands. He sent a directive to Celia that she should smuggle a journalist from a top-ranking American publication into the mountains for an interview. Celia passed the demand onto M-26-7 agents in Havana, where the *Granma* veteran Faustino Pérez had been sent to oversee operations, and within a few days the proposal was being shopped around. Soon a decision that would change the fate of the revolution was being made in a newsroom in midtown Manhattan.

CHAPTER 12

Back from the Dead

(February 1957)

A T 5:30 PM on Friday, February 15, the telephone rang in a suite of the Sevilla-Biltmore Hotel on the edge of Old Havana. "You will be picked up in an hour," intoned the voice on the line in accented English. "Be sure you are ready." The guest, fifty-seven-year-old *New York Times* journalist Herbert Matthews, had been instructed to dress like a rich American tourist on a fishing holiday—not a difficult task, given his dry academic demeanor. (Matthews's biographer, Anthony DePalma, describes him as "a tall man, thin, half-bald, a simple dresser, silent as a tomb, precise as a Swiss watch.") One of the most famous war correspondents of his generation, Matthews had just finished packing his knapsack with the essentials for the excursion: hiking boots, a warm coat, a small box camera, and a jaunty black newsboy-style cap. His English-born wife, Nancie, who was also going partway on the trip, was unimpressed by the short notice. She was getting ready to dye her hair and said that it was impossible to be dressed in an hour. Matthews reminded her that they weren't going to a ritzy beach resort; they were taking a secret all-night drive with revolutionaries. Fashion was not a top priority.

To Nancie's annoyance, the M-26-7 agents didn't turn up in an hour. Nor in two. To pass the time, the Matthewses walked around the corner to the Floridita bar-restaurant, a favorite of their good friend and Havana resident Ernest Hemingway, to have a frozen daiquiri and a plate of fresh stone crab.

Finally, later that evening, a Plymouth sedan rolled up driven by Javier Pazos, a banker's son turned activist, along with a couple introduced as Marta and Luis. Only later would Matthews learn that the attractive and spruced-up "Marta" was Liliam Mesa, another of the adventurous socialites who had become a Movement supporter. ("The extent to which the women of Cuba were caught up in the passion of the rebellion was extraordinary," Matthews later wrote, "for like all Latin women they were brought up to lead sheltered, nonpublic and non-political lives.") "Luis" was Fidel's old comrade in arms, Faustino Pérez. As the car rumbled onto the dark Carretera Central—the two-lane Central Highway that runs the length of the island—they chatted about the rebellion and sang Cuban songs. Matthews was thrilled at the adventure, Nancie tired and irritable.

The coming weekend would qualify as one of the great turning points of the guerrilla war, as three major dramas unfolded. The first and most famous involved the *Times* reporter. But Fidel had also invited the top leadership of M-26-7, known as the National Directorate, to meet him in the Sierra Maestra to discuss how the rebellion might recover from its disastrous start. Celia would be hiking into the mountains at the same time as Matthews, along with Haydée Santamaría and her new husband, the lawyer Armando Hart, who had both flown in from Havana. Joining them from Santiago would be Frank País and Vilma Espín, a striking young woman who had become a key underground organizer in the city. The twenty-six-year-old daughter of a wealthy lawyer for the Bacardi rum company, Vilma had studied chemical engineering at MIT in Boston and could also serve as an English translator. The high-powered pair from Santiago was also bringing cigars, candy, and ham as presents for the guerrillas; as a cover while they drove to the trailhead, they filled their car trunk with bottled drinks and a boxed cake so they could tell soldiers at checkpoints that they were going to a wedding.

The third great drama that would occur on that fateful weekend is the least known; the guerrillas would stage their first and most traumatic trial, meting out "revolutionary justice" to a traitor in their midst.

MATTHEWS'S JOURNEY, THE modern answer to Stanley's cross-Africa trek to find Livingstone, was the result of convoluted logistical planning. No sooner had Fidel requested an American journalist than M-26-7 agents put out feelers to the only permanent stringer in Havana, Ruby Hart Phillips of the *New York Times*. Phillips was a fast-talking, chain-smoking reporter who burbled with as much nervous energy as a character out of *His Girl Friday* (although, to dodge the rampant sexism of the 1950s, she used a byline "R. Hart Phillips" to obscure her gender). The initial contact was made through a pillar of the Cuban establishment: Javier Pazos's father, Felipe, the former director of the National Bank of Cuba and one of the country's leading economists. When they met, the fifty-eight-year-old Phillips almost blew things immediately. "You have contact with Fidel Castro?" she blurted out in her office, to the horror of Pazos. Luckily, the Batista censor who was posted at the *Times* to monitor telephone calls and cables did not overhear her faux pas.

Phillips understood that it would be a major coup to land the first interview with Fidel. Modern print reporters can only be nostalgic for the power of the press in the 1950s, when eyewitness stories, syndicated around the world, could have enormous impact. But she was worried that Batista would have her deported if she wrote the story herself. Instead, she sent a cryptic cable to the New York office asking to bring in an outsider. Herbert Matthews, who had covered almost every major news story of the twentieth century, was the obvious choice. He had lived in Paris in the 1930s, reported on the Spanish Civil War with his buddy Hemingway, and been imprisoned in Italy during World War Two. What's more, he had a rare interest in Cuban politics. It was Matthews who had written the *Times* editorial marveling at the "mad" *Granma* landing in December.

In Havana, Matthews leapt at the chance to break the story that Fidel was alive. Despite his reserved manner, he was a romantic at heart and felt an urge to lend support to this quixotic "youth rebellion" (as Phillips described it) against the repugnant Batista. But Javier Pazos was visibly taken aback by Matthews's age and apparent frailty. With his tailored suit and a pipe clenched between his teeth, he looked more like a staid Princeton don than a hard-bitten war correspondent capable of hiking into the sierra.

"Will you send for someone from New York?" Pazos asked politely.

"No," Matthews replied tersely. "I'll go myself."

ON THE ALL-NIGHT drive to the Oriente, soldiers at roadblocks took one look at the dapper Matthews and Nancie in her white turban and waved them on. The group spent the next afternoon resting at a safe house in Manzanillo, then, after dark, a jeep driven by Celia's most trusted farmhand, Felipe Guerra Matos, arrived to conduct Matthews and Pazos along the first stretch of the trail. (Nancie remained in Manzanillo; Liliam and Faustino would hike up separately with the other M-26-7 top brass.)

They began their trek into the dripping forest at midnight. According to the driver-guide, Matthews promptly slipped on a rock while crossing a stream and fell. *"El Americano* has fucked up!" Guerra yelled to Pazos. He rushed over and gave Matthews his hand, worried that he had broken a leg or twisted an ankle. But the reporter simply got up with a carefree laugh, his pipe still clenched between his teeth. By good fortune, the knapsack containing his camera had not gone under.

When they reached the rendezvous point, nobody was there to meet them. The Cubans scouted the area for two hours, whistling softly to find their contact, while Matthews sat dozing on a muddy bank until mosquitoes woke him. At last, a new guide materialized from the darkness. It was 5:00 a.m. on the morning of Sunday, February 17, by the time they all arrived at a farmhouse where a small group of guerrillas was waiting for Fidel. The property was considerably lower and more exposed than other rebel hideouts, but Fidel had decided that its relative accessibility made it worth the risk.

The guerrillas laid down a blanket for Matthews to rest in a clearing. Raúl broke the ice by asking "How are you?" in English, but could not understand the American's answer. Luckily, Matthews's Spanish was good from his Civil War days. Over a breakfast of dried crackers and coffee, the men chatted in hushed tones about their lives. Fidel had already briefed them on what to tell the reporter. One man explained that he had volunteered because soldiers had dragged his brother from his home and shot him dead. ("I'd rather be here, fighting for Fidel, than anywhere in the world now," he declared.) Another talked about playing baseball in the US.

Fidel made his appearance in the first rays of dawn like a character in a Western. The bushes parted with a spray of morning dew and he strode into the clearing wearing a fresh set of fatigues and khaki cap, his beloved rifle on his shoulder. By way of introduction, he proudly showed Matthews the weapon's telescopic sights, boasting that he could pick off soldiers with it at 1,000 yards. For the next three hours the interview was conducted in Spanish with Vilma as backup translator. With his instinctive theatrical flair, Fidel crouched by Matthews's side and spoke in a whisper, making every word seem an urgent, intimate confidence.

Fidel stage-managed every aspect of the meeting carefully. In fact, if he had not become a revolutionary, he would have had a stellar career in advertising. He wanted in particular to convince Matthews that the rebel army was far larger and better organized than it was. His eighteen battered guerrillas had cleaned themselves up as best they could, although many still wore torn uniforms and boots held together by wire; one man had to walk sideways so that the reporter would not see that his shirt had no back. In one fine touch, a breathless messenger interrupted the interview with news from the "second front"—which didn't exist. ("Wait until I'm finished," the *comandante* coolly ordered.) Fidel spoke loftily about his various platoons of "ten to forty" guerrillas who were roaming other parts of the Sierra Maestra, although he would not say the exact number "for obvious reasons."

Fidel later said that he carried out an even more outrageous deception, ordering his men to walk in circles through the forest around the camp, changing uniforms as they went, to give Matthews an inflated view of their real numbers. Anthony DePalma, who wrote the most detailed account of the meeting, defends Matthews's reputation: he considers such play-acting "unlikely" given the topography of the farm, although he admits that only Fidel knew the real truth. Still, it hardly seems beyond the realm of possibility. When Fidel declared that the rebels had fifty telescopic rifles on hand, for example, Matthews accepted the exaggeration without question.

Whatever the reason, Fidel's gambit worked. Matthews gained the impression that the rebel army totaled several hundred men across the sierra, which squared with the figures he had heard from Ruby Hart Phillips and US embassy sources in Havana. Part of it may also have been wishful thinking. The older man was drawn to the feisty underdogs in Cuba, just as he had been to the embattled Republicans in the Spanish Civil War. (As Fidel later confided to Che: "The gringo showed friendliness and didn't ask any trick questions.")

As proof that the interview had indeed occurred, Matthews asked Fidel to sign his notes. The signature still survives on a trimmed piece of paper in the Columbia University archive: a single carefully penned line, *Fidel Castro, Sierra Maestra, Febrero 17 de 1957.* Matthews then asked a rebel soldier to take a photo of them both. He flew with Nancie back to Havana, where they dined with their celebrity friends Ernest and Mary Hemingway at the Finca Vigía, the writer's "lookout house" on the rural fringe of the city. In a cab to the airport the next morning, Matthews debated the best way to get his notes through Cuban customs. If the officers saw Castro's signature, the pages would be confiscated. Nancie offered to smuggle them in her girdle. After take-off, she slipped into the plane's restroom to remove them. Matthews began writing his story on board.

THAT SAME HISTORIC weekend saw a meeting that would prove just as significant for the revolution. It had occurred not long after dawn on Saturday, as Celia was climbing up a mountainside with Frank País—she wearing a white shirt and slacks, he in full battle regalia of khakis, rifle, and helmet. As they groped through light fog, they ran into Fidel and his bodyguard Ciro Redondo. It was the first time Fidel had met the legendary "Norma," whose rural support network had saved his life. Thus began one of the great collaborations of revolutionary history, whose importance has been forgotten in the loving attention given to, say, the bromance of Fidel and Che. Sadly, nobody recorded the conversation between Celia and Fidel that morning, so we don't know whether there was an instant attraction. However, a lovely photograph survives of Fidel showing Celia his pride and joy, his telescopic rifle. A gun aficionado herself, she is looking on with genuine delight. The slender, dark-haired "doctor's daughter" was in many ways the perfect match for Fidel: seven years his senior, she was entirely comfortable with the outdoor life and (more importantly) she shared Fidel's monomania for the cause.

In late afternoon, Fidel began the M-26-7 summit meeting in a makeshift hut. Celia, Raúl, Che, Vilma, and Frank were now joined by the Movement's other top leaders, including Haydée, Faustino, and Armando Hart. Many were old friends who had not seen one another since the Mexico days. "Hugs exchanged, general happiness," Raúl noted in his diary. "We passed a very happy day eating the candies they had brought us." The meeting of Fidel and Celia was not the only incipient romance at the picnic. Raúl briefly notes the presence of "V-A Espina" (Vilma Espín), "the friendly *santiagueña* who has been so useful to the Movement."

She would later become his wife, but at the time, Vilma was more interested in meeting the mysterious leftist doctor Che Guevara, whom she and the others had assumed was in his forties or fifties because of his education and breadth of experience.

"Let me look at your face," she recalled saying to the Argentine. "Ah . . . but . . . you are a very young man. How old are you?"

Che said he was twenty-eight.

"We all thought you would be an old man! You don't have an Argentine accent."

"That's because I'm international," he joked.

Vilma couldn't help noticing that Che's trousers had become unstitched at the crotch and revealed his underpants. She and the other women got to work patching them on the spot. Che made his own observations of the group in his private journal. For a start, he noted that the candies Celia brought the guerrillas "provoked, naturally, a series of indigestions." He also wrote that he was impressed by Celia and Vilma, but with a dire lack of chivalry dismissed the socialite Liliam Mesa as little more than a guerrilla groupie: she was, he thought, "a great admirer of the Movement who seems to me to want to fuck more than anything else."

Pleasant though the reunion was, both Frank and Celia were shocked by the shape of the rebel army. As far as they could see, the tiny force was a grimy shambles, and there was an excellent chance that Fidel would be trapped and killed. Over a dinner of chicken stew, rice, and *malanga* root, the pair tried to convince him to give up the armed struggle and start afresh in Mexico. They were startled by Fidel's response: "We only need a few thousand bullets and a reinforcement of twenty armed men and we'll win the war against Batista!" They were dumbfounded by his confidence, but Fidel refused to budge. He insisted that to leave the sierra now would make the Cuban people lose faith in him. Frank and Celia reluctantly agreed to equip new recruits and funnel them up from Manzanillo.

Privately, they still had their concerns. Fidel was disorganized, capricious, and petulant. Celia in particular was astounded to learn that he stomped on his spectacles whenever he flew into a rage; the sheer logistics of replacing them made such lack of self-control bizarrely childish. Frank was also worried by the obvious lack of discipline in the army. Even their weapons were filthy with mud and grease. While they were chatting, he started to casually clean their guns, a silent rebuke that the guerrillas took to heart.

But most dangerous were Fidel's lapses of judgment, Frank felt. He trusted people too easily.

FRANK'S OBSERVATION WAS borne out by the third drama of that pivotal weekend, the trial of the peasant guide, Eutimio Guerra. Short, wiry, and brimming with good cheer, Eutimio had been a favorite with Fidel and his men ever since he had first welcomed them to his farm near Pico Caracas, plied them with suckling pig and coffee spiced with cognac, and let them sleep in his cockfighting arena. He seemed the very embodiment of the "noble peasant" who was going to carry the revolution to victory, and soon became their trusted full-time guide. Fidel particularly admired Eutimio's almost supernatural ability to slip through enemy lines and return with such treasures as condensed milk, cigars, and working flashlights.

The guerrillas never seemed to notice that Eutimio's absence coincided with a string of unlucky incidents, including the bombardment that had almost decimated them on January 30. Fidel's suspicions were only aroused by accident when a farmer reported that he had seen 140 soldiers gathered nearby and casually added that Eutimio was with them. Incredulous, Fidel realized that the army was perilously close to surrounding their camp. Seconds later, bullets began to whistle around them. A recruit standing next to Fidel was shot in the head and killed instantly. In the desperate rout that followed, Che lost his medicine, his books, and even his rifle. The guerrillas remained on the run for four days.

Eutimio's road to betrayal had in fact begun in late January, when he was arrested by the army and offered an unenviable choice: they would either hang him from the nearest tree or give him a reward—$10,000 cash plus prime farmland—if he would turn informer. Choosing the latter, Eutimio became responsible for the guerrillas' run of "bad luck." The air attack of January 30 had been eerily accurate because he was in the spotter plane, pointing out their exact location to the pilot. Eutimio also came shockingly close to murdering Fidel. On one unusually cold night, he slept alongside the *comandante* in a hut and even shared his blanket, with his pistol resting inches from Fidel's head. Che later blamed Eutimio's "cowardice" for not pulling the trigger. More likely, Eutimio knew that he would not escape alive if he murdered Fidel in a camp surrounded by sentries.

Now, a few hours after Matthews left on Sunday the 17th, a guerrilla ran into camp yelling, "The prick! The prick! The prick is here!" Eutimio was hiking towards them, oblivious to the fact that his betrayal had been exposed. The rebels pretended to greet him warmly until the muscular Ciro Redondo gave Eutimio a bear hug from behind and refused to let go, while another man disarmed him. "But what's going on?" Eutimio said. "Have you gone crazy?" When they frisked him and found two pages folded in his breast pocket, the peasant visibly paled. "Don't read those," he begged. "Shoot me first." They were safe conduct passes issued by the army.

Eutimio was brought before the assembled guerrillas in handcuffs for the first revolutionary trial in the Sierra Maestra. Standing in an open field, Fidel cross-examined him; then Ciro launched into a sermon in the tone of a wounded friend, explaining the pain his betrayal had caused. The death of their *compañero* in the army ambush meant that mercy was impossible. Heavy clouds had gathered; now light rain turned into a thunderstorm. Fidel ordered the death penalty but did not choose an executioner. Instead, he simply walked away to get out of the rain under a tree. The other rebels fell into awkward silence; nobody was willing to carry out the sentence.

It was Che who finally stepped forward. "The situation was uncomfortable," he noted in his diary, "so I ended the problem giving [Eutimio] a shot with a .32 in the right side of the brain." He clinically added that the "exit hole" was on "the right temporal [lobe]." Lightning was crackling so loudly that the gunshot was drowned out. The execution, biographer Jon Lee Anderson notes, was one more element in Che's growing mystique. He already had a reputation for reckless bravery, as if to compensate for his asthma. Now he was displaying a ruthless clarity of vision. From that moment forward, it was Che who would cold-bloodedly enact the most difficult decisions.

But Che was more shaken than he let on. In his diary he records what seems like a hallucination: as he was trying to take a watch from Eutimio's belt, he heard the dead man say to him: "Yank it off, boy, what does it matter?" Che also records of that night: "We slept badly, wet, and I with something of asthma." It was the start of a respiratory attack that would last ten days. In public, Che kept up more of a front. As he later wrote of the incident in the rebels' underground newspaper, the "timid stage of the revolution" was at an end.

ON FEBRUARY 24TH, Herbert Matthews's story was splashed across the front page of the Sunday *New York Times:* CUBAN REBEL IS VISITED IN HIS HIDEOUT. Its first line set the positive tone: "Fidel Castro, the rebel leader of Cuba's youth, is alive and fighting hard and successfully in the rugged, almost impenetrable fastnesses of the Sierra Maestra . . ." For M-26-7, it was a PR triumph of the first order. Readers learned that Batista's elite troops were locked in "a thus-far losing battle" with the guerrillas, while Fidel himself was painted as a cross between Pancho Villa and James Dean. He was "quite a man—a powerful six-footer, olive-skinned, full-faced," Matthews wrote, whose "brown eyes flash." Matthews's compliments pile up: "The personality of the man is overpowering"; Fidel displays "extraordinary eloquence." He is also the very picture of idealism and moderation. "Above all," Fidel is quoted as saying, "we are fighting for a democratic Cuba and an end to the dictatorship." He then assures *Times* readers that he and his men harbor "no animosity towards the United States or the American people." Matthews was not entirely uncritical, noting that Fidel had little grasp of economic issues and was no military genius. But the conclusion was resounding: "From the looks of things, General Batista cannot possibly hope to suppress the Castro revolt."

It was an astonishing plug for an eighteen-man army that had only one minor victory to its name. The story and its two follow-up articles were a resounding blow to the dictator, making a mockery of his claims that Fidel was dead and that the Sierra Maestra was encased in a "ring of steel" through which no rebels, let alone middle-aged foreign journalists, might pass. Government censors tried to block the story within Cuba, cutting the piece by hand with scissors from every copy of the *Times* on sale. But the story had its own life and was smuggled onto the island. Movement supporters in New York made over 3,000 copies and mailed them to every address in the Havana social registry. Translations into Spanish were eagerly pored over and passed hand-to-hand from university halls to restaurant kitchens. (The only guerrillas who may have been less than thrilled were Raúl, who was dismissed as "slight and pleasant," and Juan Almeida, whose name was misprinted as "Ameida" and was unflatteringly described as "a stocky Negro" with a "ready brilliant smile and a willingness for publicity." The story was so widely read that a girl in a remote sierra village would later compliment Almeida on being more svelte than El Señor Matthews had reported).

Batista then managed to make himself look even more foolish when he ordered his minister of defense to denounce the article as a fabrication. Because no photo had been published showing Matthews and Fidel together, the meeting was merely "a chapter in a fantastic novel." The next day the *Times* duly printed a shot from Matthews's camera, showing Fidel lighting a cigar next to the journalist, who was poised in his black overcoat and newsboy cap, notebook in hand.

In one stroke Fidel and his fortunes had been resurrected. From now on he would be seen as a romantic hero, the Robin Hood of Cuba, while Batista was typecast as a lying buffoon. One New York magazine would later run a cartoon of Fidel with a caption taken from one of the newspaper's most famous slogans: "I Got My Job Through the *New York Times.*" The ever-thoughtful Celia sent a thank-you note to Ruby Hart Phillips in a hand-woven basket lined with mountain moss and adorned with orchids.

CHAPTER 13

Havana Vice

(Spring 1957)

T HE INTERNATIONAL SPLASH caused by the *New York Times* story
was both inspiring and threatening to other Cuban revolutionaries. Fidel was now the public face of opposition to Batista. But the
26th of July Movement remained only one small part of the rich pageant of Cuban subversive activity: the island was seething with underground organizations plotting to seize power. There were armed
cadres around the universities; factions jockeying within the military
(one group at the naval base of Cienfuegos planned mutiny); exile
paramilitaries scheming in the United States. None of this was coor-
dinated or even very consistent. In Miami Beach, the bitter ex-president Prío dipped into his millions to fund almost any conspirator who
knocked at his penthouse door. The Cuban Communist Party, meanwhile, displayed an unexpected indifference to any form of violent
insurrection; its officials regarded Fidel as a middle-class dilettante
and snootily dismissed his revolt as "adventuresome."

There was even a fissure within the ranks of M-26-7 itself. The
members in Havana and the lowland cities formed a faction dubbed El
Llano, "the plains," and they had very different ideas on how to seize
power than the guerrillas in the mountains (dubbed La Sierra).

Nobody seriously believed that Fidel and his motley crew could overthrow Batista's military machine by themselves. His impact on Cuban politics was still symbolic at best. A national strike seemed far more potent—but even that, from the viewpoint of Havana, was a stretch.

To the casual observer, the cosmopolitan capital was untouched by the discontent that was growing elsewhere in Cuba. American tourists flocked in record numbers to the "Pearl of the Antilles," which had become shorthand for decadence and erotic pleasure, much as Berlin had been in the '20s or Shanghai in the '30s. To the rum-soaked partygoers, Fidel and his men might as well have been in the Himalayas. For $68.80, Americans could take "party flights" direct from Miami to Havana with live mambo bands and complimentary pink daiquiris on board; shuttles would then speed them from the airport to the buzzing Tropicana nightclub to admire the *diosas de carne*, "goddesses of flesh," and luxury casinos owned by the likes of Meyer Lansky, "the Jewish godfather." Even a normally astute observer like the English novelist Graham Greene found himself seduced by Havana's louche sensuality. Greene was a particular fan of the raunchy Shanghai Theater in Chinatown, where long-legged dancers threw themselves at the audience "like a nudist camp gone berserk," and the legendary Superman would line up twelve silver dollars to measure his impressive *chorizo* on stage, then perform live sex acts. Like most foreign visitors, Greene never lost sleep over Batista's nightmarish terrorism or the distant sound of police sirens and bombs going off in the night.

Only occasionally did political violence intrude on the holiday idyll. Not long before Fidel landed in the *Granma*, a top SIM officer was gunned down while leaving a Mario Lanza concert in Havana, and some panicked tourists injured themselves when they ran into mirrors trying to flee. A month later, on New Year's Eve, a bomb went off in the Tropicana cabaret and a Cuban teenage girl lost her arm. (The owners later alleged that she was carrying the explosive herself and it went off accidentally.) But the most dramatic act of revolution in Havana was brought about in late March by Fidel's main political rival, a twenty-four-year-old architecture student named José Antonio Echeverría, who was head of the radical Directorio Revolucionario, "the Revolutionary Directorate," or DR. Peeved by the *Times* article, Echeverría decided to steal Fidel's thunder with a daring plan: he would stage an armed attack on the Presidential Palace in the center of the city and gun down the dictator. This would not only decapitate the regime, he reasoned, it would eliminate M-26-7's very raison d'être.

José Echeverría ranks high on the roster of Cuba's unlikely revolutionaries. A plump, jovial figure, he stood out on campus for his devout Christian faith and refined fashion sense. He had such rosy cheeks that he was nicknamed La Manzanita, "Little Apple," but to his student followers he was known more often, with great affection, as El Gordo, "Fatty." Clever and charismatic, he had no problem luring conspirators—almost all of them students, with the odd artist thrown in—to his ambitious assault. Perhaps unsurprisingly, the result was as haphazard as if a bunch of Stanford PhD candidates decided to assassinate the US president today. On the afternoon of March 13, more than eighty armed DR members set off in cars for the Presidential Palace. One, Faure Chomón, recalled the world moving as if in slow motion as he drove in busy traffic down La Rampa, "the Ramp," the boutique-lined stretch of 23rd Avenue that descends from the upscale Vedado district to the ocean. He was fascinated that the shoppers and tourists were going about their business entirely oblivious to the firestorm that was about to erupt in the city. Chomón and his friends were openly carrying rifles and grenades, but the pedestrians who saw them assumed they were secret policemen. Inside a red truck marked FAST DELIVERY, two dozen other students were squeezed together in suffocating heat. Echeverría, perspiring profusely, took off his favorite jacket and joked that he didn't want to see it riddled with bullet holes.

Just after 3:00 p.m., Batista's guards at the Palace—an over-the-top neoclassical pile from 1920 whose decorations were created by Tiffany's of New York—were surprised by cries of "Long Live the Directorate!" followed by a barrage of wild gunfire. The students burst into the marble-lined interior and started shooting their way up the broad staircase. Things went awry from there. Many of the assailants' guns proved faulty and jammed. Grenades failed to explode. One student had made bombs from seven sticks of dynamite, which "made a terrifying racket," he recalled, but did little damage. Another lost his glasses but grabbed a machine gun anyway and started firing blindly. When a telephone rang, someone picked it up in the middle of the battle. "Yes, it's true, the Palace has been taken, Batista is dead!" he yelled. "We Cubans are free!"

Chaotic though it was, the attack very nearly succeeded. The students fought their way into the Hall of Mirrors, a replica of the Grand Salon in Versailles, and then into Batista's office. Sitting on the dictator's desk was a cup of coffee, still warm. They had missed their target by seconds. On hearing the first shots, Batista had taken a private stairway to the fourth floor and barricaded himself with his bodyguards. The students tried to retreat, but by then tanks had rattled to the scene, and the army launched a counterattack. Many were cut down in the streets; Chomón was shot in the hip; only fifteen escaped. "All I could smell was gunpowder, blood and death," a survivor recalled. "That terrible odor clung to me for two weeks."

Echeverría himself was leading a second attack to seize a popular radio station. He estimated that he would have 180 seconds of air time before he was cut off, so had rehearsed a speech of exactly that length. "People of Havana!" Echeverría boomed. "The Revolution is in progress! . . . The dictator has been executed in his lair!" He finished the delivery on second 181—a feat of timing that the Soviet Russian poet Yevgeny Yevtushenko would later eulogize in his poem "Three Minutes of Truth." But Echeverría was speeding away from the studio in a Ford when the police intercepted him. He was killed in a shoot-out. In total, more than thirty-five of his followers also perished that day, and SIM took the opportunity to arrest, torture, and execute dozens more suspects. One respected politician was simply gunned down, gangland-style, outside his house.

The March 13 attack was yet another bloody fiasco to add to Cuba's list of failed uprisings and elevated the Little Apple into its crowded pantheon of martyrs. It was also a major dent in Havana's reputation as a carefree vacation getaway. In the pitched battle outside the Palace, several bystanders were wounded, and an American tourist—a thirty-eight-year-old office worker from New Jersey named Peter Korinda—was killed by a stray bullet on his hotel balcony. The *New York Times* covered the assault on the front page, reporting that flights to Havana had been canceled, nightclubs were closed, and sidewalks ran red with blood. *Life* magazine published a photo spread showing civilians cowering in doorways as wounded soldiers were carried past Sloppy Joe's bar.

Fidel heard news of the attack on his little transistor radio. He denounced it in a statement as "a useless spilling of blood" and declared that he was against assassination and all forms of terrorism. The life of the dictator did not matter. He was just one man; it was the system M-26-7 was fighting. Still, capitalizing on the bad publicity, supporters in the US printed a leaflet demanding tourists to boycott the island. They reported that the luckless Peter Korinda had not been killed by "a stray bullet" but an armored car that had deliberately pumped two hundred rounds into his room. "Thousands [of Cubans] are being imprisoned and shot daily without benefit of trial," the leaflet summed up. "This regime of terror will have to come to an end soon."

SIX WEEKS LATER, Batista gave a triumphant interview to an Associated Press journalist in his bullet-pocked palace. Sitting behind a new desk in a chamber hung with red and gold drapes, he declared in excellent English that he was no despot. "I think the only dictatorship around here is that which my beloved wife and four sons exert upon me," he chortled. He had only suspended the constitution "to protect the people," he explained, and dismissed Fidel as a "natural criminal" who led only a handful of men. ("I do not understand why he has been compared to Robin Hood as he has been in some newspapers.") When the reporter asked if Batista kept a gun handy after the attack, he laughed, "Why not?" He then pulled a pistol from his drawer and squeezed off four shots. When an alarmed attaché rushed in, Batista revealed that it was a cap gun.

"Just practicing," he giggled.

CHAPTER 14

"The Bitter Days"

(March–April 1957)

MEANWHILE, IN THE Sierra Maestra, the guerrillas were living like desperate nomads. The small band may have become minor celebrities in the US, but in the months after the *New York Times* interview they were changing camp daily, usually after punishing twelve-hour hikes, and often only one step ahead of the army. They were also perilously short of supplies, going without food for days at a time. That the fragile revolt failed to be extinguished entirely was largely due to the efforts of the detail-oriented Celia, who after meeting Fidel threw herself into the task of funneling matériel from Manzanillo to the mountains. In the process, she became "the soul, heart and life of the rebellion," as one of her admirers put it. Privately, Celia longed to be the Movement's first female guerrilla, following in the footsteps of the heroic nineteenth-century Cuban women who had fought for independence, but she could see that her logistical talents behind the scenes were needed far more. The *chicos* in the sierra were full of passion and drive, but they were sorely lacking in organization.

Her top priority was to help increase the guerrillas' sadly depleted numbers. Under orders from Frank, Celia overcame the resistance of macho Cuban males unaccustomed to taking orders from a woman and began creating a secret transit base for new recruits. (Many were

M-26-7 agents who were *quemado*, "burned"—in other words—had their covers blown. Frank also insisted they should be "politically sophisticated.") After a few days of location scouting, Celia stumbled on an unlikely piece of real estate: an abandoned plantation house outside Manzanillo within full view of a busy road and only a quarter mile from a military prison. Like Frank cruising in his flaming-red Dodge, this would be hiding in plain sight. ("Let the soldiers protect us," she joked.) The key attraction was a morass of thorny trees—the same bristling *marabú* that had given Celia refuge when she was on the run from the police. Tall, dense, and hostile, the thicket offered splendid protection, and became known in the Movement as the *marabuzal*—which was also Cuban slang for "a convoluted mess."

The *marabuzal* was soon converted into a barracks Tim Burton might have envisioned. Animal trails were widening into bristling tunnels and clearings into spiky "dorms." By night bats swooped overhead, while a brown boa that could grow ten feet in length, the Majá de Santa María, writhed through the underbrush hunting rodents. No reveille call was ever needed, since hundreds of birds created a cacophony before dawn. Celia herself took up residence in the derelict plantation house nearby, stockpiling uniforms, tinned food, and medicine in her "central warehouse," a drafty upstairs chamber. Like a haunted army surplus store, Celia's stock was updated as the war developed. In one letter smuggled from the sierra, Raúl politely asked her to make sure any knapsacks she bought had straps at least two and a half inches wide, otherwise they would tear apart with the heavy loads, spilling bullets and food into the underbrush.

EXPERIENCING CELIA'S RECRUITING system was a surreal affair, as we can learn from the vivid recollections of Eloy Rodríguez. The fresh-faced nineteen-year-old M-26-7 activist was taking his rooster into a cockfighting ring one morning in early March when a friend tapped him on the shoulder and whispered: "Are you ready to go into the mountains?"

"You can count on me," Eloy replied.

He clearly did not understand the urgency. The police were staking out Eloy's home. He had to leave immediately.

Without saying good-bye to his family, Eloy signed a pledge of allegiance Frank had drafted for all new recruits and was bundled into a waiting car; only later would he learn that the cherubic, snappily dressed woman at the wheel was Vilma Espín, who calmly bluffed her way past a military checkpoint with her upper-class hauteur. (Vilma could often intimidate Cuban men; on one occasion, when her purse containing snapshots of herself and Fidel in the Sierra Maestra was seized by policemen, she shamed them into giving it back without opening it, saying it contained "intimate women's things.") None of the recruits were told where they were going until the last minute—a nerve-wracking adventure for the provincial boy Eloy, who had learned how to dynamite bridges and destroy electricity plants but had never been away from home.

Vilma deposited him at a house outside of Manzanillo, where—of all things—a noisy children's party was underway. As sugar-charged seven-year-olds raced past, a housewife cheerfully presented him with a slice of cake. It was the home of Felipe Guerra Matos, Celia's right-hand man, who hosted parties for his son, Pupi, as a cover for the comings and goings of M-26-7 recruits. As 1957 progressed, the lucky Pupi would sometimes have birthdays three or four times a week. It was "an endless fiesta," Eloy discovered, "where the children, unaware of the dramatic situation they were covering up, delighted in gobbling down sweets and soda."

After dark, Eloy and another volunteer were driven to the ghostly *marabuzal*, where Celia gave them tetanus and typhoid shots by the light of a kerosene lamp. She then lectured them on the difficult task ahead—"You are going to live the life of a vagrant; you have to prepare for the worst"—and left them to hang their hammocks in the dark. But the *marabú* thorns slashed their hands, and the pair decided to sleep on the hard ground. Eloy fought off homesickness, particularly when food arrived the next morning. At first he thought it was a practical joke when he received the daily ration of five spoonfuls of rice, two of *picadillo* (a ham and egg hash), and two slices of yucca. "That's it," the squad leader laughed. "In the sierra, you eat when you can."

Slowly, the number of recruits increased until the thicket was crowded with hammocks. Fidel wanted to return his numbers to the magic eighty-two of the *Granma.* (The figure had such talismanic resonance that veterans of the landing would introduce themselves as "one of the eighty-two.") But the schedule was pushed ahead by the DR's ill-fated attack on the Presidential Palace on March 13, which prompted a burst of army repression all over Oriente. Two nights later, in the middle of a rainstorm, fifty-two men in hand-sewn uniforms with M-26-7 armbands and berets climbed into the backs of two trucks, which lumbered along unpaved back roads until mud slowed their progress to a standstill. Led by Guerra, the men stumbled along dark forest trails overnight until they were finally met by the enigmatic Argentine, Che Guevara. Che gave the new recruits his personal take on the "elementary guerrilla training" he had learned in Mexico. His first lesson—"The most important thing is to shoot them and don't let them shoot at you"—got a big laugh. But the men's high spirits were tempered by the grueling ten-day march that followed, and dashed entirely when they finally met the celebrated Fidel and his main force. The *New York Times* story had led the volunteers to expect a robust army of hundreds, but they found less than twenty guerrillas, all of whom were a sorry sight. "These men had long hair, beards, ripped uniforms, a sack for a backpack," recalled Eloy. "It was a deplorable situation . . . We saw them and our hearts sank to our feet." Even worse, Fidel informed them in his welcome speech that the war might last "five, ten, fifteen, twenty years." Most of them had thought they were signing up for twelve months.

Fidel's veterans were just as unimpressed by the greenhorns. Barely half of the fifty-two recruits had weapons. Their knapsacks were weighed down with "useless" items like towels, and they complained constantly about the discomforts of sierra life. Many even rejected their one daily meal as unpalatable; particularly despised was one of the culinary staples in the mountains, boiled green banana tossed with butter and salt. In his diary, Raúl noted with dry humor that they had also arrived just as "a novelty was added to our guerrilla lives— flea infestations." For the new men, the evening ritual became to take off their clothes and pick for vermin. Still the fleas were not as bad as the *macagüeras*, Raúl thought, flies whose bites would get infected when scratched.

CHE AND JUAN Almeida were impatient to keep up the momentum after the victory at La Plata, and urged another raid; the Sierra Maestra had become so quiet that an army colonel in mid-April told the *New York Times* that the guerrillas had given up the fight. But Fidel felt that the new recruits were still too raw. At this stage, the aim of the Rebel Army (as the men now called it, capitalizing the title) was still simple survival, and with the increase in numbers, food shortages had become critical. The coming weeks would be recalled as the days of *vacas flacas*, "lean cows," a biblical reference to a period of want from the story of Joseph and the pharaoh.

Prized provisions were traded like currency: yucca for sweet potato, chocolate for cigarettes, milk for sardines. Fluctuations in supply could alter the exchange rate. The truly famished might swap an expensive cigar for a single banana skin, which was then sautéed and devoured. The officers and men shared the same rations, which consolidated morale, although the gourmand Fidel flew into a rage when he returned from the field late one night and found the rice and beans he had been expecting for dinner had been eaten. On another occasion he refused a meal because it was poorly cooked, retiring to his hammock, Che noted, "with an air of offended majesty." Fidel begged Celia to send more palatable supplies, "especially the packets of cream-of-pea soup with ham. Each one makes four cups of thick, delicious soup; I received only six packets, we need large quantities."

Training the volunteers progressed slowly. As the column trudged onward, guns would go off accidentally, ammunition was lost, arguments began. Che's biographer Jon Lee Anderson compares the Rebel Army's progress to "an episode in a Keystone cops movie." Che was harshly critical of the new men, but he had his own embarrassments. On one occasion he went on a solo night mission to buy three chickens from a farm and became lost for twenty-four hours. In fact, the spring months of 1957 were for Che "the bitter days," he later wrote. His asthma was aggravated by the lint of hammocks stitched from burlap sacks. He was forced to sleep on the ground, which only made him sicker, until Fidel gave him an upgrade to a high-quality canvas version.

Che's physical condition improved considerably when a rural herbalist supplied him with a local remedy: dried sweet-pea leaf, which opened the lungs when smoked. Many in the rebels' orbit were also marijuana farmers, including a favorite guide named Molinero. The drug had long been part of the sierra's underground economy, although there is no evidence that the guerrillas partook.

IN LATE MARCH the rebels welcomed some memorable recruits: three teenage Americans who had run away from home to bear arms for the revolution. Chuck Ryan, age nineteen, was the oldest and cockiest. The first time he encountered the ramshackle guerrilla force, he walked up to Fidel and asked point-blank in English: "Where's the army?" The exotic trio were all rebellious sons of naval officers at the US base in Guantánamo Bay. The Massachusetts-born Ryan qualified as an elder statesman; the others were Mike Garvey, a fifteen-year-old Brooklynite who styled his hair in an Elvis Presley pompadour, and

Vic Buehlman, described as "a tall husky youth," age seventeen and raised in Virginia. These younger two still attended high school at "Gitmo." They had first heard stories about M-26-7 from Cuban girls while hanging around a beachfront brothel for GIs and became caught up in the adventure. Their first modest act of support was to buy arms from Guantánamo's sports store and smuggle them out of the base in barrels of flour. When they read in the *Times* article that Fidel was gathering reinforcements, they ran away to join up without leaving farewell letters for their parents. (As Garvey later recalled, "We just went off base and we didn't come back. I didn't give a damn.")

Frank and Celia immediately realized the media value of the gringo teens. They were given special treatment in Manzanillo, hosted in a comfortable house, and even permitted to make friends with local youngsters until front-page "missing" photos in local newspapers prompted Celia to have them smuggled into the sierra. When they met, Fidel was unfazed by Chuck's blunt question about his ragtag brigade. "He said, 'This is it,'" Ryan recalled. "'We are all people dedicated to the principle of liberty or death.'" That was good enough for the boys, who were quickly won over by the leader's charm and passion: "He was . . . a revolutionary trying to overthrow an evil dictator. That's what it was all about for me. Good versus evil."

Within days Fidel sent off a promotional package to the *New York Times.* It included a snapshot of the wholesome, all-American youths, wearing their M-26-7 uniforms and berets, and cradling their guns with toothy smiles. An open letter (supposedly from the boys but probably in part dictated by Fidel) asked President Eisenhower not to revoke their US citizenship for joining a foreign army. It included a stilted "special oath": "I am inspired in the same ideals of liberty and democracy that drove the founders of the United States of America to declare their independence on July 4, 1776." This was the same "cause of liberty," the letter pointedly added, that Eisenhower himself had championed in command of the Allied armies in Europe "against the tyranny of the Nazifascist [sic] Axis." The oath devoutly concluded:

"Acting like this, I will serve the destiny of Cuba, America and the world. So help me God."

Over the coming weeks, the Navy brats were popular enough with everyone in the Rebel Army but the medic Che, who felt he was wasting time on "their many maladies." According to Ryan, Fidel would tease them about the aloof Argentine, saying *"Muy malo. Muy malo. Communista!"* They mostly stood guard duty, since the gringo kids were too valuable to lose. After the *Times* ran a story on them, their presence piqued the interest of many in the US, including the CBS TV editors in New York. Print journalism was already becoming passé in 1957; the "new medium" of television was the way of the future, and Fidel would prove to be a natural.

CHAPTER 15

The Revolution Will Be Televised

(April–May 1957)

Herbert L. Matthews was far from the only reporter in Manhattan who sympathized with the underdog; CBS in particular was filled with progressive correspondents drawn to Fidel's cause. The presence of the three American runaways was just the news hook that a roguish television newsman named Robert Taber needed to convince his superiors to send him and a cameraman into the Sierra Maestra. With the cumbersome video equipment, it would be a far more ambitious expedition than Matthews had undertaken, and potentially more dangerous; weeks earlier, two NBC journalists from Birmingham, Alabama, posing as geologists had been arrested by the Cuban military and only released when the US embassy intervened. But M-26-7 was now committed to getting Fidel on the air. The potential PR benefit was enormous: CBS TV was able to reach more than 60 million people with each broadcast, and its radio division at least as many more.

Of the many *yanqui* romantics attracted to Cuba's cause, the wiry thirty-seven-year-old Taber had the most swashbuckling biography.

A tough Chicago kid who had been in and out of reform school, Taber ran away from home as a teenager, riding the rails and taking part in a string of armed robberies in Cleveland. He spent several years in the Ohio state penitentiary and was paroled to serve in the merchant marines during the Second World War—all before he had turned twenty. As a grown-up juvenile delinquent, Taber moved to New York and landed on a career as a freelance journalist as the best way to avoid boredom, working for *Newsday*, the *Brooklyn Eagle*, and the *Long Island Star Journal*. He became a war correspondent for CBS in the early 1950s, and made a name for himself covering post-colonial conflicts in French Africa while living in a luxury hotel in Casablanca with his wife, an elegant Manhattan model, and young son. Taber became disillusioned with the US while reporting on the 1954 coup in Guatemala, where he watched jets roaring over the capital's main plaza with American markings on their wings. Washington's brazen support for the overthrow of a democratically elected government defied the country's noblest ideals, he felt, an echo of the McCarthyism that had wreaked havoc among his friends back home.

For Taber, the idea of filming the idealistic Fidel was irresistible. In mid-April he flew to Havana with cameraman Wendell Hoffman—a strapping, six-foot-four-inch farm boy from Kansas who had taught himself the cutting-edge technology of video. There was no chance of sneaking their 150 pounds of gear through Cuban immigration, so they declared to airport officials that they were two Presbyterian missionaries doing a documentary on the island's rural faithful. Haydée Santamaría met them with a driver and accompanied them on the sixteen-hour overnight trip to the Oriente, this time in a car that had been specially refitted to hide the camera equipment under the broad leather seats. In Manzanillo they met Celia and loaded the bulky Auricon camera and tripod onto a mule; the newsmen lugged the other equipment on their backs. The group of six, including Haydée, Celia, and two armed male *compañeros*, then trekked 150 miles by night into the heart of the sierra.

A few days later, word reached Fidel that the army had surrounded the farmhouse where the American journalists were resting, and Camilo was dispatched with a platoon to rescue them "at all costs." The guerrillas ran along trails and riverbeds for almost seven hours straight, but it turned out to be a false alarm. When Haydée spotted the rebels approaching through the trees, she was convinced they were enemy soldiers until they saw Camilo's flashing smile. "Camilo had marvelous teeth," Yeyé recalled. "I don't remember anything else."

ON THE SAME day Celia brought Taber into Fidel's camp, she realized her dream of becoming a guerrilla. Fidel formally inducted her into the Rebel Army. From now on she could march and fight by his side. (Haydée, her feet oozing blood and suffering from asthma, was more of a city girl). The guerrillas were stunned to learn that a woman intended to join them full-time. They were still trudging for ten to twelve hours a day through the jungle and changing camp almost daily. Celia was rake-thin and elegantly coiffed; many rebels assumed that in the long term she would live in a village with a campesino family. (As one recalled: "We couldn't imagine someone as fragile as her being able to stand such a hard life.") But she didn't flinch. Over time, the men were relieved to find that Celia moved among them effortlessly. They also noticed that her presence improved Fidel's mood: as he basked in the attention, his mood swings became less extreme.

Celia now threw her planning skills, polished by decades of caring for her father, into looking after Fidel. On the surface, her role appeared domestic. She would get up at 5:00 a.m. to prepare his coffee. She mended his clothes and ensured they were clean. She repaired his boots and confirmed that new spectacles were always on order in case he threw a fit, and that good cigars were on hand. She would organize his correspondence and appointments, and would only retire at night when Fidel was ready for bed. But Celia was far more than an aide, secretary, and lover. She discussed every detail of the war with Fidel, and very quickly became his closest confidante and advisor. It was an early triumph for women's liberation in Cuba. The strutting male guerrillas quickly began to recognize Celia's peculiar genius and deal with her directly on a range of daily issues. Her orders were on a par with Fidel's. For his part, Fidel believed that Celia's feminine presence and small acts of thoughtfulness made the men dress and behave better; it also cut down on their swearing.

BY THE TIME the CBS journalists arrived, Fidel had achieved his goal of commanding eighty-two men, even if most of them were urbanites who still found wilderness life a struggle. He instructed them on how to behave on camera for Taber and Hoffman and, after the first day of filming, celebrated by giving out an extra ration of condensed milk, the guerrilla equivalent of the British Royal Navy's prized tot of rum. Fidel decided that they should conduct the key interview with him at the summit of Pico Turquino, Cuba's highest mountain, in front of the bust of José Martí that Celia and her father had lugged up there in 1953. It was a strenuous climb, with a wheezing Che the last to summit, but it offered postcard-perfect coastal views. The ever-curious Fidel measured the peak's height with his altimeter, clocking it at over 6,500 feet.

Hoffman left soon after with the videotape, burying his camera by the side of a road for safekeeping so he would draw no unwelcome attention at the airport. Taber stayed on in the sierra to shoot still photos for *Life* magazine. When he did depart, Fidel asked Taber to take home the youngest two American runaways, who were healthy but emaciated. It would put a serious dent in US sympathy for the revolution if either was injured, Fidel felt. The guerrillas gave the teens a rousing send-off, singing the Cuban national anthem and breaking into applause. Che was less sentimental. He felt the young gringos "simply could not stand the rigors of our campaign." ("We felt a sort of affection for them," he sniffed, "but in the end we were glad to see them go.")

From Guantánamo, the two boys were promptly shipped back to the US to resume their high school studies. Before they left, Camilo had asked them to visit his wife in San Francisco—which Buehlman eventually did, without telling his parents.

AT 6:00 P.M. on Sunday, May 19, Taber's thirty-minute documentary *Rebels of the Sierra Maestra* hit American airwaves. Publicity stills of shouting guerrillas raising their rifles had whipped up interest for weeks beforehand; in New York, a crowd of six hundred Cuban supporters gathered to watch the special in a midtown hotel, while ex-president Prío was given a private preview in Miami. The show was also seen on Cuban televisions—the island had the second highest per capita ownership of TVs in the world, after the US—and, taking advantage of a rare lapse in censorship, was transcribed in *Bohemia* magazine soon after. The issue became so popular that it had to be reprinted, and eventually reached around 1 million Cubans, about one-fifth of the population.

The documentary was so positive towards Fidel that he might as well have directed it himself. It vividly conveyed the difficulties of sierra life and the guerrillas' youthful idealism, culminating in the scene filmed on Pico Turquino where the men burst into patriotic song together. The result crystallized for tens of millions of viewers the image of Fidel as Latin America's Rebel with a Cause. Taber's son Peter recalls basking in reflected glory at his Manhattan elementary school the next morning: "I was in the fourth grade and half the kids in class had seen it," he said. "They were in awe."

The Rebel Army now seemed more real in the media than it did on the ground. Fidel decided it was finally time to end the weeks of inactivity. A large shipment of arms had landed by boat on the coast of

Oriente, many rescued from DR caches in Havana. The treasure trove included three tripod-mounted machine guns, nineteen semiautomatic M1 Garand rifles (the standard US Army issue in World War Two and Korea, named after its designer), and 6,000 bullets—enough to equip most of the Rebel Army's now 136 men. Celia claimed one of the new rifles, to the envy of some male combatants. Che was given a submachine gun. Although he had always carried a rifle, this officially elevated him from his background role as medic to a frontline fighter.

Fidel offered the latest batch of volunteers one last chance to go home—nine did so—then started marching with 127 men. The resulting battle, Che would later write, would have "the greatest psychological impact in the entire history of the war."

CHAPTER 16

Baptisms of Fire

(May–July 1957)

The enemy advances, we retreat; the enemy camps, we harass;
the enemy tires, we attack; the enemy retreats, we pursue.
—SELECTED MILITARY WRITINGS OF MAO TSE-TUNG

BEFORE DAWN ON May 28, teams of guerrillas crept through a ghostly sea mist near the remote fishing village of El Uvero, weaving past a darkened lumber yard to encircle a fortified army barracks. Inside, guarded by four sentry posts, some sixty soldiers were sleeping to the steady rumble of the distant surf. It was a far larger enemy force than the Rebel Army had ever faced; even though they outnumbered the military two to one and had the element of surprise on their side, the guerrillas' almost complete lack of experience made it an agonizing moment. Fidel was stationed on a steep hill above the village, Celia by his side, squinting through his rifle's telescopic sights and trying to identify the telegraph equipment in the main building. He needed to knock out communications with the first shots so the soldiers could not call for reinforcements.

The barracks had only one open window, which Fidel deduced was to ventilate the telegraph set. He squeezed off the first rounds at 5:15 a.m., which found their mark, knocked out the machine, and signaled to his men to start their attack. Unfortunately, he had fired several minutes too soon. The guerrilla platoons down below had not reached their positions, and it was still too dark and misty to see. But suddenly, they could identify their targets from the flashes from the barracks as the sixty panicked troops started shooting blindly at them in the darkness.

What Fidel had planned as a hit-and-run surprise attack ended up being a bloody pitched battle. The guerrillas perforated the main army structures and sentry posts with barrages of gunfire and made several attempts to seize them, without success. These assaults were led by Che with a bewildering indifference to his own safety. He remained unscathed, but soon a steady stream of rebel wounded was limping to the rear. Juan Almeida was hit in several places. One near-lethal bullet was deflected by a metal spoon Almeida was carrying in his chest pocket; another hit a can of condensed milk in his trousers, whose contents soon oozed white and red. Up on the hill above, a man kneeling near Fidel and Celia, Julio Díaz, was hit in the eye and killed instantly. The young American Chuck Ryan, meanwhile, dodged bullets in Raúl's platoon.

By the time full daylight arrived at 7:30 a.m., the soldiers were still holding out. The commanding officer hoped the guerrillas would either run out of ammunition or the gunfire would be spotted by a passing aircraft. But when he peeked from his hiding spot to assess the situation, he was shot in the head. A few minutes later the second in command took a white handkerchief from the dead officer's trousers and waved it in surrender.

The barracks buildings had been turned into sieves; in fact, they were so saturated with gunfire that five of the soldiers' seven pet parrots had been killed in their cages. It was a costly victory. A half dozen rebels and fourteen soldiers were dead, with thirty-five wounded on both sides. Che had to suddenly step back from his role as fighter to field surgeon, a transition made, he said, by simply washing his hands. Military patrols could now arrive at any time, so the guerrillas loaded their wounded into commandeered trucks, together with fourteen unhurt army prisoners. The other rebels clung to the sides of the moving vehicles any way they could; the hoods became so crowded, the drivers could barely see the road ahead. The convoy took a turnoff into the forest and set up an improvised hospital camp only one hundred yards from the main highway. The six rebel dead were buried in a clearing nearby.

Two critically wounded guerrillas had to be left behind at El Uvero, even though the military might summarily execute the pair. A young man named Cilleros had a bullet pass through his lungs before embedding itself in his spine, leaving his legs paralyzed. "He knew it was the end," Che wrote. "We knew it too." But they all put on a brave face as they said farewell. Che kissed him on the forehead and told him all would be well, since "we didn't want to make his last moments more bitter." Cilleros died of his injuries soon after, but the other man, Leal, who had a serious head wound, was protected by an officer who had been cared for by Che and testified to the rebels' decent behavior. Leal eventually recovered and spent the rest of the war in prison.

TODAY, A MONUMENT with a gilded rifle marks Fidel's lookout above El Uvero, offering breathtaking Caribbean views. It celebrates the rebels' first taste of genuine combat. "This was the victory that marked our coming of age," Che later wrote. "From this battle on, our morale grew tremendously." For weeks afterward participants recounted to one another the details of the firefight, exaggerating their own experiences. "We had learned how to be invincible," Fidel crowed. "We had learned how to win!" Despite renewed censorship, word of the victory caused a sensation when it leaked out in Cuba. The *New York Times* reported with pride that the teenage gringo, Chuck Ryan, had "fought bravely and well, and now is accepted as a full-fledged soldier in the rebel forces."

Two days after the battle the army prisoners were released after signing a statement attesting to their good treatment. (The guerrillas had even shared their paltry food rations.) Showing mercy to captives had become a central tenet of the guerrilla war. In time, it would have a corrosive effect on enemy morale. When released soldiers returned to their units, they encouraged others to throw down their arms rather than risk injury or death.

Most of the rebels now began hiking back into the sierra, but twenty wounded men, including Juan Almeida, were forced to stay behind under Che's command. El Uvero proved to be a watershed for the Argentine even more than for the rest of the army. Not only had he displayed near-suicidal bravery, the aftermath showcased his leadership skills. Keeping the rebel wounded safe was a hair-raising feat. The men had to keep moving to avoid patrols, camping wherever they could in damp caves and chicken coops, and foraging for food as they went. One man had to be carried on a makeshift stretcher created from hammocks strung beneath a palm branch. It took a full month to nurse the wounded and transport them to safety. By the time they met Fidel's main group, Che's charges were as ragged as castaways, but not a single man had been lost.

From then on Che's confidence increased. He shed his "foreigner's complex," as he called it—the feeling that he should defer to Cubans on all issues of politics and strategy—and his bond with Fidel became more intense. They were both intellectuals, with a vast depth of reading at their command, and would spend hours at night arguing about history, literature, and politics as the more left-wing Che tried to convince Fidel of the virtues of Marxism.

At last, two months later, on July 22, Fidel acknowledged Che's new stature by promoting him, although he did it in a casual, almost offhand way. The guerrillas were all signing a letter of support for Frank País and Celia, who had been forced to return temporarily to the lowlands to help the increasingly harried Movement leaders. When Che was about to add his name, Fidel told him, "Put '*Comandante*.'" Che was taken aback. This was the highest rank in the Rebel Army, giving him a status just below Fidel himself; it also meant he was leapfrogging above Juan Almeida, his former superior. In a slightly more ceremonious gesture, Fidel presented him with a small golden star to pin to his forage cap. "There is a little bit of vanity hiding somewhere within every one of us," Che wrote. "It made me feel like the proudest man on earth that day." Almeida, meanwhile, struggled with a pang of jealousy at having been passed over, since he had been with Fidel much longer. "I said to myself, 'I would have liked that,'" he wrote in his diary, with disarming honesty. "'But there you go.' I understood it perfectly. I gave [Che] a powerful hug and we said good-bye."

FOR THE ARMY, the defeat at El Uvero was a far more serious psychological blow than La Plata. Its commanders were forced to admit that isolated military posts could not be defended; over the coming weeks, many were closed down, starting a withdrawal from the sierra that would accelerate over time. The new tactic would be to indiscriminately bombard the mountains from the air with B-26s, sometimes using the newfangled incendiary agent purchased in bulk from the US, napalm. Whole villages were wiped out in attacks that observers would compare to small-scale Guernicas, but the raids did little to hurt the guerrillas: in the jungle, trees and mud would absorb the impact of high explosives and limit their effect to twenty-five to fifty yards.

The offhand cruelty of the Rural Guard did not relent. On one occasion the guerrillas found the mutilated corpse of Guillermo Domínguez, a twenty-five-year-old Cuban photographer who had been captured by an army patrol in early May. He had been beaten, stripped, and had his hands tied with his belt; the soldiers then bayoneted him and let him squirm for a while before blowing off his head. On another occasion the rebels went in search of a foul smell near their camp and came across the bloated body of a campesino. They were horrified to recognize him as Ángel el Cojo, a farmer who had lavished food on them in April; he too had been kidnapped and tortured to death.

Not long after, an attempt to emulate the *Granma* expedition ended in tragedy. Twenty-seven would-be guerrillas from a Cuban exile group in Florida landed on a desolate beach in the Oriente in a boat called the *Corinthia*. The force was quickly betrayed by villagers and intercepted by the army. A mass execution followed. Only one man escaped and, with nowhere else to hide, joined Fidel in the sierra.

FOR THE URBAN cadres of M-26-7, news of the victory at El Uvero provoked euphoria tinged with envy. For all its discomforts, guerrilla life felt oddly peaceful to the city-based revolutionaries who had visited the Sierra Maestra. The jungle was cold, damp, and infested with bugs, but there was a clear-cut division between friends and enemies. There were even moments of security and calm when the hammocks were stretched out at camp after dark. Cuban cities, by contrast, had become murky worlds of spies, sudden shoot-outs, and midnight police raids that make John le Carré's postwar Berlin seem tame. There was no respite: the nights of a *clandestino*, Haydée said, were passed in a state of "constant tension . . . You always had to sleep with your eyes open." This was particularly true in Santiago, which was slowly degenerating into a war zone—one reason why the guerrillas had sent their letter of support to Celia and Frank.

Army checkpoints on street corners were piled with sandbags and barbed wire, and backed up by armored cars mounted with machine guns. Violence could erupt out of nowhere. Gunfights scattered the customers of outdoor bars. Pedestrians would be seized on the sidewalk and bundled into unmarked cars. By night, police vehicles trawled the streets with floodlights, looking for saboteurs. SIM raids would be followed by the sound of mothers shrieking as young men were herded into the backs of trucks. Women wandered the city's prisons asking after missing husbands and sons. On one occasion, a fourteen-year-old was picked up and executed for putting a firecracker in a milk bottle, which somehow was taken to be a Molotov cocktail.

Disgust with Batista seeped through every social class in the

Oriente. A network of middle-class business owners called the Civic Resistance—accountants, butchers, grocers—donated cash, distributed leaflets, and provided safe houses. Pistols would be dropped at bread shops, hidden inside bags of bread rolls. Housewives would transfer ammunition in their children's dolls. The city was honeycombed with caches of arms. Vilma wrote that she used "false walls, false floors, basements, holes, gardens, backyards, special furniture, water tanks, cisterns, vaults, warehouses, hospitals, pharmacies, stores, schools and recreation centers."

This civilian support was crucial for the Movement in Santiago. An agent fleeing the police might dash into a tailor's shop, where the owner would throw a jacket over his shoulders and pretend they were in the middle of a fitting. Families took to leaving their doors open for fugitives. When dodging patrols, Haydée recalled how she would casually slip into someone's house, sit down, and ask for a coffee as if nothing were out of the ordinary. When the coast was clear, she would just as casually get up and say, "Well, see you later, thanks!"

Even on the most tense occasions, the Cuban sense of humor could shine through. *Santiagueños* liked to joke that the only businesses thriving in the city were funeral parlors, travel agencies, and the national lottery, since residents were either being killed, leaving town, or desperately gambling for money to flee. Vilma once escaped a night raid at Haydée's apartment by grabbing sensitive documents and jumping from the rear balcony in her nightgown. Her wild wet hair and getup surprised the neighbors, who joked that the Holy Virgin had dropped down from heaven. Later they suggested Vilma should wear a hairnet the next time she was out on the town. "When something didn't end in violence, it ended in laughter," Vilma recalled.

The Civic Resistance became so popular that it became the basis for an agreement Frank brokered with Fidel and moderate politicians in mid-July, promising that after Batista's defeat, Fidel would hold democratic elections within a year. This so-called Sierra Maestra Manifesto was instrumental in further broadening support for the rebellion, with all sorts of religious and social groups warming to M-26-7, including Rotarians, medical associations, theater groups—even garden clubs.

Despite the unrest, Santiago's venerated Carnival went ahead in high summer, and even encouraged a touch of revolutionary whimsy. To celebrate the fourth anniversary of the Moncada on July 26, Celia and her friend Elsa inflated balloons marked M-26-7 and floated them off a rooftop to land in front of the Manzanillo police station. But grim reality reasserted itself soon enough.

On July 30, one of Vilma's telephone operators listened in on a disturbing call to the police station: "Listen, Chief, those 3,000 pesos you promised me?" one officer said. "Okay, I'm ready to collect." Another voice added: "We got him, that filthy———. It's done, we put a bullet through him." It was the first news that Frank País had been assassinated for a $3,000 bounty.

The linen-suited charmer Frank had been arrested earlier in 1957 but released, since his pivotal role in M-26-7 had somehow remained secret. But by July, he was being hounded by SIM so intensely that he was forced to change safe houses almost nightly. It was even too dangerous to meet with his mother or girlfriend. (The women arranged to stand on a distant street corner so he could at least see them with a spyglass.) Frank's sense of isolation was radically increased when his twenty-year-old brother Josué was killed in a shoot-out with police. No young males dared attend the funeral; elderly women made up the majority of mourners. Still, they were a feisty bunch: when a suspected informer arrived, they hammered him with their high heels.

Exhausted and depressed, Frank began to behave erratically. On the night of July 29 he moved into a house he had long avoided because it had only one exit. The next afternoon Frank received an urgent call: the military were cordoning off the neighborhood and were searching door to door. What happened next was pieced together from eyewitnesses. He and the house owner, Raúl Pujol, dashed out into the street, thinking it would be safer to blend into the crowd. But one of Frank's former classmates was riding in an unmarked police car and identified him. Frank and Pujol were stopped, pummeled with rifle butts, and thrown into the back seat of the vehicle. After roaring a few blocks away to an alley, both men were tossed onto the sidewalk and shot in the back of the neck. País was twenty-three years old.

Within minutes a crowd had descended on the murder site, and as the news spread, Santiago fell into a state of shock. When the police released the corpses from the morgue, Frank's mother examined the bullet wounds and cried out: "My son was a teacher, not a gangster!" In tropical Cuba, burials are conducted quickly, and the funerals were scheduled for the next day. Frank's body was lovingly dressed in an olive-green guerrilla uniform and black tie, and laid in state, where mourners remarked on his "saintly" serenity. The funeral procession was followed by 60,000 people with emotional scenes that evoke the cortège of JFK. Crowds threw flowers from the balconies, and chanted "Death to Batista and his regime!" and "¡Viva Fidel!" Businesses closed in a spontaneous protest. Bank tellers walked off the job, cinemas were shut, bus drivers abandoned their vehicles by the sides of the roadways. Even the shoe shiners' chairs were empty.

The police left the burial alone, but other political gatherings in Santiago were ruthlessly repressed. By chance, the new US ambassador to Cuba, Earl Smith, arrived in the city that same day on his first official visit. He and his wife were greeted by mothers in black weeds who were holding placards demanding an end to US support of Batista. The Americans were appalled when firemen turned hoses on the women and riot police dragged them into wagons. Smith held a press conference to express his disapproval of the "excessive" force and ask that the arrested women be released. (They were.) Frank's funeral service was still going on that afternoon when the ambassador placed a wreath at the tomb of José Martí. It was a subtle act—Smith was hardly a radical—but the first sign that the US might be rethinking its attitude to the brutish Batista.

The members of M-26-7 would be haunted forever by the murder of the handsome young leader, who had been on a par with Fidel in the hierarchy and had a more astute grasp of national politics. The treacherous classmate who had identified Frank, Luis Mariano Randich, was quickly found and executed by an M-26-7 agent, but that did little to fill the void he left. Vilma realized that she had spoken calmly by phone with Frank only ten minutes before his death; he had given no indication that he was in danger. Celia was horrified to later receive a letter that Frank had posted the morning he died. In the sierra the guerrillas heard the news on Fidel's transistor radio. The sense of loss was visceral, even among those who had met Frank only once.

For Fidel, Frank's death left both a personal and organizational void. "What monsters!" he railed in a letter to Celia. "They have no idea of the intelligence, the character, the integrity of the person they murdered." He withdrew to himself for a night of uncharacteristic silence. ("Fidel is in a bad way," Juan Almeida noted in his diary. "The news hit him hard. I've never seen him like this.") The Movement was now rudderless in the cities of Oriente. Celia, who was still in Manzanillo on her supposedly short visit, was obliged to stay on to help.

Within the space of a few months, the two most charismatic resistance figures besides Fidel—Frank País and José Echeverría—had been killed. But the presence of a few guerrillas in the mountains still seemed to most observers an insignificant threat. Batista appeared as secure as ever.

CHAPTER 17

Scenes from the "Free Zone"

(Summer–Fall 1957)

THE REBEL ARMY had swelled to two hundred men by midsummer, organized into a half dozen platoons in separate camps. Since the victory at El Uvero, the guerrillas were feeling increasingly at home in the Sierra Maestra, and they began to carve out an area of control they dubbed El Territorio Libre, "the Free Zone." Although they continued to move camp nightly, the rebels created the embryo of an infrastructure, with permanent huts as refuges and caches of tinned food and ammunition buried at strategic points. They soon set up their own bakery, a field hospital, and even a "bomb factory" where they manufactured land mines and grenades using TNT from unexploded airplane shells with shards of condensed-milk tins as shrapnel. The ever-inventive Fidel took a hands-on role: working with a captured lathe, he designed a makeshift mortar, then tried to develop "a kind of bazooka" with projectiles crafted from corrugated iron.

The guerrillas also became more integrated into sierra society. Eutimio's betrayal in February had shaken their confidence in the *guajiros*, but it soon became obvious that he was an exception, as the mountain communities supplied them with consistent support, often at great peril. As Fidel wrote: "The word 'people,' that has been pronounced so many times with such a vague and confused sense, has become a living reality here, a marvelous thing. Now at last, I know what 'the people' is."

In turn, the Rebel Army became more trusted. In stark contrast to the Rural Guards, who left a trail of executed farmers and torched houses, the guerrillas maintained a respectful code of conduct. They religiously paid for food—Fidel would overpay rather than bargain—while Batista's soldiers simply confiscated whatever they wanted. Their strict respect for local women struck a deep chord. And every time they eliminated a murderous overseer (often leaving a hand-painted sign that read EXECUTED FOR BETRAYING THE PEOPLE—M-26-7), their popularity grew. At one stage the guerrillas even put aside their guns and helped with the coffee harvest.

Instead of inducing fear and suspicion, the rebels were now embraced. The American photojournalist Andrew St. George hiked into the sierra on assignment for *Look* magazine, and his stories are a vivid source for this period. He added cinematic detail to Fidel's image as a Caribbean Robin Hood, writing that wherever the guerrilla leader wandered, peasants would pop out of the bushes "dangling the gift of a hen, even a poem. He talks endlessly to them about their crops, their health, their families." Like a politician on the stump, Fidel took the time to explain the revolution's goals, ask about the campesinos' hardships, and win each individual over.

The army's price for betraying Fidel varied wildly: one peasant said he had been offered a mere $300 and two cows, a far cry from the $10,000 Eutimio was promised. Later in the summer Batista upped the ante considerably, putting an official reward of $100,000 on Fidel's head. But as 1957 progressed, it became increasingly unlikely that there would be any takers. After a rebel platoon captured one remote army outpost in Bueycito, villagers even emerged to celebrate with them in the streets, with cold beer and sodas donated by the local bodega owner.

The near-famine days of spring faded as the campesinos secured the guerrillas' supply lines, with one muleteer gaining the nickname "the

Food King" for his ability to deliver tinned goods. Each of the six rebel platoons chose a cook who could work with the limited range of ingredients. The creative culinary solutions now included stews made of horsemeat, with leftovers salted and turned into *tasajo*, a version of jerky; when rehydrated, it had a texture similar to corned beef. Guerrillas from the cities found horse "exquisite," Che claimed, but peasant volunteers were mortified. For farmers, the very idea of devouring a working farm animal was a crime: it was as if they were "committing an act of cannibalism while chewing the old friend of man." They would have their revenge when they taught the city slickers to eat a sierra delicacy, snake. The boa often ended up on campesino tables in lean times. (The recipe: Cut off the head four inches from the neck, then hang the snake by its tail from a branch to drain the blood. Skin and gut. Chopped into six-inch pieces, the flesh can be roasted on sticks over an open fire or fried. The result was tough, sinewy, and full of tiny bones, but not without flavor and a good source of protein. True gourmands would bread the snake chunks with flour first, but this was a luxury rarely enjoyed in the mountains.) Camilo, who loved practical jokes, would offer nervous new recruits pieces of snake cooked up on his little gas burner, telling them it was "cat meat" to see their horrified reactions.

The only staple that never ran out was coffee, which was available in every hut, although percolation could be basic, with the grains strained through a spare sock.

In the remotest camps, fireside meals might be accompanied by music from a transistor radio or the quiet strumming of a guitar. Even small fiestas were not unknown. After midnight on August 12, a few veterans of the early struggle—Juan Almeida, Universo Sánchez, and Guillermo García—came to toast Fidel on his thirty-first birthday with a bottle of brandy.

NEW RECRUITS DRIFTED in from all over Cuba, including intrepid women, mostly still M-26-7 agents whose lives had become too "hot."

A routine was developed for fresh arrivals: They would be interrogated to make sure they were not spies, given some cash to send to their families, and provided a several hours of "political training." After a couple of days, they would also be offered a chance to go home. By then, any illusions about guerrilla life had been crushed out of them by endless hikes and sodden conditions: summer was slightly warmer in the Sierra Maestra but it was also the rainy season. Even dry nights remained surprisingly frigid and sometimes so dark that the guerrillas had to use glowing coals to find their way. Trying to relieve himself one evening, Juan Almeida lit a match but fell down a fifteen-foot cliff, nearly killing himself; he spent several days recovering.

There were also more organized attempts at reinforcement. Celia dispatched a second group of eighty-eight men from the Oriente via her thorny transit camp, the *marabuzal*, including a nephew of one of Batista's ministers and an ex-army officer. They turned out to be far less disciplined than the first. En route, they devoured their rations, argued among themselves, and got lost. They lightened their forty-pound packs by tossing supplies in the bushes, including half-finished tins of milk and even, inexcusably, ammunition. ("That is monstrous!" Fidel wrote when he found out.) Only twenty had guns, and they were terrified of a surprise army attack. After two weeks the portly old peasant leader Crescencio Pérez managed to track down the sixty-six who were left—the others had deserted—and straighten them out, but the mishaps continued. No sooner had they reached Fidel's camp than the ex-army officer accidentally shot off his gun, forcing the entire group to relocate. Many were suspicious that he was an undercover agent, and the man would have been executed, Che said, if it was not for his genuine look of "surprise and consternation." (The firearm accidents continued, until the inevitable tragedy occurred in late summer when an eighteen-year-old named Enrique Somohano shot himself while cleaning his rifle. The bullet passed through his lung and, despite quick medical attention, he died the same day.)

To whip them into shape, Fidel took the new recruits to climb Pico

Turquino; at the majestic summit the excited first-timers engraved graffiti on the base of the José Martí statue. With his supernatural energy, the *comandante en jefe* developed a personal relationship with each volunteer and spent every waking minute asking his men's opinions on every little matter. ("How do you feel? Did you sleep well? How was the food last night?") At the end of any day's march, no matter how exhausting, he gave a speech analyzing the landscape they had traversed and explaining his strategy.

As the camaraderie of the Rebel Army grew, members took the Cuban love of nicknames to extremes. Some were simply diminutives, reflecting the affectionate Latin habit of adding -*ito* to virtually every moniker—Carlito, Juanito, Guerrita, and so on. Others were more original. The guerrillas soon included Lalo and Yayo, Pepe and Paco, Chichí, Chicho, Chuchó, and Chino. There was Sabú, Vilo, Nano, Nandín, Kiko—Tano, Titín, Tita, Tatîn—Popo, Pepín, Pancho—Quico, Quique. One rebel soldier was nicknamed Cantiflas, after a Mexican comic actor, another Baby, for reasons unknown. One thin woman was Arbolita, "Little Tree." Celia teasingly called her stressed-out assistant, Felipe Guerra Matos, El Agitado, "the agitated one."

One of the most beloved newcomers was Roberto Rodríguez, El Vaquerito, "the Little Cowboy," who got his nickname from the ornate riding boots Celia gave him when he arrived in camp barefoot. Combined with a broad-rimmed straw hat, the boots made him look like a Mexican cattle hand. Indifferent to danger, he became a leader of Che's "suicide squad," which was given the most difficult tasks. El Vaquerito was cherished for his constant, almost childish good humor and his tall tales. Friends tallied up the stories of his adventures and figured he must have lived twice as long as his twenty years.

Still, despite such quirks, the Rebel Army was a barbaric-looking bunch. Their ranks were peppered with fearsome-looking reprobates, shady characters, and street kids in trouble with the law, and few paid attention to sartorial elegance, mixing and matching their ragged uniforms with *guajiro* garb, blue jeans, and captured army outfits.

(Che compared their appearance to "pirates.") The veteran male guerrillas were almost all bearded by now—the impish Raúl was one of the few who could not muster facial hair. They swore almost constantly, and reeked more than ever of sweat. Even Che, El Chancho, admitted that personal hygiene was an issue, as "our bodies gave off a peculiar and offensive stench that repelled anyone who came near." One reason Celia wore mariposa flowers in the sierra was that their perfume masked the stench of body odor. (Another, more official reason, was their historical association: Cuban women in the nineteenth-century independence movement used garlands of the white mariposa, or "butterfly" lily, to smuggle anti-Spanish messages.)

The beards became a badge of identification, and it was now that the guerrillas came to be known simply as *los barbudos*, "the bearded ones." Fidel also saw a practical advantage: as he later explained to the Spanish journalist Ignacio Ramonet, shaving wasted fifteen minutes of a man's life every day. "If you multiply that fifteen minutes . . . by the number of days in a year, you'll see that you devote almost 5,500 minutes annually to shaving. An eight-hour day of work consists of 480 minutes, so if you don't shave you gain about ten days that you can devote to work, to reading, to sport, to whatever you like." It also saved a fortune in razor blades and soap. The only downside, Fidel admitted, was that gray hairs sprout first in a beard. Clean-shaven men can "hide their ages better."

THE EDUCATED GUERRILLAS continued to give literacy classes to poor farmers. They also provided a traveling health care system. Doctors were rarely seen in the Sierra Maestra, and from his earliest days, Che would set up a rustic clinic whenever they arrived at a village, taking up office in a corner of a thatch-roofed hut. He found it a dispiriting experience, since he saw the same illnesses resulting from generations of malnutrition, parasites, and overwork. On one occasion, he wrote, a little girl watched him for hours and then complained to her mother: "Mama, this doctor tells everyone the same story." It was true, Che admitted to himself: "People in the Sierra grow like wild flowers, unattended. Then they fade away, constantly busy at thankless tasks."

The guerrillas themselves were plagued by dental problems, especially Fidel, who had poor teeth to begin with. Leaving their toothbrushes behind in Mexico had proved unwise. Fidel constantly complained about toothaches and begged Celia to send a dentist from Manzanillo. ("It's the limit," he joked weakly. "Now that we have food, I can't eat. Later when my teeth are all right, I won't have any food.") In late June she did send a dentist's bag, and Che assumed the mantle of "tooth-puller." Without painkillers, he resorted to swearing and intimidation to make rank and file patients submit. (He dubbed it "psychological anesthesia.") His skills were sketchy at best. In his memoirs, he recalls being unable to extract a rotten canine from one unhappy "victim," saying he would have needed dynamite to remove it. Che sagaciously did not attempt to apply this treatment to himself, leaving his own toothaches until the end of the war; Fidel also avoided him.

Over the summer, several more doctors joined the Rebel Army, releasing Che to concentrate on the military duties he preferred. The medical profession in Cuba had been sympathetic to the Movement from its earliest days. Doctors were regularly confronted with evidence of police torture and were targeted if they spoke out or testified in court. Many took refuge with the guerrillas. Word of their presence ensured that a parade of sick villagers would converge on their camps every night, turning each one into a "mobile emergency room," according to Almeida. There would be "kids with diarrhea, kids with infections, kids with infested pimples, people with cataracts, people who need molars removed," he marveled in his diary. (Almeida found the evidence of rural neglect added to his revolutionary zeal: "The heart burns up before so much human misery . . . It pains me that in the middle of the 20th century such things occur in Cuba. No, a thousand times no!")

Doctors were also on the front lines during combat. Their tropical MASH units treated the wounded on the spot where they fell. Medics joked that they carried their surgeries in their backpacks and had mules as their ambulances. Operating tables were often the forest floor. Wounded men might go under the knife on bare hillsides, with IVs of saline solution hung from tree branches. Other first aid was more perfunctory: when Che was wounded in the foot, a friend removed the bullet using a razor blade.

A NEW PHASE of the guerrilla war began in September, when Comandante Che set off with his own hundred-man troop to create a permanent base in a valley called El Hombrito. His was the second "column" of troops, as rebels now dubbed their larger contingents, but Fidel decided to call it "the Fourth Column" to confuse the enemy and exaggerate their numbers. The idea was in part to give Che a break from the constant movement that exacerbated his asthma attacks. He threw himself enthusiastically into building his "extra-revolutionary society" with its own pig and chicken farms, a shoe factory, and a saddle workshop, as he had taken to riding a little mule. The camp printed its own newspaper, *El Cubano Libre*, to which he contributed as "the Sniper." When the army destroyed the structures in December, Che re-created them in La Mesa, adding a field hospital, a slaughterhouse, and a small cigar factory, to feed his addiction.

In this community-building endeavor, Che relied on another strong-willed woman, Lidia Doce. Her recruitment is another of the forgotten milestones of Cuban feminism: she was forty-two years old, twice divorced, and the mother of three adult children when Che found her working at a bakery in the hamlet of San Pablo de Yao. One of her sons had joined his column at El Hombrito, so Che asked Lidia to help organize the camp. She soon did so, ordering his men around with a notoriously sharp tongue. (Che called her "tyrannical.") He then asked Lidia to carry secret messages to Movement leaders in Santiago, a dangerous mission she executed with such aplomb that she was elevated to the trusted position of "executive courier"; from then on she carried the Rebel Army's most sensitive documents, risking execution if she were captured.

Che's column was notorious for its strict discipline enforced by a special police unit. No diaries were allowed in case they fell into enemy hands and yielded crucial information. (Only Che was above the directive.) Fires could only be lit after dark, and a bucket of water had to be kept nearby to douse it if a plane flew over. Any minor lapse while on guard duty was harshly punished. The men were wary of Che, but they begrudgingly admired his personal austerity. Like Fidel, he shared every danger and would not eat until the men had their share. Even so, the stress was too much for some. One lieutenant picked up his revolver and shot himself in the head in front of his stunned comrades. After this, Fidel decided to balance out Che's toughness by appointing the happy-go-lucky Camilo Cienfuegos as his second-in-command. The constantly grinning Camilo, who looked more like a rumba dancer at a Havana nightclub than a soldier, proved the perfect foil to Che, lightening his mood with jokes and banter, and spouting quotes from his favorite book, *Don Quixote*.

Not that Che entirely lacked a sense of humor; he was often noted for his Argentine sense of irony. He dubbed new volunteers to his column *descamisados*, "shirtless ones," after the working masses championed by Evita Perón in his homeland, and made fun of his own foreign origins: "Steal a dollar from an Argentine and he'll kill you," he liked to say, "but steal his woman and he'll sing you a tango."

Che was also becoming increasingly flamboyant. On one occasion, Raúl met him at 1:30 a.m. riding through the moonlit jungle on a white horse ahead of a captured army jeep and truck piled with supplies. Little wonder that photographers would soon be seeking out the inscrutable Argentine almost as often as they did Fidel.

※

As 1957 PROGRESSED, the emboldened guerrillas honed their improvised strategies into a distinctive style of irregular warfare that would
later be echoed by the Vietcong in the jungles of Southeast Asia. To
pin down vastly larger enemy forces, the guerrillas would descend on
the enemy's weak point then melt like ghosts into the jungle, only to
strike again at another vulnerable spot (a tactic Raúl nicknamed
muerde y huye, "bite and flee"). The soldiers were often barely trained
recruits led by officers fresh out of the classroom, and the rebel tactics
eroded their spirit. Repeatedly ambushing the vanguard could derail
an entire battalion, Fidel and Che found. Homemade land mines
placed on the trail would scatter the first patrol, whose members
could then be picked off individually. Or snipers would shoot one soldier in the leg, and when his companions dropped their weapons to
carry him to safety, guerrillas would pounce from the foliage and capture them all. Even if the soldiers got away, the shouts and chaos
would demoralize the others. Thus, wounding an enemy conscript
was far more effective than killing one, Fidel instructed his men.
Eventually, terrified soldiers would refuse to take the lead and, as Che
rejoiced, "an army without a vanguard cannot advance."

The army's attempts to pursue the guerrillas were futile. By getting
to know every wrinkle in the landscape, the rebels could "run like
water through the enemy's fingers," as Fidel put it. Each entrance to
the sierra, he boasted, was "a little Thermopylae," where a small company could hold off an adversary force many times its own size.

Che would later write a classic handbook for budding partisans,
Guerrilla Warfare, which—quite apart from handy tips on how to
hang a hammock and what type of plate to buy—expanded on his favorite strategies, each of which took advantage of mobility and surprise. There was "the so-called minuet," a dance-like maneuver where
some twenty guerrillas would creep up on an enemy from the four
points of the compass. When the first group of five men opened fire,

the soldiers would rush towards them shooting randomly into the forest. That contingent would retreat while a second attack was launched from another direction. "The army will repeat its action and the guerrilla band the same," Che instructs. The result confuses, immobilizes, and demoralizes the enemy, as well as wastes its ammunition. This tactic was especially effective after dark, when soldiers would often panic. ("The guerrilla fighter grows at night, and the enemy feels his fear growing in the darkness.")

The rebels continued to experiment with homemade ordnance in their thatch-roofed armories. Their most striking success was a grenade launcher officially called the M-26 but more vividly nicknamed "the Sputnik." A sawed-off shotgun mounted on a bipod provided a solid launching apparatus; the "grenade" was a Molotov cocktail attached to a cylindrical stick. Using an empty shotgun cartridge, the flaming, kerosene-filled bottle could be projected up to one hundred yards and exploded like Greek fire, an ancient version of napalm. It was "a weapon of extraordinary effectiveness," Che gloated, and a terrifying sight for defendants as the projectile arched towards them—as the nickname suggests, resembling the first Soviet satellite launched in October, which they could spot streaking across the clear night skies.

Caution remained second nature. The disciplined guerrillas still spoke only in whispers both day and night, unlike the soldiers, who had a tendency to yell to one another and give themselves away. When the rebels got to a clearing, they would cross it one man at a time, at intervals, so a passing plane would think it was just a stray peasant. And the poor morale of the soldiers was an increasing contrast to the guerrillas' cheery bravado. When three army trucks were ambushed by Che's men at the sawmill settlement of Pino del Agua on September 17, most of the soldiers threw down their weapons and fled, leaving behind their wounded and four dead, a dismal performance that led to the court-martial of the commanding officer for cowardice. This was followed by a rare lapse in the guerrilla code, when a campesino whose family had been murdered by Rural Guards executed one of the wounded. When Che berated him for "savage" behavior, another injured soldier who had been pretending to be dead piped up and begged to be spared. Every time a rebel passed, he would shout, "Don't kill me! Don't kill me! Che says he doesn't kill prisoners." The soldier was taken to a field hospital and released when he had recovered.

There were also setbacks. In late August, Fidel and his men made a night assault on an army camp near the Palma Mocha River that seemed successful. But at dawn they were aghast to see 250 soldiers dug into trenches in the hills around them. Several guerrillas were killed as they beat a hasty retreat. While he was carrying their vital 50-millimeter machine gun, a hulking twenty-year-old named Pastor Palomares was hit in the legs and lower body. As he lay dying on the riverbank, Palomares whispered to his platoon leader that his wife was heavily pregnant and begged for Fidel to raise the child. The rebels were forced to abandon Palomares's body, but farmers found and buried it a few days later. By then his right hand had been chopped off. The army had hoped this athletic, bearded character was Fidel himself and, unwilling to carry the whole corpse, had taken the appendage away for fingerprinting.

CHAPTER 18

Revolution on $300 a Day

(Summer–Fall 1957)

CELIA'S RELATIONSHIP WITH Fidel had blossomed during her two-month stint with the guerrillas in spring—at least as much as it could while camping in the raw mountains among dozens of odiferous guerrillas traipsing back and forth in the mud. (Imagined scenes of bodice-ripping passion on the mossy jungle floor are unlikely, according to Celia's biographer Nancy Stout: "There were always bodyguards around. Always.") A hiccup in the romance occurred when Celia's "short" visit to the lowlands in June dragged on into the fall, as she was forced to help the new M-26-7 chief in Santiago, René Ramos Latour, code-named "Daniel," take the reins after Frank's murder. Driven into ever-deeper hiding, she changed her own code name from Norma to Aly. ("Even the dogs know me as Norma," Celia joked.) Her new choice seemed to deliberately echo Fidel's alias "Alejandro"; it was his second name but also a subtle nod towards one of his classical heroes, Alexander the Great.

For several months they carried on a unique long-distance relationship, with the pressures of underground life adding layers of tension. Their surviving letters show a volatile mix of tenderness and brisk, often querulous discussions about revolutionary logistics. After addressing her fondly as *Querida Novia*, "Dear Girlfriend," Fidel would launch into demands that Celia found capricious and thoughtless. He showed no understanding of the risks urban fighters took and constantly complained to her about the lack of support he was receiving from the Llanos, "the Plains." "The proper order should be: *All guns, all bullets and all supplies to the Sierra*," he railed. "About your order that all large armaments be shipped to the Sierra," Celia wrote back curtly, "I already said that we don't have any so we can't send them." Fidel's insistence on his own priority also implied that he was the Movement's undisputed leader, while the *clandestinos* in the cities felt they should share the decision-making, since they were risking torture and death daily.

Celia was also impatient at Fidel's chaotic leadership style and infantile tantrums. His poor choice of personnel irked her. One of his couriers turned out to be completely unreliable. ("He is such a liar and has such a loose tongue!") She berated him for whining about his teeth, telling him to take calcium tablets. (She too had a sore tooth, she said, but didn't complain about it.) And they argued endlessly about money. In response to Fidel's demand that he be sent $10,000 a month, she wrote tersely, "That seems like a lot and we don't have it." Another sloppy courier failed to pick up envelopes of cash; she even found $1,000 still sitting in someone's living room. Fidel then accused Celia of spending too much on her personal expenses, which infuriated her: "My expenses have always been paid by Papa and my brothers," she railed, every inch the middle-class rebel.

Celia's itemized accounts swelled during this period. Unlike her neat notes from earlier in the year, they now covered three double spreadsheets, scrawled, crossed-out, and smudged. With two hundred men in the sierra, the revolution had become a much more complex affair than the shoestring operation that had supported the *Granma* survivors. The list now included the expected mountain gear, office equipment, and bigger-ticket items like a jeep. The monthly total in June came to $8,706.89. It was the revolution on roughly $300 a day.

Still, despite all the stress and recriminations between Fidel and Celia, there were moments of affection: "And you, why don't you make a short trip here?" Fidel wrote. "Think about it, and do so in the next few days, days of observation and expectation. A big hug." He was also solicitous about her safety: "Look after yourself carefully! I don't know why, but I feel confident that nothing will happen to you. Our loss with Frank has been too great for it to be repeated."

In truth, life was increasingly dangerous for Celia. With unusual thoroughness, SIM had searched the offices of a sugar mill in Pilón and found that a number of coastal charts had been signed out the previous year by "the doctor's daughter"—the same set of charts that had been found on the *Granma*. It was hard evidence of her top-level role in M-26-7, and SIM soon upped the ante by targeting her family. On a sweltering day in August, trucks full of soldiers converged on the home of her elderly doctor father, stormed inside, and began to ransack the house. In an effort to intimidate him, they overturned furniture, smashed decorations, and went through his files. One officer showed him a woman's girdle, implying that Celia had been raped.

It was the beginning of months of harassment for Dr. Sánchez. When he tried to escape by train to Havana with some of his other daughters, he was arrested and only released when the mayor of Manzanillo intervened on his behalf. The family group then tried to visit their house in Cienfuegos, a port on Cuba's south coast, but found the city in uproar in the wake of a naval mutiny against Batista. (It failed dismally, but the reprisals went on for weeks; there were mass executions, including dozens of prisoners buried alive in pits by bulldozers.)

The Sánchezes finally found refuge in a relative's beach bungalow near Havana. Although Celia begged her father to stay out of trouble, he befriended Fidel's mother, née Lina Ruz, when she visited the area.

He even wrote a letter to Celia enclosing a snapshot of himself with Señora Castro—at fifty-four years old, now the merry, if deeply Catholic, widow—and, a little crazily, suggested that the pair should travel together one day to the Sierra Maestra to pay a social call on their notorious offspring.

The naval mutiny in Cienfuegos led to a purge of the officer corps all over Cuba, eliminating any moderates and leaving the military more pitiless than ever before. By late September, the intensified crackdown convinced Celia that it was time to cut loose from the lowlands and rejoin Fidel, but when she tried to hike into the sierra, the route was blocked by massive air force bombardments. For ten days she hid in a cave with eighteen other fugitives as Fidel sent out fruitless search parties. Finally some M-26-7 agents from Santiago stumbled across Celia and her sorry "caravan," as she called it, and escorted her back to Manzanillo. The last leg was in a car filled with young female Movement members. They pretended they were returning from a weekend party and carried a cake to prove it, flirting with guards at checkpoints and offering them slices of dessert.

No sooner was she home than Celia went back to business. She sent Fidel a snappy leather jacket ("I ordered you one made in olive green, very light and warm"), newspaper clippings, and notes about journalists requesting interviews. Even so, she felt neglected in her claustrophobic underground life and described herself as "more than hidden . . . I'm buried alive!" Another letter to Fidel ended on a vulnerable note: "Please write!" But when it came to the revolution, Celia did not hesitate to take him to task. In a blistering 4,000-word missive, she criticized Fidel for a range of sins. He was accepting recruits who had not been approved by René Latour in Santiago, breaking the agreement forged with Frank. He complained about lack of funds, but there was now $6,000 waiting to be picked up from different safe houses. "This is the insanity you've caused," she fumed. "I see the effort I've made over the past two months has been of no use, since you have created this state of chaos." But at the end of the letter Celia holds out the olive branch, saying that she hopes Fidel will now understand the stress she is under: "Let's reach an agreement for your well-being and my peace of mind."

IT WAS THE last time Celia would need to berate the *comandante en jefe* from afar. Less than two weeks later, on October 17, she left again for the Sierra Maestra. Her departure was prompted by news that the widow of Pastor Palomares, the guerrilla who had been killed two months earlier at the Palma Mocha River, had given birth to a girl— the perfect excuse for Celia to rush into the mountains bearing baby clothes and tinned milk, just as she had often done as a teenage caregiver working for her father. This time, Celia got through the military aerial bombardments safely. After visiting Fidel's camp, she trekked with an escort to the remote mountain cave where the child had been delivered by her grandfather, an herbalist. It was a precarious mission. At one stage an army patrol came so close that the grandfather was forced to put coffee leaves into the baby's mouth to stifle her squeals.

A few days later, the Cuban Revolution's first official offspring was baptized. Honoring Palomares's dying wish, Celia and Fidel agreed to be the godparents. They arrived at the cave with the "guerrilla priest," Father Guillermo Sardiñas, a radical Catholic cleric who had joined the rebels with such gusto that he had taken to wearing a cassock stained khaki with a woven red star. (It had been designed for him by Camilo Cienfuegos, drawing on his youthful experience working in a Havana fashion store.) The forty-year-old Sardiñas's lush black beard and the faraway look in his eyes only added to his Rasputin-like appearance.

The scene was a throwback to early Christian rites. In the grotto whose walls were dripping with tropical foliage, the celebrant anointed baby Eugenia with holy water and intoned the baptism vows.

Flanking him were Fidel, solemnly wearing Catholic medals over his uniform, and Celia, whose military lapel was graced with white mariposa blossoms. In this natural chapel, the baby's mother and her new husband looked on from the shadows, while the "congregation" was made up of menacing-looking guerrilla guards, all as heavily bearded as the priest, their ears cocked for enemy patrols. Fidel and Celia swore to protect Eugenia during and after the war. The mother then kissed the baby and left with her husband to find a new life elsewhere in Cuba.

At once quotidian and strange, the ritual symbolized the sense of stability that had settled over the Free Zone by late 1957. Father Sardiñas was the most eccentric of three Catholic clerics who now tended Fidel's wayward guerrilla flock. Raúl referred to him as El Celestial, not quite of this world, for his forgetful habits, and joked that he would wander off a cliff if it wasn't for the bodyguard assigned him. Sardiñas even lugged around a heavy "portable altar" for church services until Fidel ordered him to abandon it for slowing the column's movements. The strong Catholic devotion of the guerrillas was noted by every journalist who beat a path into the Sierra Maestra. Almost to a man, they all wore religious medals or rosaries handed out by the priests. (Only the die-hard Marxist Che was an open atheist; Fidel, despite his Jesuit upbringing, professed to be agnostic, but didn't think twice about adorning himself with sacred baubles.)

In the Sierra Maestra, priests were as rare as doctors, and baby Eugenia's baptism was the beginning of a great tradition: wherever the guerrillas went, villagers asked the three clerics to conduct weddings, hear confessions, or perform funeral rites. Over the coming months, there would be dozens more christenings—Fidel invariably chosen as godfather, Celia as godmother—and a festive atmosphere attended the arrival of the Rebel Army. Fidel would hand out sweets to children as crowds of villagers filed by to greet the "bearded ones," sell them rice and beans, and have their physical and spiritual needs attended to by the clerics and medics in tow.

※

THE BAPTISM ALSO marked the official return of Celia to the sierra, and as they attended to the wilderness ceremony, she and Fidel became the revolution's first couple. Celia now threw herself into organizing the Free Zone's first formal trials. To maintain a semblance of order, the rebels had been developing their tenets of "revolutionary justice" into a solid legal code; now Celia set up an open-air courtroom. A "contagious banditry" had broken out in the power vacuum left by the departing army, with cattle rustlers, wandering thieves, and army deserters preying on farmers at will. In this frontier environment, deceptions were easily carried out. Some thieves pretended to be guerrillas and extorted money; others forced themselves on prostitutes. Such masquerades threatened to undermine support among the peasants and had to be dealt with severely.

The trials were conducted with the formality of circuit courts in Georgian England. The American photojournalist Andrew St. George happened to be in camp at the time and featured them in a spread for *Look*. First to be prosecuted was a statuesque bandit leader with a scraggly mustache named Carlos Ramírez, although he went by the nickname Chino Chang for his touch of Oriental ancestry. For three days farmers filed through to testify against Ramírez and his twenty-two man gang, who had been terrorizing the area for months. Photos show Fidel in lawyer mode presiding over a tribunal alongside a shrewdly attentive Celia and three judges, including the former vice president of the Inter-American Bar Association in Havana.

The bandit chief was found guilty, and a compelling series of images documents his fate. The first shows him being tied to "the execution tree" in front of a six-man firing squad commanded by Raúl. The next (with the caption: "'Fuego!' Fire!") is a blur as the air is filled with smoke. In the next, Ramírez's body is shown slumped before the tree. Finally, Raúl delivers the coup de grâce. Another marauder who confessed to rape was also "sent to the tree." (The "puritanical" Fidel, notes St. George, would not tolerate "interference with women.") In total, there were twelve days of trials, held from dawn until dusk. "If we don't keep order in our liberated zone, the people suffer," Fidel pontificated. "Our revolution is tarnished."

The last trial was of a disturbing character known as El Maestro, "the Teacher," who had been impersonating Che. He would turn up at remote villages, offer to medically examine women, then sexually molest them. The former schoolteacher had fought alongside the guerrillas for several months before turning predator, and was renowned for his fine physique: he could shoulder enormous loads "like Hercules," Fidel recalled, even though his huge ginger beard made him look like "an orangutan." At one stage he had carried the asthmatic Che for days. Most campesinos knew Che by name only, so the Teacher had easily passed himself off as the "Argentine doctor." "'Bring me women. I'm going to examine them all!'" Fidel recalled of the prosecution. "Did you ever hear of anything so outrageous? We shot him."

In the field, guerrilla justice was more perfunctory. Che earned a reputation for ordering the death penalty most readily and leaving a trail of executed "bandits" in his wake. But he often second-guessed his decisions in private. In October he ordered the execution of a young deserter named Arístidio who had sold his revolver and threatened to defect to the army. Many years later, Che confessed that Arístidio might not have deserved the death penalty, but he felt obliged to make an example of him to prove that the Rebel Army was "pure and uncontaminated." Still, Che did relent on one occasion, when a trio of adolescent thieves were "sent to the tree." The boys were tied up and blindfolded, but on the shout of "Fuego!", the firing squad shot in the air. When the three realized their lives had been spared, "one of them gave me the strangest spontaneous demonstration of joy—a noisy kiss, as if I were his father." They joined Che's platoon and became his passionate devotees.

Perhaps the incident that haunted Che the most involved the death of a puppy. The affectionate little dog had become his column's

unofficial mascot, but one day it followed Che and its master, a guerrilla named Félix, into a combat zone, despite their best efforts to
shoo it away. While they were hiding from an army patrol, the puppy
started to yelp in Félix's arms, and then howl. After repeated attempts
to silence the pet they all doted on, Che wordlessly instructed Félix to
strangle it with a rope. Che recalls watching, heartsick, as the dog's
happily wagging tail grew frantic, slowed, and then fell limp.

The act weighed heavily on them all. Around the campfire that
night, while one man was strumming a sentimental tune on a guitar,
another dog sauntered past and picked up a bone Félix had dropped.
It then fixed the men with "a meek yet roguish gaze," Che recalled. A
melancholy mood fell over them: "There in our presence, although
observing us through the eyes of another dog, was the murdered
puppy."

CHAPTER 19

Love in the Time of Diarrhea

(Fall 1957)

Q UITE APART FROM the physical hardship, there was a personal cost to the guerrilla life. An insight into the stresses during this precarious, nomadic phase in 1957 is provided by the unpublished field diary of Juan Almeida, the thirty-year-old black construction worker who was also a prolific poet and songwriter. Buried in the Office of Historical Affairs in Havana, the journal has never been cited by historians even in Cuba, perhaps because of its air of raw confession. As platoon leader, Almeida led some twenty men around the sierra, constantly on the move for months, and his musings—scribbled in the lull of dawn and dusk at camp every day—are laced with doubt and soul-searching. Almeida had left behind a girlfriend in Mexico City but had not heard a word from her since landing in the *Granma*. Wracked by nostalgia, tormented by solitude, he poured out his feelings and composed tearful love verses. (*"Did I love you? I don't know!... Did I shiver in your arms? Yes, like a leaf in the breeze."*) But his longings weren't always directed to his distant *novia*: as he wove from village to village, Almeida developed a crush on almost every eligible female he met. Shopgirls, farmers' daughters, comely *guerrillera* volunteers—all became the potential objects of his affection. Recounted with winning candor, his frustrations are woven through the more practical reports on guerrilla life that we are familiar with from the diaries of Che and Raúl, including the obsessive catalogs of foodstuffs and clinical notes on bowel disorders.

One week Almeida falls for two Seventh-day Adventist girls. ("But nothing happened. We said good-bye.") The next he flirts with a pretty teen who visits his camp with her mother. ("I saw in her eyes something beautiful, like a glimpse of the Sierra.") In August he was captivated by the first three young women to officially join the Rebel Army after Celia, including the steel-nerved Geña Verdecia, who had smuggled dynamite and bullets under her skirt to the guerrillas in the early days. ("She still has the same effect on me as the first time we met.") Receiving a letter from his family in Havana filled Almeida with yearning ("I am guarding it like something sacred"), as did remembering his sister's birthday. An amorous night with a village girl named Esperanza did nothing to help. ("I confess I made love to her because I felt lonely, so immensely lonely.") As ever, he was forced to leave the next day with his men. ("God knows what tomorrow will bring.") Another dating opportunity was provided when some villagers mingled with the guerrillas at an isolated bodega. ("Contact with women. Pretty and ugly.") But his hopes for a liaison with a mulatta named Xiomena were dashed. ("Such a disappointment.")

The most promising encounter was with a tender-hearted farm girl named Juana, who had nursed Almeida while he was recovering from his wounds after the battle of El Uvero. He had thought of her often, and written poems about her. ("*And why in my sorrow does the memory of that woman's face come?*") In mid-October he finally passed near Juana's village; he dallied in his old flame's house so long that his platoon left without him, and he had to be fetched by messenger. But the romantic idyll had by then gone awry: while they were lying in bed and listening to music, Juana opened the medal of the Virgin of Guadeloupe hanging around Almeida's neck and found a photograph of his Mexican girlfriend inside. "Now she treats me distantly . . . with something more like sisterly affection," Almeida sighed in his diary, adding unconvincingly: "Anyway, it's better like that."

EVEN THE ASCETIC Che had to admit that endlessly roaming the sierra had its downsides. "There are periods of boredom in the life of every guerrilla fighter," he observes in his handbook *Guerrilla Warfare*. The best remedy for ennui, Che helpfully suggests, is reading. In fact, visitors to the mountains were often struck by the rebels' literary leanings: it was common in the jungle camps to see men hunched over books in every spare minute.

Che recommends edifying works of nonfiction despite their annoying weight: "Good biographies of past heroes, histories, or economic geographies" will distract men from vices such as gambling and drinking. An early favorite in camp, improbably, was a Spanish-language *Reader's Digest* tome on great men in US history, which the CBS journalist Robert Taber noticed was passed around from man to man (possibly for his benefit). But literary fiction did have its place, especially if it fit into the revolutionary framework. One big hit was Curzio Malaparte's *Skin*, a novel recounting the brutality of occupied Naples after the Second World War. (Always convinced of victory, Fidel thought it would help ensure good behavior amongst the men when they marched into Havana.) A dog-eared copy of Zola's psychological thriller *The Beast Within* was also pored over with an intensity that can only impress modern bibliophiles. Raúl recalled in his diary that he was lost in "the first dialogue of Séverine with the Secretary General of Justice" while lying in ambush one morning, only to be startled by the first shots of battle. To keep his mind active, Raúl also kept up his French studies throughout the war, switching tutors from Che to El Francés, "the Frenchman," Armando Torres, who had once studied in Paris.

Hours at night could also be whiled away listening to storytellers. Two rustic poets even took to holding verse competitions, the guerrilla version of poetry slams. A peasant named José de la Cruz called himself "the mountain nightingale" and composed epic ballads in ten-verse *guajira* stanzas about the adventures of the troop. Like a Homer of the jungle, "Crucito" sat with his pipe by the campfire and spouted his comic lyrics while denouncing his rival, Calixto Morales, as "the buzzard of the plains." Tragically, this oral tradition was lost to posterity when the troubadour Crucito was killed. There had not been enough spare paper to record his verse.

But the most beguiling snippet for literature lovers is Fidel's assertion that he studied Ernest Hemingway's 1940 classic *For Whom the Bell Tolls* for tips on guerrilla warfare. Papa's tome, Fidel declared during an interview with Ignacio Ramonet, allowed him and his men "to actually *see* that experience [in the Sierra Maestra] . . . as an irregular struggle, from the political and military point of view." "That book became a familiar part of my life," Fidel added. "And we always went back to it, consulted it, to find inspiration."

"Ernesto," as the famous American expat was fondly known in Cuba, had written the novel based on his experience as a correspondent in the Spanish Civil War in 1937, and its pages are filled with descriptions of combat behind enemy lines. He had hammered out the manuscript on a Royal typewriter in room 511 of the Hotel Ambos Mundos in Old Havana, never imagining that a similar war would begin in his adopted home. Although it was released when the Cuban guerrillas were children, they grew up very aware of the bestseller (in translation as *Por quién doblan las campanas*), not to mention the 1943 Hollywood version starring Gary Cooper and Ingrid Bergman. Fidel first read it as a student; he says he reread it at least twice in the sierra.

When it comes to specific tactics—the art of ambush, for example, or how to manage supply lines—*For Whom the Bell Tolls* doesn't offer much insight. There are a few straightforward tips about, say, attaching strings to grenade pins so they can be detonated from a distance, or descriptions of the ideal partisan hideout. But the novel is a perceptive handbook to the psychological element of irregular warfare. The hero Robert Jordan is forced to navigate an alien world filled with exotic personalities and possible betrayals, much as Fidel's men did in the Sierra Maestra. Translated to their Caribbean setting, there are many parallels between the novel and the Rebel Army's situation, from the importance of keeping a positive attitude among the troops to Robert Jordan's rules for getting along in Latin culture: "Give the men tobacco and leave the women alone," mirroring Fidel's unbreakable rule that village girls never be molested. (Of course, it's a rule that Robert Jordan breaks in the novel. His torrid affair with the alluring Maria includes a detailed forest romp that can only have impressed the affection-starved Juan Almeida.)

Although Hemingway surely would have been flattered that the Cuban rebels were poring over his golden prose, he was surprisingly silent about the revolution. His fishing boat captain, Gregorio Fuentes, boasted afterward that he and Ernesto had smuggled guns for Fidel in the *Pilar*, but it appears to have been a tall tale concocted for tourists. In private, Hemingway was disparaging about Batista, and in one letter called him a "son-of-a-bitch." But his only public protest came when he donated his Nobel Prize medal to the Cuban people: rather than let a government body display it, he left it in the Iglesia de la Caridad del Cobre for safekeeping. (It is still there, in a glass wall case.)

Even Batista's own intelligence service found it hard to believe that Ernesto was neutral, and several times soldiers searched his Havana mansion for weapons while he was away traveling. On one occasion the intruders were attacked by Hemingway's favorite dog, an Alaskan springer named Black Dog (Blackie); they bludgeoned it to death with rifle butts in front of horrified servants. Blackie was buried in the garden "pet cemetery" next to the swimming pool, where he had lolled happily at his master's feet for many years. When he returned to Havana, Hemingway stormed in outrage to the local police office to file a report, ignoring the warnings of Cuban friends. A local might have been given a beating, but Hemingway's celebrity protected him—although, needless to say, no investigation ever resulted.

WHETHER INSPIRED BY Papa or not, as 1957 wore on, the guerrillas' strategies continued to be refined. In November, Almeida was put in charge of expanding the war by descending from the Sierra Maestra for the first time to burn the sugarcane fields. Fidel had long espoused the idea, but it was controversial: the first random attempts the year before had nearly caused a rift with his most powerful ally in the mountains, the grizzled Crescencio Pérez, who objected that it would destroy the livelihoods of the itinerant workers who depended on the *zafra* for their survival. Sugar was not just integral to the economy of the Oriente, Pérez protested; it was a part of its cultural identity. But Fidel was insistent. Taxes from the sugar crop were propping up Batista, he argued, and economic sabotage had always been an accepted "act of war." ("During your revolution, didn't the American colonists throw tea into Boston Harbor as a legitimate defense measure?" he asked Andrew St. George.) To prove his moral commitment, Fidel ordered his own family's fields to be torched first.

Leaflets were also distributed around Cuba asking for help from budding pyromaniacs. The first new harvest after the revolution's triumph "will be a *zafra* of freedom, a *zafra* of love. It will be YOUR ZAFRA, not Batista's." On the other side of the leaflet was a handy guide to incendiary devices—Arson 101—with cartoons in the style of *Ripley's Believe It Or Not!* Option A resembled a high school chemistry experiment: a rubber tube filled with the volatile liquid bisulfide of carbon and shards of phosphorous; when they come into contact with a cellulose sheath a chemical reaction makes them burst into flames. ("The uncontrollable fire begins in 40 minutes.") Option B was a serious step down in technology: a petrol-doused sponge is tied with a yard-long cord to a ferret or the tail of a cat, which will then run through the fields in panic, causing havoc "for up to a kilometer." ("The animal generally survives.") Plan C was even more basic but perhaps more practical: a slingshot could shoot pellets of flaming red phosphorous collected from match heads straight into the fields. The range was often over one hundred yards, the leaflet advised, and the balls will burn for half an hour.

In mid-November, Almeida and fifty men slipped into the sugar plantations. The reporter Andrew St. George traveled with them. "By dusk, the skyline billowed with smoke and flamed with a purple, neon-like glow," he wrote in *Look*. They met surprisingly little military resistance. Planes strafed the rural roads but there was no sign of army troops. After setting several devastating fires, the rebels were even able to commandeer a bus to get back to the sierra, singing "their favorite Pancho Villa revolutionary song, *Cama de Piedra* ('Of stone will be the pillow of the woman who loves me . . .')."

NOW THAT THEY were almost constantly together, the relationship between Fidel and Celia continued to strengthen. But even for them guerrilla love was no picnic: the power couple's personal feelings always took a distant second place to the demands of revolution. Celia did make the occasional stab at romance. One night, during a lull in the fighting, they were holed up in an abandoned farmhouse enjoying a cozy domestic scene almost out of an eighteenth-century Flemish painting. Fidel was reading by a fireplace, and Celia had arranged for a piglet to be roasted—the Cuban equivalent of foie gras—with a good bottle of Spanish wine. As a surprise, she had also invited the easygoing Raúl, who Celia found "the best and most affectionate person that anyone can imagine." But when he appeared in the doorway at dusk after trekking all day, Fidel took one look at his younger brother and snapped: "What are you doing here? Why aren't you with your troops?" Raúl simply turned around and left without a word. The domestic illusion was punctured. Fidel went back to reading his book.

Part Three

REVOLUTIONARY ROAD

CHAPTER 20

Fiestas in Wartime

(Winter 1957–58)

B Y THE FIRST anniversary of the *Granma* landing, December 2, 1957, Fidel's invasion had defied all expectations to become a permanent presence. The rebels had lodged in the Sierra Maestra like a persistent tropical infection—a minor scratch at first that refused to go away no matter how many times it was scrubbed or dosed with antiseptic. Over the coming months, the irritation would threaten to consume an entire limb.

Instead of the expected spate of bombings, M-26-7 decided to celebrate the *Granma* anniversary in a very Cuban fashion, by hosting a pop-up street party. Word spread through strife-torn Santiago that citizens should peacefully throng downtown for revelries "reminiscent of past days of liberty." *Santiagueños* responded with glee. Defying the sense of siege, crowds spilled from houses and offices, visited shops, and in general tried to behave "with the joyousness of other times" (as Movement leaflets invited), all under the gaze of the nonplussed military. The revelers then descended on Santiago's business district to share an enormous birthday cake. Even for revolutionaries, no decent fiesta in Cuba could proceed without frosting and candles.

※

NEW YEAR'S EVE has always been laden with symbolism, and in Cuba that year the contrasts became extreme. In the guerrilla outpost of La Mesa, Che Guevara, in one of his rare moments of playfulness, strung up a hand-painted banner from the trees: FELICIDADES 1958, "Happy 1958." A fascinating group portrait was taken of Che and twenty of his men holding the banner and grinning at the camera as if they were at a holiday camp, surrounded by a riot of ferns and palms. (On a somber note, Che is wearing the forage cap owned by his friend Ciro Redondo, a *Granma* veteran and Fidel's bodyguard who was killed by a shot to the head in a skirmish the month before).

A few miles away, Fidel issued a New Year's Eve statement exhorting Cubans to boycott celebrations that night in protest against the dictatorship. Fidel himself made only one concession to the holiday in the sierra. His Order of the Day to platoon leaders was: "Distribute cigars among your men in combat lines."

Not surprisingly, Fidel's call for a party boycott fell on deaf ears in hedonistic Havana. The streets were jammed with legions of carousers all night. Even a small explosion on the grounds of the Capitol building failed to close the open-air cafés across the avenue. Clubbing continued unabated in the Tropicana—also heavily guarded after the bombing the previous year and filled with police informants who were nicknamed "thirty threes," because they were paid thirty-three pesos and thirty-three centavos a month—to enjoy its most sumptuous shows ever, *En un Paraíso del Asia* (*In an Asian Paradise*) and *Chinatown.* Guests dined on Eastern cuisine while dancing the Javanese tinikling mixed with "Latin jazz" standards. Havana's seedy dance floors, sex shows, and brothels did a roaring trade, creating a mood of frenzied decadence that some historians have compared to the last days of the Roman Empire. Meanwhile, Batista happily hosted a lavish private soiree at the military base of Camp Columbia in Havana just as he had done every year since he took power. Foreign diplomats, Cuban police chiefs, journalists, and socialites all danced to a live band with carefree abandon.

The high-water mark for Havana's frivolous self-absorption came a couple of weeks later, when NBC's *The Steve Allen Plymouth Show* pushed the limits of video technology to broadcast live from the new Riviera Hotel. The entire episode somehow survived in NBC's archives, and today serves as a time capsule of the season's goofy hijinks. In the straight-laced 1950s, the tuxedoed Allen qualified as the hippest host on American TV, and he could flirt with edgy material about the Mob, gambling, and the city's loose morals. "Here we are in Havana, the home of the pineapple and Meyer Lansky," he cracked after a choreographed stroll through the Jet Age lobby past champagne-quaffing guests. "And it's wonderful to be here." In a carnival of kitsch, mambo dancers in ruffled shirts watched on as Allen joked about gambling. ("Where else in the world can you arrive in a place on Monday and wake up Tuesday dead broke?") The comedian Lou Costello performed a skit about a craps shark. Hollywood starlet Mamie Van Doren sang by the swimming pool as men swan-dived around her like a Busby Berkeley production. Even a ventriloquist reveled in the mood: "What were you doing out all night?" the performer Edgar Bergen asked his talking dummy, who replied: "It's a long story—and a dirty one."

The Mob connections only added to Havana's allure. American tourists delighted in glimpsing the diminutive Lansky ("the Little Man") playing gin rummy in his poolside cabana. His notoriety had gone up a notch after the sensational murder of his former partner in the Cuban casino trade, the Sicilian-born gangster Albert Anastasia, three months before. In the middle of the morning, two gunmen had calmly walked into the midtown Manhattan barbershop while Anastasia's face was swathed in hot towels and emptied their pistols into the mobster. In Havana, rumors spread that Lansky had ordered the hit because Anastasia was demanding too large a share of gambling profits. Not long after *The Steve Allen Plymouth Show* aired, Lansky was met on a visit to Miami for questioning by the FBI; he was then picked up by police as he stepped from his airport taxi in New York, where he had traveled for medical attention for his ulcers. Detectives complained that Lansky was "not helpful"—he stonewalled every question about his business interests, perhaps not surprising for a man who told the IRS he worked as the Riviera Hotel's "kitchen manager"—so the officers hit him with a trumped-up charge of vagrancy and he spent the night in a precinct jail. When he was bailed out by his lawyer the next day, a Cuban government minister solemnly declared that Lanksy would not be allowed back to Havana so long as he was facing criminal charges. The Little Man was unfazed and the case was soon thrown out of court.

"Batista played a little joke on me," Lansky later said. "And when I returned to Cuba, Batista and I had a good laugh over the whole thing."

THE STEVE ALLEN PLYMOUTH SHOW made no reference to Fidel and his guerrillas; in January, 1958, Cuba still qualified as America's fantasy playground. The number of *barbudos* holed up in the mountains had increased to three hundred, but that was hardly more than an annoyance compared to Batista's host of 40,000 plus troops (including 35,000 soldiers and 5,000 in the navy and air force), which outnumbered them well over one hundred to one. But their very survival was starting to have an outsized influence on Cubans' minds. Citizens of all classes were appalled by Batista, who in his New Year's Eve broadcast had glibly promised to hold democratic elections within six months. Only the most gullible—like the US ambassador, Earl Smith—believed it would ever happen. Even moderate Cubans began to cast around in despair for a way out.

Within weeks Havana's cheerful facade started to crack. In fact, in the annals of revolution, February and March 1958 would be remembered as a "golden age" of urban sabotage. After dark, residents began to hear more frequent explosions, often followed by blackouts—one of which lasted for a full three days—the handiwork of both M-26-7 and the DR, which had rebuilt its numbers. ("Ah, there go the *bombitas*," became the *habanero*'s casual refrain). An oil refinery was set ablaze by the harbor, its 400,000 gallons of jet fuel billowing smoke for days. A new cinema palace was torched. Other attacks resembled performance art. A Havana bank was held up by gunmen who took no cash but ordered all the canceled checks to be burned in a bonfire on the lobby floor—an oblique performance piece intended to show that Batista could not manage the economy.

The most ambitious act occurred on February 23, when Havana was poised to stage its most glamorous sporting event, the Gran Premio de Cuba Formula One car race. A phalanx of foreign journalists had descended on the city to watch the world's top drivers in their Maseratis and Ferraris compete for the $10,000 prize; even the race route had been chosen to showcase Cuba's prosperity by snaking along the waterfront Malecón. It was the perfect stage for a low-tech stunt. With only a few pistols and escape vehicles at their disposal, young M-26-7 agents devised a simple plan to seize international headlines by kidnapping the dashing Argentine Juan Manuel Fangio— the race's most celebrated driver, five times world champion and as renowned as any rock star today.

Just before 9:00 p.m. on the night before the race, two men with revolvers hidden in their leather jackets strolled into the Lincoln Hotel, where the forty-six-year-old Fangio was chatting with his crew. While one agent covered the hotel door, the second dug his pistol into Fangio's ribs and ordered him out to the street, ordering stunned guests to stay inside until five minutes had passed. "There are four men with machine guns pointed at the door," he lied. Outside, Fangio was bundled into a waiting car—the rally driver would later remember it was a green 1955 Plymouth—which roared into the darkness with a dramatic squeal of tires.

The spectacular abduction was a huge embarrassment for Batista and prompted a desperate police manhunt. The Gran Premio went ahead without Fangio, but in an unrelated accident a car spun out of control and plowed into the crowd. Seven were killed, dozens injured, and the race was canceled. Fangio was released at midnight that night. At a packed press conference, he declared that he had been treated very amiably by M-26-7. Moving between three comfortable middle-class houses, he had dined on steak and potatoes, slept soundly, and been allowed to watch part of the race on TV. In fact, Fangio had become a convert to the revolution after Fidel's top man in Havana, Faustino Pérez, had visited him to personally explain the reasons behind his abduction and apologize for the inconvenience. Fangio referred to his daredevil captors as "my friends, the kidnappers," and declared: "If what the rebels did was in a good cause, then I, as an Argentine, accept it." It was a coup de théâtre. The rebels could not have hoped for a better endorsement if Fangio's fellow Argentine, Che, had written the script.

Young, principled, brave, creative—Fidel and his band of roguish followers were handily winning the PR war and were well on the way to becoming A-list celebrities. In February, *Look* magazine ran Andrew St. George's sympathetic interview with Fidel, describing him as the "now legendary rebel chief." (In a rare moment of restraint, Fidel only inflated the Rebel Army's numbers to 1,000.) That same month, *Coronet*, a hugely popular *Reader's Digest*-style magazine, went one better by publishing an essay written by Fidel himself, entitled "Why We Fight." It was accompanied by an ink portrait of the bearded comandante en jefe pensively scribbling in a hut like a tropical philosopher-king. Both publications included Fidel's by now ritualistic political points, asserting his democratic intentions, his aversion to communism, and his affection for the American people while protesting the US government supplying arms to Batista. (Washington's official policy was that arms could only be supplied for "hemispheric defense" against foreign forces, not for use against a country's own citizens.) It wasn't only Americans who were enchanted. Not long after, Fidel graced the cover of the chic *Paris Match* magazine, practicing with a revolver above the now-inevitable caption, "the Robin Hood of the Sierra." Photos inside showed him and Celia reading together by candlelight in camp, the Latin American answer to Sartre and de Beauvoir, and the comely Vilma smiling at the camera with a flower in her hair, anticipating Haight-Ashbury by a decade. Meanwhile, Batista was photographed looking slick and shifty in his tailored European suit talking up the Cuban economy at a press conference with a greedy smile. His two chubby, bratty-looking sons were featured lounging insouciantly in the Presidential Palace, one of them picking his nose.

The stylish images in *Paris Match* made a contrast to the grisly local news—for example, that the police in Santiago had kidnapped two sixteen-year-old schoolboys. The discovery of their bullet-riddled corpses led to student and teacher boycotts around the country. Havana University had already been closed for months; now almost all primary and secondary schools—private, public, and Catholic—shut their doors in protest. Word of SIM atrocities spread despite Batista's ham-fisted censorship, with his small army of clerks still physically hand-cutting critical articles from foreign publications. When *Bohemia* republished a photo spread about the guerrillas, Batista's agents confiscated 25,000 issues in Havana, while soldiers in Santiago snatched copies from the hands of people in the street. Meanwhile, Batista hired a PR firm in Washington to keep the stream of "fake news" churning. Tapping into America's Cold War obsession with communism, he continued to denounce Fidel as "a tool of Moscow," although his evidence— for example, that he had murdered six priests when he was a student in Bogotá—was easily exposed as a fabrication. A new tactic was to play up Che as a foreign red agent, depicting him as a pathological murderer with a fondness for slicing prisoners' bellies open with a bayonet.

CIA investigators had gone looking for communism in the Movement on many occasions but found nothing. In mid-1957, after meeting with Vilma and other middle-class supporters, agents went back to Washington convinced that Fidel had no real interest in radical politics. The reality was that M-26-7 relations with the Cuban Communist Party, the PSP, were icy at best; the two groups considered themselves rivals. Unfazed, Batista simply cranked up the level of fantasy. In January an English magazine earnestly "reported" that Soviet troops were being landed in Cuba via submarine to join the Rebel Army. Fidel mocked the gullible article: "The editors are very badly informed," he wrote. "The Russian reinforcements are received by means of remote-controlled intercontinental ballistic missiles." What's more, he added, the Soviet space dog Laika from Sputnik 2 was living with him in the sierra, "and the magazine failed to mention that."

To counter this fog of fake news, Radio Rebelde made its first broadcast from the Sierra Maestra on the same night the race driver Fangio was released. The ever-diligent Che had already created a "media unit" to print his newspaper *El Cubano Libre* on a mimeograph machine; now he had found a technician who could tune the camp's radio transmitter, which had been sitting disused for months. *"Aquí Radio Rebelde,"* began the first twenty-minute broadcast, a catchphrase that would become the newscast's enduring signature. ("Rebel Radio here, the voice of the Sierra Maestra, transmitting for all Cuba on the 20 meter band at 5 and 9 nightly . . .") At last, the rebels would have a voice to skirt the regime's curtain of censorship.

CHAPTER 21

"The Fuck-up"

(February–April 1958)

THERE WERE STILL plentiful reminders that the guerrillas were utterly outnumbered and outgunned. Their first attack of the new year, led by Che on February 16 on the sawmill garrison at Pino del Agua, devolved into a costly firefight in which Camilo Cienfuegos was wounded twice while trying to rescue a dropped machine gun. (One bullet passed through Camilo's thigh, the other his abdomen, but miraculously missed any vital organs.) Just as Che was about to lead another risky assault, he received a note from Fidel reining him in. "I do not think anything suicidal should be done," Fidel wrote. "I seriously urge you to be careful. You are not to take part in the fighting yourself. That is a strict order." Fidel knew that Che would never attack without personally participating, and he reluctantly withdrew. A few weeks later another terse missive from Fidel about some missing ammunition gives a sense that things were often barely under control: "This is a complete fuck-up," he railed. It was a phrase that Fidel would have plentiful opportunities to use in the coming months. M-26-7 was about to gamble all its unlikely success on a plan to bring down Batista in one bold stroke.

Aside from the military missteps, everything seemed to be going the revolution's way. Reports from Havana were unexpectedly encouraging, as the kidnapping of Fangio was followed by one sabotage success after the next. Popular outrage at the regime had been further galvanized by the sickening torture of a fifty-year-old schoolteacher, a mother of three, who had been violated by SIM agents with a soldering iron. After she denounced the regime from the hospital, the police were only stopped from arresting her again by Catholic nuns who formed a barrier around her bed. The rebels' confidence grew, creating what the journalist Carlos Franqui called "a climate of illusion, the illusion of victory." In short, M-26-7 was starting to believe its own PR.

On March 10, the sixth anniversary of Batista's 1952 coup, Radio Rebelde also reported a breakthrough in the guerrilla war. Raúl left that day with sixty-five men to start an entirely new theater of operations in the Sierra Cristal, a mountain range in the northeast of Oriente, not far from the Castro family farm. Managing this "second front" was a huge responsibility for the twenty-six-year-old, and his departure was an emotional one. "*Caramba*, brother," Raúl joked to Fidel, "I feel like a child who has left his father's arms and started walking on his own." Together with Camilo and Juan Almeida, he was promoted to the rank of *comandante*, on a par with Che, and his troops were given shiny new rifles that had arrived by light plane from Costa Rica, another first for the Movement. "For me, for all of us, Raúl's departure was sad," Celia admitted, in part because she found the good-humored younger Castro brother an emotional support when handling the volatile Fidel. Raúl's 120-mile journey across the Oriente included a dangerous drive in commandeered trucks along a section of open highway—the first time rebels had used motorized vehicles—but his men managed to arrive undetected.

Like a cell dividing, a new "Free Zone" now formed in the Sierra Cristal. Raúl's forces easily overwhelmed the few army outposts and "liberated" the far-flung region; hand-painted signs soon went up at roadblocks declaring it "Free Territory of Cuba—Trespassing Prohibited." The mountains were more densely populated than the Sierra Maestra, and Raúl saw no reason to stay nomadic: his troops took up residence in the villages and enjoyed an almost domestic stability. He proceeded to build rebel schools, hospitals, and courts; he imposed taxes; he even became involved in marketing farm produce. "They enjoy a better standard of living than here," Celia wrote enviously to her father after learning about their cozy setup. "They always [sleep in] houses and beds . . ." They even had their own cars and working telephones. She, too, began to dream of a more secure base.

The final piece of good news that spring was a surprise gift from the United States. The day after Raúl arrived in the Sierra Cristal, Washington halted one of its arms shipments to Batista, a batch of 1,950 M1 Garand rifles, and placed all future sales subject to review. The immediate reason for the volte-face was to protest yet another shameless suspension of the constitution, this time to silence a crusading judge who was pursuing a murder indictment against a police thug. But within the US government, there had been rumblings of concern about their old military ally and his homicidal habits for months. The tentative arms embargo was a symbolic rap on the knuckles for Batista intended to push him to reform, although he could easily find weapons elsewhere. (Britain leapt in quickly with sales of Hawker Sea Fury fighter planes, and the US did not stop training his troops and security forces.) Behind the scenes, Fidel's media blitz had won him many fans in the State Department and even many in the CIA had a soft spot for his cause. As the Agency's head of operations in the Caribbean later put it: "My staff and I were all *Fidelistas.*" In mid-1957 the CIA even put out feelers to arrange a meeting with the *comandante en jefe.* It never occurred but, according to Fidel's biographer Tad Szulc, the CIA channeled $50,000 in secret funds to the Movement over the next year. The US was hedging its bets.

All this convinced Movement leaders in Havana that victory was nigh. Prompted by their confident reports, Fidel broadcast a wildly ambitious ultimatum on Radio Rebelde: if Batista did not step down by April 1, M-26-7 would declare "total war." There would be a nationwide general strike. Cuban cities, he declared, would be engulfed in flames. Fidel was staking his reputation as a revolutionary on a single roll of the dice.

IN RETROSPECT, THE plan for the April uprising seems culled from history classes on the storming of the Bastille. Armed cadres in Havana were assigned to strike key targets, but that was only the spark for a mass uprising. Support from grateful citizens was expected to be complete. Workers would stay home from factories, judges would step down, lawmakers would refuse to serve. Seeing the people united against "the tyrant," the army would desert en masse to the revolution. The whole of Cuba would rise up as one and force Batista to flee.

The idea seemed much less far-fetched at the time. As the April 1 deadline for "total war" approached, a sense of crisis pervaded Cuba. In the Oriente, transport became paralyzed by saboteurs: several intercity buses were held up and set on fire, then an entire train. Every day a warehouse or rum distillery went up in flames. In Havana, March 16 was called the "Night of One Hundred Bombs" for the sheer number of explosions. Police officers were shot at. Gunmen wounded a corrupt minister when his car stopped at a traffic light.

Foreign journalists became caught up in the drama, talking up the impending "showdown" between Fidel and Batista as if it were a prizefight. ("It has long been obvious that the struggle in Cuba centered on these two determined and courageous antagonists," opined the *New York Times* in a breathless editorial entitled "Cuba in Torment," which was almost certainly written by Fidel's fan Herbert L. Matthews. "The battle seems to be approaching its climax.") The medical and legal associations demanded that Batista step down. Even the Catholic Church offered to mediate his departure, to Batista's genuine dismay. (He was a pious man, although he also consulted Santería occultists on political decisions in rites that involved the sacrifice of white doves and goats.)

In a fit of optimism, M-26-7 distributed leaflets offering *habaneros* helpful step-by-step instructions on how to become instant insurgents: "Have provisions ready for several days. When the strike order comes, sabotage the place where you work. Abandon work. Do not return until the government falls." The to-do list went on: "Barricade all streets with old furniture and garbage cans. Prepare Molotov cocktails."

The downside of this tense buildup was that Batista had ample time to prepare for the worst. Security was beefed up in Havana. Strikebreakers were organized. The dictator declared that "loyal" workers were permitted to carry firearms, and no criminal charges would be pressed against anyone killing a striker. As the April 1 deadline came and went, Cubans waited for the Movement to declare the revolt. The days rolled on through Easter; uncertainty pervaded the country. ("Fearful Cuba Awaits Conflict," reported the *Times*.) As if preparing for a hurricane, panicked citizens stripped the stores of candles, kerosene, and tinned food.

The general strike, when it occurred on Wednesday April 9, shook the Movement to its core. Operatives seized a radio and broadcast a call to action at 11:00 a.m., "a time when only housewives were listening," the humiliated Faustino Pérez later admitted. In Havana, few workers downed tools. Not a single factory or business closed for more than a few hours; by midafternoon even bus drivers were back on the job. Many trade union leaders were on the Batista payroll, in any case. Others were members of the Communist Party, which had offered to join the strike but been turned down by the Movement's middle-class leaders. The few badly planned commando raids around the capital caused some short blackouts, but most assailants were easily gunned down by police. It did not help that some had been told to strike at noon and arrived an hour late.

In the Oriente, the strike went marginally better, with fires in the streets of Santiago and work disruptions that continued for two days.

But the only large enterprise to completely shut its doors was the Bacardi rum distillery, where the 1,200 workers had been told to stay home because their president, José "Pepín" Bosch, had already been forced into exile in Miami for his pro-Castro sympathies.

As the strike crumbled, SIM began eliminating Movement activists with unusual efficiency. In Havana, underground cells, opposition lawyers, Civic Resistance members—all were swept up under the merciless direction of Colonel Esteban Ventura. The police chief was dubbed "the assassin in the white suit" for his finely tailored linen ensembles, but also "the Himmler of Cuba." One visitor to his HQ found it "like one of the circles of hell. People were lying in the cells with broken legs, bleeding and moaning for help." Ventura told his minions: "I do not want wounded men or prisoners, only dead." It wasn't an idle threat. Journalists overheard a policeman asking a dispatcher where to take one prisoner. "Cut out the double talk," the radio crackled. "Kill him." A human rights lawyer who tried to defend victims was seized and beaten to death himself.

Some two hundred Movement members were killed in the aftermath of the failed strike. Fidel put a brave face on it—"The whole of Cuba is erupting in an explosion of anger against these assassins, these bandits, these gangsters," he railed on Radio Rebelde—but it was a stunning setback, and an international loss of face. Fidel's call for "total war" now seemed farcical; the uprisings had been poorly planned and attracted almost no popular support. The army stayed loyal to the government. As the *Times* put it with admirable understatement, "Batista has undoubtedly won the first round." Clearly, Fidel's support was "waning." To add insult to injury, it ran a photo of Fidel lying on his back in the sun, idly reading a book, like a college student on spring break. *Life* magazine was even more biting, declaring that Fidel's much-ballyhooed strike had "fizzled" because the rebels were really "soft-handed amateurs." It ran a photo spread of Batista in his den, the fortified estate on the rustic edge of Havana, now back in complete control of Cuba. The reporter described with admiration the dictator's seventeen-hour workday: He slaved for his country in chambers filled with kitschy Louis XIV-style furniture and porcelain statues of tigers, and only took time out to celebrate his son's eighth birthday with family and well-wishers. (Everyone sang "Happy Birthday" in English, presumably for the journalist's benefit; Batista the family man gave $15,000 to an orphanage in his son's honor.) Overnight, Fidel and his uprising seemed to be drifting into irrelevance, and within M-26-7 itself, recriminations and despair set in.

"We've lost a battle, not the war," Fidel told his supporters, adding that the revolution had bounced back from near-catastrophe many times before, each time becoming "stronger, more necessary, more invincible." But in private, Fidel confessed to Celia that it was a "great moral rout" and bitterly reproached himself for letting others take control of strategy: "I am supposed to be the leader of this movement, I have to take responsibility in the eyes of history for the stupidity of others, and I am a shit who cannot decide anything." As Carlos Franqui noted, "The false sense of victory [before the strike] was now followed by a false sense of defeat."

Batista was delighted. Reenergized, he decided to wipe out the pesky guerrillas once and for all.

CHAPTER 22

Sierra Shangri-la

(Spring 1958)

THE TRAUMATIC DEFEAT in the cities was followed by grim news for the sierra. Fidel's informers within the military reported that an all-out offensive was planned against the guerrillas in the summer, a blitzkrieg of more than 10,000 government troops. The heroic narrative of the insurgency since the *Granma* landing, with Fidel and his upstart band growing stronger by the month, was now on the verge of being derailed. If bookkeepers at Havana racetrack had been asked, they would have laid long odds against the Rebel Army surviving the season.

With a month to prepare a defense, Fidel decided that he needed a permanent base. After more than a year of peripatetic existence, the guerrillas were settling down. He summoned the rural talent at his disposal—the campesinos who knew every furrow of the landscape—and asked them to select the most defensible location. The new general command post, it was decided, would be hidden on the flanks of Pico Turquino, accessible by a single trail so steep that it felt like alpine gear should be used. Officially known as the Comandancia General de La Plata, it would become the strikingly beautiful capital of the independent jungle republic.

Construction had a hit-and-miss, Tom Sawyer flavor. The first wooden cabin for Fidel was overseen by a Radio Rebelde announcer who had no experience as a carpenter. Returning from a mission, Celia took one look at the clumsy structure, which was barely more substantial than a tree house, and declared that she would take over as architect, interior designer, and landscaper. Issuing her orders on small slips of pink paper, she invited more competent artisans to the site, including a boatbuilder she knew from Pilón. Skilled farmers were chosen to cull trees from different corners of the forest so gaps in the canopy wouldn't be noticed from the air. Two dozen cabins were soon erected, their thatched roofs all given additional camouflage by layers of twisted branches. (As Hemingway had instructed in *For Whom the Bell Tolls,* a partisan hideout should be as well hidden "as a bear's den.") The near-daily deluges made foot trails treacherous, so Celia had branches laid down and handrails installed. Picturesque gardens and vegetable patches were also laid out beneath forest overhangs.

To furnish the cabins, Celia upgraded her mule transportation system into a full-fledged freight service, with teams of a dozen mules traveling up to sixty-five miles across the Free Zone. This FedEx of the Sierra Maestra now had salaried drivers and a strategic network of hidden storage sites. Along with munitions, the mule teams brought armchairs, cupboards, and gasoline generators; their shipping triumphs even included iron bed frames, hospital mattresses, and a refrigerator. Driving the teams remained a dangerous job. One night, Che found a long train of executed mules in a clearing, along with a murdered muleteer; the grisly scene, illuminated by a full moon, reminded him of an Indian ambush in a Western film. Another mule driver who had escaped was still hiding in the bushes. The terrified man acknowledged Che and walked off without a word.

By late April a visitor to the Comandancia would stumble from the precipitous trail covered in sweat from the nearly 100 percent humidity to find one of history's most beguiling military complexes. Burrowed across a square mile of jungle, the HQ's organic, all-wood aesthetic gave it an otherworldly, Tolkienesque air. The first building one encountered was the field clinic—HOSPITAL MARIO MUÑOZ, as a hand-painted sign said, named after the doctor who had been murdered at the Moncada—with a bright interior, two rows of beds with crisp linen, and its own pharmacy. There was a separate office for the camp dentist, a bearded professional named Luis Borges who had taken over from Che and used a pedal-powered drill when he wasn't out fighting. (Celia was an early patient, which encouraged the cavity-plagued Fidel.) The path then led to the admin offices, a sewing factory, and the press center, where the rebel newspaper, *El Cubano Libre*, was mimeographed by hand.

The highest structure, reached by another steep scramble, was the new home for Radio Rebelde, which transmitted via an antenna that could be raised and lowered unseen by passing planes. Carlos Franqui, the witty, self-taught reporter from Havana, livened up the nightly radio newscasts by inviting a local family of musicians, the Medinas, to play. Their lyrics were improvised to suit the bulletins in a popular style called *punto cubano*. The alluring actress Violeta Casal also made her way to the sierra. Beloved for her starring roles on stage in classics like *Medea* and Noël Coward's *Blithe Spirit*, she became Radio Rebelde's first female announcer, adding a touch of glamour to the news team.

But the true heart of the Comandancia was La Casa de Fidel—Castro's cabin—a spacious two-room structure Celia had designed for them both. Perched on stilts above a burbling stream, with large windows propped open by poles to let in a cooling breeze, it was a nature lover's refuge that would have suited a Cuban John Muir. The kitchen had a charming dining table and a gasoline-fueled refrigerator used to store medicine, although it had several bullet holes from when it was hit by air force planes during delivery. In the bedroom, two comfortable armchairs were placed next to an ample double bed with a decent mattress; seen from the pillows, the window was as filled with jungle foliage and flowers as a Rousseau painting. But the cabin's whiff of luxury wasn't only for the couple's personal comfort. Celia believed it important for visitors to see Fidel well established and secure—acting, in fact, as if the war were already won. She would serve guests fine cognac, Montecristo cigars, and coffee even as enemy aircraft strafed randomly overhead.

Next to his casa was a clearing where Fidel could work at a small table with a willow chair, listen to the radio, and read the newspapers. It became the piazza of the rebel base, where the guerrillas would hold meetings and receive orders. Even so, everyone kept up their old habit of speaking in whispers for safety. After dark, silence fell on the entire outpost. Night was when an assassin was most likely to slip into camp; instead of banter, the only sounds were the creaking of frogs and steady dripping of rain in the forest.

HAVING A PERMANENT base freed Fidel up to plan defense strategies against the impending Armageddon. Bunkers were dug along the spine of the mountain range and trenches in the lower, more vulnerable areas. The trails were booby-trapped: the guerrillas' handmade explosives, made from old milk cans, were hung in garlands from branches and could be set off from a distance using detonators. Experiments with these "aerial grenades" were "terrific," Fidel enthused to Che, who had been pulled from the front lines to train new recruits: each one "sends projectiles downwards and on all sides as if it were a sprinkler," and could riddle a tree with "lethal fragments" 150 feet away. Fidel removed a seven-hundred-foot cable from an abandoned TV antenna and discovered how to set off three bombs at once. ("I wonder what effect [that] would have on a marching column of soldiers.")

As the date for the offensive neared, some of Fidel's ideas betrayed a bunker mentality. At one stage he asked Celia to find him large supplies of cyanide and strychnine, evidently to poison the water supplies if they were forced to abandon the Comandancia. She focused on a more practical task: installing a telephone system using battery-operated handsets stolen from backcountry plantation roads. The first line was laid to Las Vegas de Jibacoa, a village directly below the HQ and a key point of defense. Installation was rudimentary, with the cord hidden in bushes, but the communication link would prove to be a crucial tactical advantage.

Celia even took time out to create her own historical archive. She had always been convinced of the value of documents: while she was in Manzanillo, Raúl had couriered her the first five notebooks of his war journal for safekeeping. Celia sealed them in a glass jar and buried them in a rice paddy. Now she ordered the guerrillas to make copies of their correspondence and file them with her for posterity. The men were mystified: she kept them hidden beneath a trapdoor in her and Fidel's cabin, a serious security risk if the Comandancia was ever siezed. Fidel himself was not enthusiastic but bowed to Celia's peculiar archival wishes.

One happy result is that today we have copies of the notes sent between the two revolutionary lovers when Celia was traveling. They reveal how much Fidel relied on her. "I need a fountain pen," he said at one stage in early May. "I hate being without one." (He had two pencils but they shredded the paper, he complained.) A few days later: "I'm eating hideously. No care is paid to preparing my food . . . I won't write any more because I'm in a terrible mood." He asked for painkillers, a toothbrush. He needed rifle grease, gasoline. On May 17 he wrote in a querulous tone: "I have no tobacco. I have no wine. I have nothing." He recalled that a bottle of rosé, "sweet and Spanish," had been left in someone's farmhouse. "Where is that?"

THE ATTENTION OF the US press had drifted from Cuba after the failure of the April strike—Fidel was no longer on the front pages, and had fallen out of most newspapers entirely—but energetic Latin American reporters now beat their way to his mountain aerie. They were often in far more genuine danger than North Americans, who could be sprung from prison with a word from the ambassador if needed. One twenty-three-year-old Ecuadorian, Carlos Bastidas, spent several weeks at the Comandancia and broadcast on Radio Rebelde under the nom de plume "Atahualpa Reccio," a reference to the ancient resistance leader of the Incas. Back in Havana in May, he was sitting in a bar on the Prado, when a police officer named Marrero Suárez—alias Gallo Ronco, "the Hoarse Rooster"—started insulting him, punched him to the ground, and shot him dead in front of horrified customers.

Around the same time, a young Argentine named Jorge Ricardo Masetti arrived in the sierra to tape the first radio interviews with his countryman, "El Che." Masetti had tracked down one of Che's student friends, Ricardo Rojo, in the Café La Paz, the bohemian hangout in Buenos Aires, for a letter of introduction. (The note addressed "Querido Chancho" ["Dear Pig"] and was signed "The Sniper," a nickname Che had since purloined for his byline.) Masetti noticed that Che spoke with an odd impersonality about his experiences, declaring that "I consider my fatherland not only Argentina but all of America." The interview delighted Che's parents when they heard it back in B.A.: their son was not just alive and well but famous, and as Ernesto Senior said, "fighting for a cause that was recognized as just." Masetti took a recorded message from Che back from the Sierra Maestra to the family in Buenos Aires and helped Che's father raise money for M-26-7 by hosting dances.

Che's wife, Hilda, also heard Masetti's broadcasts in Lima, Peru, where she was living as a Movement fund-raiser with their child Hildita. Being married to a guerrilla in the Cuban wilderness had stretched the definition of "long-distance relationship." The couple had been able to smuggle a few letters to one another via the underground, but when Hilda wrote in February that she was ready to come to the Sierra Maestra—Hildita was now two years old and could stay with her family—it took months to get a response. When the reply did come, Che told her that it was far too dangerous.

The real reason Che did not want his wife around may have been that he had finally succumbed to an entanglement, with an eighteen-year-old blacksmith's daughter named Zoila Rodríguez. An eyewitness to their first meeting, Joel Iglesias, a teenager who acted as Che's aide-de-camp, described Zoila as "a black girl, or better said a *mulata*, with a really beautiful body . . . A lot of women went crazy over [Che], but he was always very strict and respectful . . . but he liked *that* girl." Zoila herself later recalled that Che arrived at her farmhouse one afternoon to get his mule shod; her father was away, so she performed the service herself. She noticed him looking at her as she worked, with "a stare a little bit naughty." They kept talking over coffee. "I liked him very much, above all his stare. He had such beautiful eyes, and a smile so calm that it would move any heart, it could move any woman." A few weeks later, she agreed to move into his rustic military school in Minas del Frío, working in the camp kitchen and the hospital. They chatted often about plants and birds. "A great and beautiful love arose in me and I committed myself to him, not just as a fighter but as a woman."

THREE WEEKS AFTER the general strike, Fidel once again demonstrated his uncanny ability to turn a disaster to his advantage. While most of M-26-7's internal struggles are of no more consequence than mayoral elections in 1920s Poughkeepsie—the litany of verbose manifestos and byzantine alliances can be exhausting to keep up with—the fiasco led to a high-level summit that would define the future of the revolution. Fidel had never wanted to share power with members of the Movement in the cities—the Llanos, or "plains," faction. Now he had the ammunition to argue that he and the guerrillas were the revolution's only real hope.

On May 3, eleven M-26-7 leaders made the trek to a farmhouse in Los Altos de Mompié for a marathon face-off. They included Celia, Haydée, Vilma, Faustino Pérez, and René Ramos Latour, the M-26-7 head in Santiago. Reflecting his growing prestige, Che was invited even though he had no official position. Raúl, stuck far away in the Sierra Cristal, weighed in by letter that the "divorce" within the Movement must be ended.

Details of the powwow were largely kept secret until Che revealed them in a Cuban military magazine *Verde Olivo* (*Olive Drab*) six years later. The "exhaustive and often violent" debate began at 6:00 a.m. and continued through constant thunderstorms for twenty hours straight. Che gave the opening address, tearing into the incompetence of the April strike planners, and Fidel followed up with an even more scathing harangue. "The smoke from cigarettes and cigars irritated my eyes and nearly suffocated me," Vilma later recalled, "but I didn't want to leave even for a second to breathe. I didn't want to miss a single word of Fidel's." By the end of the debate at 2:00 a.m., the disgraced urban leaders Pérez and Latour had both been replaced by Fidel's personal choices. Fidel himself became the Movement's general secretary. From then on, Che wrote, "there was only one authoritative leadership, the Sierra, and concretely one single leader, one commander in chief, Fidel Castro."

It was also agreed that Vilma would return to Santiago as underground organizer, one of M-26-7's most dangerous positions. After the meeting, she sat exhausted under a tree and watched the lush dawn: the brilliant tropical sun exploded over forests freshly washed with rain and lit up a sliver of blue ocean on the horizon. While she meditated, "swollen with emotion and peace," she had a vision of herself hiking nearby with Frank País nine months earlier. While crossing a river, Frank had declared out of the blue, "We have been chosen to sacrifice ourselves." It was as if he was predicting his own death. Vilma herself was now staying only one step ahead of SIM. She had lost her favorite safe house and now slept wherever she could after dark, always on the verge of being betrayed. Being in the sierra, she said, was more like a "vacation."

IN MID-MAY, AERIAL strikes intensified around the Free Zone. One town, Cayo Espino, was wiped out totally. Strafing turned the houses into "colanders," Celia said after she rushed to the scene to help; whole neighborhoods were flattened. Advance army patrols arrived, committing random atrocities. Then, on May 25, Batista's offensive began in earnest. "Send ammunition and cartridges of any kind, as a world of *casquitos* is upon us," Fidel wrote, using the derisive nickname "little helmets" for the soldiers. The situation in the Sierra Maestra was now "urgent, a matter of life and death, in which upon every weapon the survival of the revolution depends." The biggest troop movement in Cuba's history had begun.

CHAPTER 23

Operation "End of Fidel"

(Summer 1958)

T HE ARMY HAD tried so often to dislodge the guerrillas without success, it had become a professional embarrassment. This time there was to be no doubt, as Batista threw Cuba's entire military juggernaut into the Sierra Maestra. To make sure his officers got the point, the invasion was dubbed Operation FF—Fin de Fidel, "End of Fidel."

IT WAS ONE of the most unevenly matched campaigns in modern history. Seventeen battalions swarmed into the mountains in a three-pronged assault to create a stranglehold around the guerrillas. The 10,000 soldiers were backed by tanks and helicopters; aerial and naval bombardments would pound civilian supporters into submission; and an amphibious landing would seize the south coast. The whole operation was led by the army's most competent commander, General Eulogio Cantillo. Against this onslaught, the Rebel Army at first fielded 280 men, with some 200 guns between them. Only a fraction carried modern weapons, mostly captured US-made M1 Garands, while the rest sported shotguns, low-caliber hunting rifles, and antique Winchesters. Each rebel was given about fifty bullets. Some of them had no boots, and even Fidel's uniform was now threadbare: "I look like a beggar," he complained to Celia. Almeida's and Camilo's platoons were recalled to reinforce the fragile lines, bringing the Rebel Army up to (it was later calculated) a grand total of 321 men. Fidel, with his love for classical references, compared the odds to the stand of the 300 Spartans against the Persian hordes at Thermopylae— although the biblical saga of David and Goliath must have also sprung to mind.

No sooner had the invasion begun than Fidel received a polite message from General Cantillo suggesting the guerrillas surrender. Cantillo was known to be one of Batista's few humane officers, so Fidel replied in civil fashion: "I think highly of you . . . I appreciate your noble feelings towards us, who are, after all, your compatriots, not your enemies, because we are not at war against the armed forces, but the dictatorship."

Seventy-four straight days of fighting followed. The guerrillas came close to annihilation on several occasions, but thanks to the veil of censorship, the outside world had little idea what was going on unless they tuned in to Radio Rebelde, leaving most to speculate that the revolt was quietly fading away in the mountains.

The situation looked hopeless on paper, but the rebels used every trick at their disposal. The mines and booby traps paralyzed the advance. Snipers held off hundreds of soldiers advancing in single file through narrow passes. And the sierra residents provided near-instant "combat intelligence." Batista's men could not move a yard, it was later said, without a sweaty farmer arriving to report it. All this sapped the army's delicate morale. Two-thirds of the *casquitos* were still unseasoned conscripts. The army's numerical advantage was squandered by inefficiency, with pointless saturation bombings, false starts, and misguided troop movements. By contrast, the rebels were obsessively careful with their resources, squeezing off their rounds one by one and rushing their only heavy machine gun from point to point so quickly that the army believed they had three or four.

Fidel and Celia traveled together by jeep along tracks carved into cliffs, speeding from crisis to crisis to cajole the men and shore up tattered defenses. At night they drove without headlights, using a torch for river crossings. They had a driver but were rarely accompanied by bodyguards, since they now had complete confidence in the safety of the Free Zone. Celia's pockets bulged with letters, which Fidel would dictate at any moment. Her role as the conduit for his impetuous thoughts was now an accepted part of the command chain. Despite the telephone line, most platoons still received orders via a blizzard of notes, often on the torn-out pages of schoolbooks, and Fidel's hand-drawn maps. Shreds from this urgent back-and-forth have survived in the Havana archives. One typical note to Ramón Paz, a key lieutenant on the front lines, begins: "How many messages I've sent you today! And always, even before the instructions reach you, the situation changes . . ." Fidel then added a rudimentary sketch of river valleys and trenches resembling a collapsed spiderweb.

Che was now the top *comandante* in the field, even though he often gave himself asthma injections in the thick of battle. Fidel himself was forced to keep his distance. Forty veterans had signed a plea that he retire from active combat, as he was too valuable to lose: "Do it for Cuba," they urged. He chafed at the new role. "I miss those days when I was really a soldier," he complained to Celia. "I felt much happier then. This struggle has become a miserable, petty bureaucratic task for me." On another occasion: "I'm fucked . . . There are twenty little problems to resolve." Some of these problems were little indeed: "Tomorrow have them fetch the cheese. Today, they're bringing honey; it's for dessert. Sugar has to be divided. The box must last for two weeks."

FIDEL LATER WROTE an 850-page account of the ten-week operation, covering thirty battles in exquisite detail. June was the bleakest month. The Rebel Army was often in disarray, with scenes that were far from heroic. As the scale of the summer offensive dawned on the guerrillas, there were many desertions and cases of insubordination. The low point came on June 19 when rebels defending the strategic village of Las Vegas de Jibacoa, the key to the lower stretch of the Sierra Maestra, threw down their rifles and ran for it, abandoning a valuable detonator cable and bomb, and leaving the trail to the Comandancia entirely exposed. Che wrote with bitter irony to Fidel that "your order not to waste ammunition has been fulfilled" by the unseemly retreat. Fidel was furious at the "shameful" news; he redoubled the order that Las Vegas was to be defended "inch by inch."

Until this point, Fidel had been willing to give ground so he could strike back later from a position of strength. But the rebels now controlled only about four square miles and could fall back no farther. In the most desperate moment of the war, he assigned forty men to hold Las Vegas and the key crest of the sierra. Again and again soldiers tried to cross the Santo Domingo River a few hundred yards below and were beaten back by sniper fire, directed by Fidel staring down at the enemy with binoculars. After dark the guerrillas experimented with psychological warfare, setting up loudspeakers to blare the national anthem interspersed with withering speeches. Fidel told the conscripts not to die for a corrupt regime that cared nothing for them: soldiers were risking their lives for $30 a month, while Batista and his hyenas reaped millions in luxury.

The ridge was held, but on June 27 the rebels finally had to abandon Las Vegas. Che was riding into the village on his little mule, blissfully ignorant of his danger, when he was intercepted by the last rebel leaving, saved from capture by minutes.

FOR CELIA, THIS defeat was made more bitter by personal loss. Three days earlier she had heard on the radio that her beloved father had lost a long battle with lung cancer in Havana. Che heard the same broadcast and sent her a tender missive whose poetic economy might be a template for all sympathy notes: "Celia: I suppose you've learned of your father's death. I wouldn't like to be the bearer of bad news. Between us there is no space for formal condolences; I only remind you that you can always count on me. A brotherly hug from Che."

Only much later did Celia learn that SIM agents had infiltrated her father's funeral in Havana thinking—incredibly—that she might turn up in disguise. It was a waste of manpower that echoed the pointless bombing in the sierra. When guests arrived at the religious service in a chapel beneath the Havana Hilton, located next to the Polynesian Room restaurant, they were appalled to see sharpshooters lining the roofs nearby. IDs were checked by police at the door and the crowd was stacked with thickset Batista goons. One of Dr. Sánchez's's closest friends, a wealthy sugar magnate, angrily dialed the dictator's personal number and told him the police presence was disrespectful: "I'd be very grateful if you'd take care of it," he said, and hung up without waiting for an answer. Minutes later a SIM officer walked in and clapped his hands twice. The strangers left.

Che had celebrated his thirtieth birthday two weeks earlier, on June 14, presiding over the trial of a guerrilla officer accused of abusive behavior. (Che stripped him of his command.) Earlier in the summer he had spoken briefly to his mother in Argentina via radio. An affectionate letter was soon smuggled to his camp, filled with domestic news of his family and how they all missed him. In a moving passage Señora Guevara wrote about her own loneliness and how distant Che had seemed on the radio call. ("I don't know how to write you, or even what to say to you; I have lost the measure . . . So many things I wanted to say, my dear. I am afraid to let them out. I leave them to your imagination.") Whether Che felt a twinge of homesickness or not, he threw himself with even more energy into combat and criticized himself for any instinct of self-preservation: "Personally, I noted something I had never felt before: the need to live," he wrote after one near-fatal skirmish. "That had better be corrected at the next opportunity." This survival instinct was a failure Che harshly attacked in others—the source of weakness, cowardice, and desertion. He had to purge all traces of it in himself.

CHAPTER 24

Raúl Goes Rogue

(July 1958)

I F BILLY WILDER had ever written a light comedy about a hostage crisis, it might resemble the saga that now unfolded on the "Second Front." While Fidel and his men clung on in the Sierra Maestra, Raúl grabbed international headlines when he ordered his men to kidnap fifty North American citizens in the Sierra Cristal.

The drama began at dawn on June 26 when Raúl's commandos infiltrated the grounds of the Moa nickel mining site and politely ordered ten American and two Canadian executives and engineers onto a bus. They then roared off with nineteen company vehicles loaded with food and medical supplies, including a valued array of metal-framed hospital beds. Before they left, a guerrilla turned to an engineer's wife and told her amiably that the prisoners would be treated well and "returned in a few days." The reason for the kidnapping, he added, was that the United States, despite assurances of an arms embargo, was continuing to supply Batista's army in secret and even refueling his bombers at Guantánamo Bay naval base.

The tension escalated the following night when twenty-eight US Marines from Guantánamo Bay Naval Base were dozing on their chartered bus after a casual day of R & R, all in civvies and happily tipsy from visiting the bars and boudoirs of the town. At 9:30 p.m.

their Cuban driver was roaring along a plantation road, when the headlights picked up a group of bearded men at a roadblock ahead. The guerrillas climbed onto the bus and ordered the driver to head into the Sierra Cristal; the cheerfully soused Marines didn't even realize they had been hijacked until they were transferred to waiting trucks. Ten more Americans were picked up from local mines and a United Fruit Company sugar mill, bringing the total haul to forty-eight US citizens and two Canadians.

"Operation Anti-Aircraft," as Raúl called the kidnap plan, was a last resort. The villages of the Sierra Cristal had been pounded without mercy by Cuban air force B-26s since Operation End of Fidel began in May, and the situation was becoming desperate. Although this breakaway wing of the guerrilla army had increased to two hundred men, padded with urban fighters fleeing Santiago after the failed April strike, they were isolated and almost out of ammunition. As Vilma later put it: "We were lost." The only way to stop the bombing, Raúl felt, was to draw attention to US complicity in Batista's war machine. He declared that all American citizens in the Oriente were subject to seizure. Then, after the kidnappings, he invited US newsmen to visit him in the sierra and see the truth for themselves. As the *Times* stringer Ruby Hart Phillips later wrote, "It was a brilliant idea."

Ernest Hemingway, who was in Havana at the time, saw the comic side of the situation. He called up friends at the US embassy and asked when the rebels were going to start kidnapping FBI agents. Raúl, he joked, would be hosting more Americans on the Fourth of July than the ambassador himself.

Not everyone took the situation so lightly. Initial meetings between guerrillas and hostages were abrasive. Raúl's right-hand man, the former doctor Manuel Fajardo, recalled "those gentlemen thought that we Cubans were savages." One "overweight" sugar executive complained: "My children will be wondering where Papa is, and their papa is in the Cuban jungle." Another asked what Fajardo would do if he just walked out of the guerrilla base, since there was only a handful of guards. "I said that I wasn't planning to use just a pail of water to stop him," Fajardo retorted, and warned that the roads were booby-trapped. As proof, he bandaged up a guerrilla and told the Americans he had stepped on a land mine. ("That's how we held on to them.") Two hostages slipped off anyway but were turned in by a farmer when they asked for water.

Relations improved rapidly when the Americans realized that they would be housed in bucolic comfort. *Los invitados especiales*, "the invited guests," as they were addressed, were billeted in charming residences with clean sheets and soft mattresses, and fed healthy farm food; the luckiest servicemen ended up in an old aristocratic plantation house attended by servants and a private chef who prepared steak and french fries. The liquor supply—rum and beer—was kept up for all. The mood soon became so jovial that, as one Marine later put it, they were all "buddy-buddy." To keep spirits high, the Cubans took the hostages on swimming trips and rainforest hikes. As Hemingway guessed, the rebels also put on a Fourth of July party, with a lunch of barbecued pork and machine guns fired into the air to simulate firecrackers. A baseball game between kidnappers and hostages was interrupted when an air force plane passed overhead and everyone ran for cover, although the score at the time left little doubt about the probable outcome: Rebels, 10; Invited Guests, 4.

But it wasn't all fun and games. The guerrillas also took the Americans on harrowing tours of bombed-out villages where the hospitals were full of maimed and burned civilians. One group was shown the corpse of a three-year-old boy. Raúl had a box full of bomb fragments; one piece read: PROPERTY OF U.S. AIR FORCE.

FIDEL HEARD ABOUT the kidnappings on the radio. By all accounts he was first incredulous, then livid: Raúl had unilaterally put at risk his image in the US, so carefully honed over the last eighteen months. Now there was a good chance, he felt, that Batista's agents would murder Americans and blame the violence on the rebels. (Fidel might also have been annoyed at Raúl for stealing the limelight; many US press reports would emphasize that Raúl's territory was ten times larger than Fidel's.) Even the hard-line Che thought the move a dangerous display of "extremism." Within the US, shrill calls were made for the president to show "some Yankee guts" by sending in the Marines. But Eisenhower, in his first-ever statement on the Cuban Revolution, announced that he was not going to do anything "reckless." The sense of impotence presaged the Iran Hostage Crisis of 1979–81. The goal was not to go in with guns blazing, Eisenhower explained patiently, but "to get live Americans back."

Publicly, Fidel behaved like a diplomat. On July 3 he declared in measured tones on Radio Rebelde that, while Raúl's actions were "understandable," he should immediately release the hostages. A sterner private note was couriered to the Sierra Cristal, although it took nearly ten days to get there: while Raúl was surely "managing the affair with great tact," Fidel wrote, "keep in mind that in matters that have weighty consequences for the Movement, you cannot act on your own initiative." Though he counseled caution from his brother, Fidel himself was hardly immune to anger at the US-assisted bombings. Only a few weeks earlier, on June 5, he had seen one of his friend's farmhouses destroyed, and shot off a furious letter to Celia containing one of his most quoted passages: "When I saw the rockets that they fired on Mario's house, I swore that the Americans are going to pay for what they are doing. When this war is over, I'll start a much longer and bigger war of my own: the war that I'm going to fight against them. I realize that will be my true destiny." But the note was scribbled in anger, and he more often seemed genuinely convinced that the American people misunderstood the situation in Cuba.

Raúl was in no rush to release his hostages; for him, the crisis was a win-win situation. The Americans were the perfect human shield. Aerial bombardments stopped almost overnight in the Sierra Cristal—a crucial respite that allowed him to regroup and rearm his battered forces. The effective cease-fire lasted for three weeks, making each *yanqui* as valuable, Raúl joked, as a 50-millimeter antiaircraft gun.

EVEN FIDEL SOON had to admit the crisis had its upside: the rebels had deftly attracted the world's attention again. For months since the April strike, foreign newspapers had been suggesting that M-26-7 was "through." Now, overnight, some thirty American reporters flew down to Cuba to take up Raúl's invitation. The race for a scoop provoked some hair-raising measures. Two gung ho stalwarts, Robert Taber and Andrew St. George, chartered their own light plane together in Florida. Their wily plan was to parachute directly into Raúl's HQ, but as they flew over the Sierra Cristal they encountered tropical storms and became lost; when they ran out of gas, the pilot safely made a dead-stick landing in a jungle clearing. Guerrillas yelled at them from the forest that the field was mined.

"The rebels were glad to see us," St. George recalled, "but at the same time they were obviously disappointed that their land mines hadn't gone off. They asked us, 'Why didn't you blow up?'"

More sober reporters traveled overland from Havana, smuggled by M-26-7 agents through the army cordons to a dusty village called Las Calabazas, population 400. The outpost, they found, was like a "Wild West town," with horses tethered to posts, naked children playing with chickens in the unpaved streets, and no plumbing. This American press corps soon ranged from high-profile correspondents for glossy national magazines such as *Life* to a staff writer for the more obscure *Battle Creek* (Michigan) *Inquirer.* (Of the thirty US reporters who tried, only eleven made it to the sierra. The others made the mistake of traveling via Guantánamo Bay, where they were "taken hostage," they complained, by the US Navy, which enforced Batista's ban on journalists in the Oriente. They were forced to cover the whole thing from behind barbed wire on the base.)

Like the hostages, journalists were taken on guided tours of both idyllic swimming holes and bombed-out villages, where they became "international witnesses" to US depredations. Bodyguards always followed fifty feet behind—"for the reporters' own safety"—although they could come and go as they pleased with their own jeeps and drivers. A squadron of Latin American and European newsmen soon joined them, until there were so many that every movement by the guerrillas was followed by a cacophony of camera shutters. To manage the multinational scrum, "the Frenchman" Armando Torres was appointed the Las Calabazas "press officer."

THE INTENSE PRESS coverage means that we have a wealth of eyewitness detail about the peculiar interlude in the Sierra Cristal. The first flurry of excitement was the arrival from Santiago of the US negotiator, Consul Park F. Wollam. A tough Foreign Service officer since World War Two, he had made a daring solo journey by jeep with a *guajiro* guide and a driver cradling a shotgun. At one stage the vehicle got stuck in a hole so big it had to be pulled out by an ox. Later Wollam was forced to dive into a pigsty for cover when a Cuban air force plane strafed the road. He watched it drop a bomb near a Baptist church, giving credence to rebel claims that Batista's planes shot anything that moved, and scrawled a message to send back to his superiors: "Call them off!!!!" Not long after, his guerrilla guide pointed at a passing flock of birds. "The rebel air force," he laughed.

Mud-splattered and bruised, Wollam was annoyed to find that Raúl was not even in Las Calabazas yet. Taking up residence in a wood-frame house he dubbed "the Calabash Hilton," he accepted with good humor the dusk mosquito invasions and crack-of-dawn rooster calls, and joined the American journalists sneaking off to bodegas for the occasional rum. He was so adaptable that the press corps fondly dubbed him "the consul in a T-shirt." His vice consul, Robert Wiecha, a former army colonel and undercover CIA agent, was more prickly. Traveling separately, he arrived in one camp at 3:00 a.m. and superciliously refused to stop for the night. The guerrillas promptly informed him that he was under arrest. "This is very serious," Wiecha blustered. "Do you know what you are doing?" The tension was defused when someone produced a bottle of Bacardi rum. They all then sat beneath a lantern chatting about politics—recognizing the American obsession, they assured Wiecha they were not Communists—and the next day took him to visit rebel-run schools. Wiecha was so impressed that when he later returned to Santiago, he sent five hundred notebooks and pencils for use by the children.

RAÚL FINALLY ROARED into Las Calabazas leading a convoy of four brightly colored jeeps seized from the mining companies, to the cheers of his gathered men. He had developed his own distinctive look, with shoulder-length hair, a thin mustache, and a ten-gallon Texas cowboy hat. Although he had only just celebrated his twenty-seventh birthday, he had come into his own as a leader and exuded confidence, joking with his soldiers as he walked. "You see me as I am now, happy and free," he confided to *Life*'s Lee Hall. "But when I meet the United States Consul I will be very serious indeed." By his side was his "attractive" (Hall noted) MIT-educated political advisor, Vilma, who had traveled from Santiago to translate. The youthful, gun-toting pair swaggered about like a tropical Bonnie and Clyde.

At the Calabash Hilton, the two American officials were waiting at a raw wooden dining table crawling with flies. Raúl gave them a theatrical bow and said grandly, *"Buenos días, señores."* Negotiations continued for days, often over the sound of kids playing at their feet and rain pounding the corrugated iron roof. The consul presented a formal letter from Secretary of State John Foster Dulles denying that the US was giving aid to Batista. Raúl countered with photographs of

Cuban air force bombers being refueled in Guantánamo. They had been obtained by Movement agents on the base, while a sympathizer in Cuba's US embassy had forwarded a letter confirming that three hundred American rocket warheads were currently en route. (The warheads, Washington later lamely claimed, were replacements for "defective" earlier shipments already paid for.)

"How do I know you will keep your word?" Raúl berated the consul at one point, evidently relishing the situation. "I want some high official [from the State Department] to come to Las Calabazas and give me solid guarantees you will keep hands off 'our' war." Fidel's gift for the theatrical clearly ran in the family.

Despite the wrangling, the guerrillas were portrayed sympathetically by the American journalists. They conveyed Raúl's disarming apology to the "parents, wives and sweethearts" of the hostages, and described the guerrillas as endearing hosts. Photo spreads showed the rebels hanging out amiably with their supposed captives, sharing cigars. After a friendly clothing accessory swap, many guerrillas went about wearing US Marine insignia on their caps, while the Americans sported M-26-7 armbands like holiday souvenirs. A crewcut Navy airman named Thomas R. Mosnes from Iowa appeared in *Life* lying on his "prison" porch, taking an untroubled siesta. He had been abducted on his twenty-second birthday, he told reporters, but was having a ball: "I always wanted to come up here [to the sierra], anyway. I am just like one of them. They treat me very well." The rebels had even given him a pistol and nicknamed him "Cowboy" because he slung the holster low on his hip.

Airman Mosnes's commander at Guantánamo Bay publicly groused that kidnapped servicemen should not be lounging around in Las Calabazas drinking beer. Mosnes was having a suspiciously "fine time," he complained, and had better get himself back to the Navy base "to straighten himself out." The young airman became so friendly with his captives that Raúl suggested he join the Rebel Army—one reason why the consul made sure he was the first military man to leave. The idea of a *yanqui* guerrilla was certainly not far-fetched: in fact, one of the camp guards, Charles W. Bartlett Jr.—"Charlie"—was actually a twenty-year-old Navy machinist's mate from California who had jumped ship in Guantánamo and was now with Raúl's rebels.

RELUCTANTLY OBEYING FIDEL'S orders, Raúl began releasing hostages in small groups, starting with five married civilians. A daily ritual developed. With no radio contact, Consul Wollam laid out two lines of lavender material in a field as a signal that a rescue helicopter should be sent. (A US observation plane flew overhead at 10:00 a.m., noon, and 4:00 p.m. daily.) The first copter to arrive brought all of Las Calabazas out to watch. They were soon a daily sight, with Navy pilots battling high winds, torrential rain, and the threat of vultures slamming into their windscreens. A rebel "honor guard" would offer a fond farewell to the departing "guests." There were warm embraces from the Cubans, and the Americans gave the guerrillas their leftover toiletries as gifts. The next day, photos of released prisoners would appear in US newspapers, often posing in cotton shirts with goofy grins. They fell over one another in their praise for their captors. One plantation manager declared: "I lived like a millionaire without a cent in my pocket." Another: "These people are fighting for freedom!" The most succinct remark: "He's a swell guy, that Raúl Castro."

The hostages were treated with "a courtesy and friendliness that in other circumstances might have been considered amusing," the *New York Times* admitted. Nobody was in any rush to leave. "Hell, a few days won't hurt us," a mining executive chortled when asked if the delays bothered him. "We are all rebel sympathizers anyway."

Raúl dragged his feet on releasing the last Marines, confessing to Robert Taber that he knew there would be "all hell to pay" when his human shields were gone. The delay allowed the consul to helicopter back to Guantánamo for a hot shower, and gave reporters time at leisure to observe "the strange world of Raúl Castro," as Lee Hall put it in another *Life* photo spread: "To me Raúl seemed partly heroic, partly melodramatic and partly sinister." Hall displayed special interest in Raúl's "consorts," a condescending reference to the women guerrillas. Vilma was shown with a tommy gun above the jaunty caption: "Once [a] U.S. student, she also savvies guns." Her mix of femininity and radicalism was astonishing for readers in the Doris Day era: "In blue jersey pedal pushers, plaid skirt, a red kerchief tied around her thick black hair, she looked like a counselor at a Western girls' camp," Lee noted, and yet Vilma's MIT-honed intellect was intimidating. She could discuss the minutiae of nickel extraction then debate political philosophy with Raúl or foreign policy with the journalists. ("All [the US is] interested in is business," she once snapped at Hall. "It's Wall Street, that's all.")

HALL CONCLUDED WITH disappointment that there was no budding romance among the coed guerrillas in the Sierra Cristal. Vilma had her own room, with four guerrillas hanging their hammocks in front of her door as apparent chaperones. "For all the female companionship Raúl and his companions get they might as well be monks," Hall sighed. But unbeknownst to him, Raúl and Vilma were becoming closer behind the scenes. It was during the summer hostage crisis, Vilma remarked later, that they began "going together."

They seemed an unlikely match. Raúl, the career rebel, had been raised running wild on the farm in Birán; she was the cosseted attorney's daughter, raised on classical ballet and high society balls in Santiago. Their dating history was patchy. After their first meeting in Mexico City—Raúl and Fidel had both welcomed Vilma at the airport with an orchid; Raúl invited her on a "date" to go on shooting practice in the countryside, but it had fallen through—they had run into one another again in the Sierra Maestra in February 1957. But Vilma admitted that she barely noticed the younger Castro until she went up to the Sierra Cristal the next year and found him in command. The pair never spoke about the details, but when it came time for her to return to Santiago, Raúl forbade it. He had already written to her fellow operative "Anita" that the city was too dangerous: "When I think that if Frank had done the same [fled to the sierra], we would still have him fighting by our side, I insist every time more that the *rabilarga* [a nickname for Vilma taken from a long-tailed, azure-winged Cuban bird] should come here. If they capture her they are going to cut her to pieces, and you yourself will die of remorse and heavy conscience. Then the Movement will have lost two great *compañeras*."

Raúl's instinct was correct. Soon after, telephone operators in Santiago overheard two SIM officers saying that the M-26-7 agent code-named "Debora" had been identified as the schoolteacher Vilma Espín, and they should "grab her." She was *quemada*. From now on, Vilma would be Raúl's permanent aide-de-camp, soon trading her plaid skirt for a khaki uniform, red-and-black armband, and black beret. Vilma was relieved to escape the near-unbearable tension of the urban underground, with its constant risk of "dying shoeless," as the expression went, in a police cell. Her cover was far more publicly blown when the two issues of *Life* magazine came out in the US with her photo splashed all over them. Batista's agents clipped the pages and passed them around to army officers with instructions to identify any people or buildings for possible reprisals.

Raúl released the last Marines on July 18 in a deal brokered by a veteran *Chicago Tribune* journalist, Jules Dubois. A few days later Raúl entered in his expenses ledger: "$1,400 for the Americans," covering incidentals such as rice, beans, and beer.

CHAPTER 25

The Comeback

(July–August 1959)

THE MOST LASTING CONSEQUENCE OF the hostage crisis was to draw attention to the army's apocalyptic offensive in the Sierra Maestra, which was running into unexpected trouble. Batista's censorship had imposed a complete news blackout, except for the usual fabricated press releases nobody paid attention to. (In the most egregious one, the military reported two hundred guerrillas killed with only one soldier wounded "in the hand"; Cubans joked that Batista had "the bulletproof army.") But by July, Radio Rebelde's reports that the mass invasion was faltering drew the attention of the gaggle of foreign journalists who had flown to Cuba. M-26-7 agents spirited several up to meet Fidel in the Comandancia, including NBC producer Morton Silverstein, who took back one of Castro's hand-drawn battle maps to be published in the *New York Times*. Even the army would soon have to admit that something was going seriously awry in their "End of Fidel" campaign.

Despite the early setbacks, Fidel's plan of falling back until he was ready to counterattack paid off on June 28 when an army patrol was ambushed at the Yara River. The vanguard was engulfed by a sixty-five-pound TNT explosion, then cut down by snipers. It was a total rout, and the Rebel Army's first clear victory. Soldiers left behind their weapons, their wounded, and their dead. Twenty-three were taken prisoner, along with fifty rifles, ammunition, and—an item that would turn out to be even more valuable—an army radio transmitter with its codebook. The captives were then transferred to a holding camp rebels dubbed Puerto Malanga, "Tuber Port," a play on the name of Batista's notorious prison in Santiago, Puerto Boniato ("Sweet Potato Port").

Although the army had clawed its way into rebel-controlled territory around Las Vegas in June, the deep sierra was proving far more daunting. In its dense jungles and gullies, patrols leading the two main pincer movements could be isolated and picked off. The conscripts were showing signs of exhaustion. But then in early July a new danger appeared when the third, amphibious prong of the invasion was launched. Supported by naval bombardments, 1,000 troops stormed the rocky beaches of the south coast, where the Sierra Maestra dips precipitously down to the Caribbean Sea, and surged inland to encircle the guerrillas.

As luck would have it, the landing was led by one of Fidel's fellow law students from Havana University, Major José Quevado. On the spur of the moment, Fidel sent him an affectionate note, lapsing into the informal *tú* form of Spanish: "Dear friend, it would have been difficult to imagine when we knew each other at college that one day we would be fighting one another . . ." He concluded: "I sent off these lines without thinking about it . . . just to greet you and to wish you, very sincerely, good luck." Quevado later admitted that he was perplexed and unnerved by the amiable missive, which was signed, "Your friend, Fidel Castro."

The ensuing Battle of El Jigüey would prove to be Batista's Stalingrad. Quevado's men successfully hacked their way over one high ridge, but after heavy fighting were forced to retreat into a river valley. Instead of surrounding the rebels, the soldiers were trapped themselves. The air force tried to parachute in food, but the guerrillas intercepted the drops. Fidel used the captured radio transmitter to sow confusion, since the army high command (with extravagant incompetence) had failed to change the secret codes. He ordered a recruit with acting talent, Braulio Coroneaux, to transmit fabricated reports "in a desperate tone—that there are men starving to death in the mountains, that the rebels are still in the camp . . . and that for God's sake they should send reinforcements, that there are many wounded." The ruse worked and the air force swooped down to bomb their own men with napalm. "Now the guards run like hell every time they hear a plane," Fidel exulted.

Twice Quevado tried to break out in vain. ("I control them completely," Guillermo García gloated. "They even have to shit in their trenches.") And it was at El Jigüey that the guerrillas honed psychological warfare. All through the night, loudspeakers blasted the maddeningly cheerful mariachi strains of "La Cucaracha" followed by a bland announcement: "You have now heard some pretty music. The battle begins again." (The effect on troops huddled in the darkness, one officer admitted, was "devastating.") On other nights, the guerrillas would fall silent and hide, pretending they had left; but when the soldiers began to explore, the barrage of gunfire would erupt. Fidel offered his old college mate Quevado—this time using the formal form of Spanish address, *usted*—an "honorable, dignified surrender." Like his half-starved soldiers, the major himself was suffering from serious malnutrition. Fidel sent him some food so that he could be strong enough to meet him for negotiations, but he vomited it up. When Quevado finally arrived on horseback, Fidel greeted him like an old comrade and began chatting about their student days. The officer was dumbfounded: his first reaction was that Fidel was "crazy." This was "the worst moment of my life," Quevado recalled; he was sick and humiliated, and here was Fidel behaving as if they were back at the college café. Celia, ignoring a bomb that fell nearby, led the major to a cave to discuss surrender terms. Quevado was permitted to keep his pistol and even visit his men in the prison of Puerto Malanga by himself—"like a gentleman." He would remain a prisoner at the Comandancia, where he was provided with food and cigars for several months, until he finally gave up and joined the rebels.

The last 150 soldiers at El Jigüey threw down their arms on July 21. "Try to have lunch prepared" for the surrender, Fidel told Che. He also wanted a record of the historic occasion: "Not one photo has been taken of anything. Could you do something about this? It's a pity!"

QUEVADO'S SURRENDER WAS a shocking setback for the army, and Batista's censors desperately tried to keep news from spreading. There were now 253 hungry soldiers in Puerto Malanga, a quarter of them wounded. The number was far more than the rebels could deal with, so Fidel contacted the International Red Cross to broker a prisoner return. He did not ask for an exchange, since the army left no rebel captives alive to swap.

The messenger chosen to arrange the cease-fire—a dangerous solo mission across enemy lines—was an extroverted seventeen-year-old girl known as Teté. Delsa Esther Puebla had experiences far beyond her years: she was only fifteen when she began transporting dynamite for the guerrillas beneath her crinoline dress in a special girdle nicknamed La Engañadora, "the Deceiver," after a hit pop song. Forced to flee her hometown Yara in July 1957, Teté was in the first group of three women to arrive in the Sierra Maestra. (The others, met by Juan Almeida, were Geña Verdecia and Ileana Rodés.) When they first arrived, one of the males asked: "What is this *mocosa* [snot-nosed kid] doing here?"—providing her with a permanent nickname. But Fidel was genuinely delighted: "The women have arrived!" he declared. "Now the guerrilla forces are really growing."

Twelve months later, Teté's negotiating role involved a new level of risk. Che, who was overseeing the prisoner return, reasoned that Batista's trigger-happy soldiers would probably just shoot a male guerrilla on sight, but would hesitate to gun down a *guerrillera*. Even so, he sat her down to prepare her for the worst: "All right, Teté, three things can happen," she recalled him saying. "The [army] can accept the truce and everything's fine. Or they can kill you. Or they can take you prisoner and take you to Bayamo." The latter option might involve torture, rape, and execution. Even after this dubious pep talk, Teté signed on.

At dawn on July 24 she let down her long, tawny hair to make her gender obvious, mounted a mule, and set off for the enemy camp. She was in uniform but unarmed and carrying a white flag tied to a long stick. The mission was expected to only take a few hours, but delays began immediately when aerial bombing forced her off the trail. When Teté finally approached the sentries, they were confused by the strange sight of a woman in khakis; unable to think what else to do, they let her past. As she rode through the muddy outpost, soldiers stopped in their tracks to stare. The commander, Captain Carlos Durán Batista, tried at first to bully her. He ordered her to take her M-26-7 armband off and when she refused, threatened to arrest her. According to Teté, "he was insulting and asked me how a pretty girl like me could be with that filthy and bedraggled bunch of guerrillas." His main concern, it transpired, was keeping news of Quevado's defeat a secret from his own men to keep morale from crumbling. He wanted the troops to somehow believe that the returned prisoners were really captured rebels. But with little alternative, the captain begrudgingly agreed to a cease-fire the next day.

When Teté made it back into the guerrilla camp at dusk, Fidel, Che, and Camilo were all waiting for her anxiously. They greeted her with cheers and carried her around the camp on their shoulders. But the danger was far from over: she had to head back that same night to confirm the cease-fire. Captain Durán made her sleep in his own tent so she wouldn't talk to the soldiers, but she snuck out into the trenches after he fell asleep.

The next morning, Che arrived with the 253 prisoners marching in single file. They made, as Teté recalled, "a strange caravan." The wounded used canes or crutches fashioned from branches; the most seriously injured were carried in hammocks slung from poles. The soldiers stood gaping. Fidel recalled: "If the presence of a woman guerrilla, Teté, had been the cause for great excitement amongst the guards, even more astonishing was the surprise arrival of Che . . . [He] had already become a legend, and the soldiers relished the opportunity to see the Argentine guerrilla fighter in person."

EL JIGÜEY HAD tipped the balance of the offensive. In a confidential report to Batista, a sheepish General Cantillo guessed that the guerrillas had fielded between 1,000 and 2,000 men "of the first class, quite well armed." ("On top of that, almost every inhabitant, man, woman or child, of the high sierra is a rebel confidant, courier or informer.") He admitted that most of his own troops could not cope with the terrain; perhaps it was wiser to lure the guerrillas into the open plains. Fear of the *barbudos* was now seeping through the armed forces: rumors spread that troops in Havana would jump from the trucks when told they were going to be airlifted to Oriente.

The Rebel Army now began regaining the territory it had lost. The strategic village of Las Vegas was seized in late July, to Fidel's great satisfaction; the rest of the Free Zone soon followed. At Las Mercedes, the rebels even captured a Sherman tank, a potentially fabulous prize that induced in Fidel fantastic visions of storming like Patton across the sierra. Unfortunately, it was stuck in a deep muddy ditch, and all efforts to drive it out failed. Fidel even hired a team of oxen to pull it out, but the tank's steering system broke, rendering it useless. ("Hopes dashed," Fidel wrote mournfully. "It has been a long time since I've had such pipe dreams.")

When another 160 soldiers surrendered, the army began withdrawing from the Sierra Maestra altogether. By August 7 the last government troops were gone. Even to the guerrillas, the lopsided victory was like something out of a fairy tale. Years later, Fidel started his memoir about the campaign by saying that he couldn't decide on a title: "I didn't know whether to call this *Batista's Last Offensive* or *How 300 Defeated 10,000*, which sounds like a story from *One Thousand and*

One Nights." (He decided on *The Strategic Victory.*) In the seventy-four days of fighting, only thirty-one guerrillas had been killed; army casualties were ten times that number, with 1,000 wounded. The Rebel Army had captured a total of 443 prisoners and 507 weapons. "The offensive has been liquidated," Radio Rebelde crowed. "The biggest military effort in the history of our Republic has ended in the most shocking disaster the arrogant dictator could have imagined. His troops are in open retreat." The Free Zone was now permanent: "The Sierra Maestra, in effect, has been liberated forever."

Only now did *New York Times* stringer Ruby Hart Phillips decide she had better buy a shortwave radio to keep abreast of rebel broadcasts. Like other Cubans, she had to listen to them furtively, closing all doors and windows in her office and turning up the air-conditioning full blast to foil eavesdroppers.

ON AUGUST 13, Celia threw a surprise party for Fidel's thirty-second birthday on a forested mountainside. In perhaps her most elegant logistical achievement, she had an ice cream cake shipped up from Manzanillo; it survived the scorching summer heat by being packed in dry ice. Fidel was delighted. And yet, as he confessed to her in private: "In the middle of my happiness at our victory, the culmination of so many sacrifices and efforts, I feel sad." The summer triumph was made bittersweet by the loss of close friends. The stalwart Beto Pesant, one of the Movement's first supporters in the Oriente, was blown up by accident while he was handling an antiaircraft shell. Che was thrown a distance by the explosion, and his lover Zoila ran up to Beto, horrified. ("Beto, don't die, don't die!" she shouted until Che took her aside, whispering, "Zoila, he's gone.") Pesant's wife traveled to the front lines for the funeral: "We all cried and when I looked at Guevara he had tears in his eyes." René Ramos Latour, the former Santiago chief aka "Daniel," was hit in the stomach by mortar shrapnel in the last days of the offensive. Che dashed to the clinic "only to find a corpse at my arrival." The wound was several inches deep, he lamented, "but he could have been saved if he had had immediate medical attention."

Pedro Miret, meanwhile, had a lucky escape: he was hit in the chest by a ricocheting bullet from a strafing plane, but it didn't penetrate beyond the breastbone.

THE FINAL PRISONER return in early August had been a cordial affair: one of the negotiating army officers offered to take Fidel for a spin in his Soviet-made Sikorsky helicopter. To the shock of their bodyguards, Fidel, Che, and Celia all hopped on board and took off for an aerial tour of the Sierra Maestra, enjoying the clear day and recognizing key landmarks. "It was a Fidel-type thing," his aide-de-camp later said with a shrug. This time, the army captives were exchanged for $10,000 worth of medicine and plasma. "You may have the mountains," Colonel Fernando Neugart magnanimously conceded, "but we are waiting for you in the valleys."

There is no record of Fidel's response, but he already had other plans.

CHAPTER 26

Women in Uniform

(September 1958)

I T WASN'T ONLY Batista's soldiers who were wide-eyed at the sight of Teté in khakis. *Paris Match*, *Life*, the *New York Times*—media outlets around the world were fascinated by the women in the Rebel Army. Flicking through the publications today, there is a startling contrast between the images of the Cuban Amazons and the cheesy advertisements alongside them, which depicted ideal middle-class housewives of the 1950s polishing floors and washing dishes. The *guerrilleras* were ahead of their time, blazing a way for the incipient feminist movement five years before Betty Friedan's *Feminine Mystique* popularized the term "Women's Liberation."

The effect was even more powerful within Cuba itself, where traditional Latin culture affirmed the sanctity of marriage and role of women in the home. Visitors to sierra camps estimated the *guerrilleras* to be outnumbered by men twenty to one. But trumpeted by Radio Rebelde, their presence had an impact far beyond their numbers: their very existence seemed proof that the entire populace was being mobilized to eject Batista.

While much of the early media attention was given to high-ranking women—Celia presiding at a revolutionary trial, Haydée hiking Pico Turquino, Vilma cradling her tommy gun—there were many others in the rank and file. The majority were recruited in the cities, and were young and unattached, but some were married to fellow guerrillas. Several had children, whom they left with their families for the duration of the conflict. Their numbers, a trickle in 1957, became a steady flow in 1958, until there were enough to form an all-female brigade. Largely forgotten for decades, they would blaze the way for women in irregular armies decades later in Nicaragua, El Salvador, and Colombia and eventually for conventional armed forces in First World countries. (It was not until 1976 that women were admitted into West Point and other US military academies.)

STILL, THE REBEL Army was hardly a feminist paradise. Women who arrived in the sierra after days of grueling hiking had to contend with the macho culture of the rank-and-file men and ingrained sexism of the leaders. Having been treated as relative equals in the cities, they now found themselves relegated to domestic support roles as cooks, nurses, and seamstresses. Che pontificated that women in guerrilla camps should perform "their habitual tasks of peacetime," particularly cooking: "It is very pleasing for a soldier subjected to the extremely hard conditions of this life to be able to look forward to a seasoned meal that tastes like something." Male volunteers naturally "scorn . . . tasks of a civilian character," he adds, whereas women will tolerate them. The exception to the rule, he conceded, was that women made superior couriers to men, but only by taking advantage of sexism: they "can transport [messages] through a thousand tricks. It is a fact that however brutal the repression, however thorough the body-searches, the woman receives less harsh treatment than the man."

These antiquated gender roles crumbled before the reality of guerrilla life, especially in times of crisis. The summer offensive in the Sierra Maestra was a watershed: Teté, for example, was delivering food to the troops in the hamlet of Villa Islazul Santo Domingo when it was in danger of being overrun, so she simply picked up a rifle and

started firing. Women helped dig trenches and endured air bombardments; they kept the telephone lines working and carried orders to the
front lines. Three *guerrilleras* narrowly escaped death when a mortar
shell hit a mess hut just minutes after they had left it, killing two soldiers and the cook. But after the army's withdrawal from the sierra,
the men tried to return women to purely domestic positions. As Teté
indignantly put it: "We had already proved that women could do just
about everything. But we were still not allowed to fight."

In frustration, a dozen women appealed directly to Fidel. As an
aficionado of Cuban history, he was well aware that *guerrilleras* had
played a vigorous role in the nineteenth-century wars of independence, a memory that Celia reminded him of whenever she could. He
decided to call a round table meeting for September 4 in the Comandancia hospital, warning the men in advance that they were not going
to like what he was going to say. As he predicted, his announcement
that he would form an all-women platoon provoked a furious debate
that lasted for over seven hours. The counterarguments are an ency-
clopedia of sexism. Some men said it was foolish to arm women when
there were still not enough rifles to go around. Others protested that
if women fought, men might be stuck doing the cooking themselves.
The doctor, René Vallejo Ortiz, was the most vocal critic. He argued
that women would lose their "femininity" if they "turned into lion-
esses," adding that "from the biological point of view, women have a
cycle that can make them weak." Women's maternal instincts would
also make them stop and help wounded enemy soldiers instead of
fighting. Ortiz even argued that they were not used to the sight of
blood—an absurd suggestion, given that most of them had done stints
with him as nurses.

"If you can win this fight, you can win anything," Fidel joked to
Teté as the arguments raged past midnight. But Fidel helped them
carry the day, and at 1:00 a.m., he swore in thirteen *compañeras* as the
Mariana Grajales Women's Platoon. It was named after the indestruc-
tible Afro-Cuban mother of independence hero General Antonio Ma-

ceo, who traveled with rebel troops on campaign against the Spanish in the 1890s, and entered open battles in search of the wounded; she herself lost nine of her eleven sons in the war. Even the meeting date, September 4, had been chosen for its rich historical symbolism. It was the twenty-fifth anniversary of the "Sergeant's Revolt" that first brought Batista to power in 1933. While soldiers were drunkenly firing their guns in celebration, Fidel told the meeting, the Rebel Army was creating a new future for Cuban women.

Teté remembers Fidel taking them aside later: "*Muchachitas*, you have seen how much I had to argue for you so that you can fight. Don't make me look bad."

MOST OF THE Marianas, as they were known, were in their late teens. The oldest, Rita García, was a thirty-six-year-old widowed mother of six, who the others teasingly called "grandmother," despite the fact that she was such a fast hiker the others had to almost run to keep up. The youngest, Norma Ferrer, was fourteen, and had cut her teeth graffitiing revolutionary slogans on walls and the sides of buses in Manzanillo. (She fled to the sierra, she said, to take a more active role in society: "I found a reason to live, I found a reason to die.") They came from a variety of social and racial backgrounds. Teté had grown up in a dirt-floored hut with a leftist campesino family. Isabel Rielo had been a chemistry student and was referred to as "Doctora." Angelina Antolín, meanwhile, came to the sierra because she had nowhere else to go: she had been harassed by Rural Guards after her husband joined the guerrillas and fled for his life, leaving her three young children with relatives.

The day after the platoon was formed, Fidel took the women for rifle practice, declaring that whoever was the best shot would be made leader. He nailed a twenty-centavo coin, the size of a quarter, to a tree and they all took turns trying to hit it from ninety feet. Isabel Rielo won the honor and was given command; Teté, although she was more experienced, came second. Equipped with the relatively light M1 Garand rifles, Fidel appointed them his personal bodyguards at the Comandancia and, as a statement about women's equality, sent them ahead as his advance detachment whenever he traveled in the sierra. There was much grumbling, Teté recalls: "Some of the men would say things like, 'If the enemy soldiers toss a lizard at them, the women are going to dump their rifles and run.' But they were only jealous, because Fidel used to say, 'They are better soldiers than you are.'"

The Marianas first went into action on September 27 at Cerro Pelado, a long engagement where they were heavily shelled by mortars and Sherman tanks. They did not fire a shot, but held fast under intense pressure. This hardly ended the sexism: the women now realized that as well as fighting, they were expected to continue cooking for the men, cleaning, and getting up at dawn to make the coffee. ("We almost didn't sleep," Teté sighed.) One of their most outspoken critics, Eddy Suñol, was actually married to one of the Marianas, Lola Feria. He became apoplectic when he was told by Fidel that he had to take four women, including his wife, Lola, Isabel, and Teté, with him on an expedition into the plains. His first response was: "No, no, no and no," Teté recalled, adding: "I wanted to kill him." Only after Fidel threatened to cancel his mission entirely did Suñol reluctantly agree. "I'll take them," he said ruefully. "But it's going to be the death of them all."

The first weeks of the campaign were the most difficult, as the women were tossed straight into the austere guerrilla lifestyle. Each lost twenty pounds; even when food was later plentiful, none of them ever weighed more than 105 pounds. With only one change of clothes each and sharing a single piece of nylon to sleep under, they became accustomed to being permanently wet. Surrounded by men twenty-four hours a day, they also had to overcome their conservative upbringings. Teté recalled the awkwardness of having to deal with personal "necessities": "We had to just tell the men to turn around." Several of the women made a pact to carry an extra bullet each, which they would use on themselves if they were ever on the verge of capture.

Suñol's opinion of the Marianas was changed on October 21, when they and a contingent of male guerrillas were surprised by two trucks full of soldiers and surrounded. In the bitter firefight that followed, Flor Peréz Chávez was shot in the thigh and spent weeks in recovery; a bullet also whizzed by Isabel's head so close it "scorched" her. But the coed rebels beat the army back and captured eleven rifles. "After that, the issue was settled," Teté recalled. Eddy Suñol sent a message to Fidel apologizing for his former opposition. "When the order was given to advance, some of the men stayed behind, but the women went ahead in the vanguard," he wrote. "Their courage and calm under fire merits the respect and admiration of the entire Rebel Army—and everyone else." Ten days later, when Suñol himself was wounded at Los Güiros, far from friendly support lines, it was the Marianas who pulled a local doctor from his bed and forced him to treat their leader at gunpoint.

DESPITE FEARS THAT *guerrilleras* would become distractions for the sex-starved males, Teté recalled that the relationship on the field was usually fraternal. The Marianas were drawn into the intense camaraderie of the guerrilla bands, where a single cigarette might be passed around among twenty and the most minuscule piece of bread broken up and shared. Still, complications developed. As Isabel recalled: "Whenever men and women are together, amorous feelings can arise." The Marianas had their own camp, where males were forbidden unless invited. But, Isabel said, "Women are women and men, men. That being so, love stories sprung up, later marriages." Evita Palma took up with a guerrilla named Gonzalo Camejo, with whom she remained inseparable—"like little tortoises" as the expression went. The teenage Norma fell for a young recruit who promised that after the war he would drive her around "in a black carriage with a bouquet of flowers." She later learned that he was killed in a mortar attack. The "guerrilla priest" Father Sardiñas wandered the camps in his khaki vestments offering to make the sporadic liaisons legal, with mixed success. One straitlaced visitor reported the coed life led to "moral disintegration," although conceded it was probably no worse than regular armies. Many of the romances lasted: Teté later married a soldier she first met on campaign.

MEANWHILE, IN THE cities, women continued to be involved in the Movement on every level and took risks at least as great as men. The first death had been the eighteen-year-old Urselia Díaz Báez, who smuggled a bomb strapped to her thigh into Havana's America Cinema in early September 1957 and was blown up while trying to set the watch timer in the bathroom. By 1958, SIM agents had gotten over their conviction that women were frail and apolitical and began unleashing their brand of savagery on them. The torture of a schoolteacher with a soldering iron in March was only the start. In June, Maria and Cristina Giral, two young sisters who were part of the Civic Resistance in Havana, were caught up in a police sweep after the assassination of a Batista crony. When they didn't turn up for work the next morning, their brothers and employer searched the hospital wards. Eventually, the girls' half-naked bodies were found in the city morgue; they had black eyes and were shot in the chest, with evidence of sexual molestation. The police declared that a search of the girls' apartment had turned up guns, pamphlets, and "a book by Leon Trotsky." The sympathetic Jules Dubois of the *Chicago Tribune* arranged for the girls' employer, José Ferrer, to meet with the US ambassador, Earl Smith, who naïvely asked whether he had "gone to the police to file a complaint." "What police?" Ferrer retorted. "The same police who killed the girls?" According to Ferrer, Smith replied: "What do you want us to do, send in the Marines?"

The dangers for women were driven home again only a week after the Marianas were formed in September, when Che and Fidel's courageous "executive couriers" both vanished in Havana. The two women

had been in the capital for several weeks, and nothing appeared out of the ordinary when Che's courier, the gutsy middle-aged former store-keeper Lidia Doce, sent a playful letter to the Sierra Maestra saying she had a small puppy to bring back for Che as a gift: "I'm unhappy because I don't have my *comandante* here to give me orders," she teased. "By God, send for me soon! Because I want to see you and give you a big hug just as you deserve, even if I don't." (Her devotion to the Argentine was such that she called herself a "Che-ista.")

The night before she was to leave Havana, Lidia went for ice cream with other women agents—they would remember that she ordered a "Lolita cup," a cheeky homage to Nabokov, with two custard flans dotted with small scoops of pink ice cream—then met up with Fidel's executive courier, Clodomira Acosta. "Clodo" broke the mold of the city-educated women activists: a shy, plain-looking farm girl, she was twenty-one years old but looked only sixteen. Her tiny size belied her physical strength, and she had twice escaped from prison. (On one occasion, the police had shaved her head; Isabel joked she looked "just like Yul Brynner.") Before her first assignment, worried that Clodo's unpolished style would give her away, Celia had asked a friend in Santiago to give her a makeover: "Take Clodo to a dentist and have her teeth fixed; then get her to a beauty salon."

Lidia and Clodo's pleasant reunion took an ominous turn after dark, when a SIM informer known as "the Jeweler" was murdered and police roundups began. Unnerved by the activity, the two women took refuge in a safe house in Regla, a city neighborhood across Havana Harbor, with four male agents. It was an unlucky choice. An arrested agent known as "Popeye" cracked under torture and led police to their door. In the ensuing bloodbath, four policemen died and the surviving male M-26-7 agents were executed on the spot. Clodo and the badly wounded Lidia were bundled into a car and taken to a precinct station overlooking the waterfront. They were never seen again.

Many months later, a police officer who was present provided the most accepted account of their fate. The two women fell into the

clutches of Lieutenant Julio Laurent, the ruthless naval intelligence officer who had dispatched many of Fidel's men after the *Granma* landing. The beatings began immediately. When Lidia was knocked unconscious by a blow to one of her bullet wounds, Clodo started punching and scratching the officers. ("She was a real beast, that one," the officer reported, showing the interviewer the scar from a bite on his shoulder.) The two women were then placed in sacks and lowered by ropes into the sea. Lidia drowned on the third immersion. Clodo was near death when they shot her. Both sacks were then filled with rocks and tossed back into the waves.

ON OCCASION, THE sexism of Cuban soldiers could still be manipulated by women operatives. This was the case in one of the revolution's most daring raids, which occurred a few weeks earlier in the summer. It was put in motion when M-26-7 agents learned that one of their highest-ranking imprisoned officers, Carlos Iglesias Fonseca (aka "Nicaragua") was being transferred by overnight train from Havana to Santiago to face a new trial. The route passed the Sierra Cristal, so Raúl decided to stage a railroad holdup that would have impressed Jesse James.

The seat-of-the-pants plan began at Havana station: an innocent-looking agent, Martha Correa, peered in the carriage windows pretending to look for a friend, and established where Nicaragua was sitting, handcuffed and surrounded by guards. In the Oriente, Captain Raúl Tomassevich was put in charge of the rescue. (The rakish Tomassevich had himself escaped eighteen months earlier from Boniato prison. After stealing a pistol from beneath the pillow of a sleeping warden, he and six other inmates had locked up the jailers, put on civilian clothes, and calmly walked out the front gates. "Perhaps if we had planned a classic escape, digging a tunnel, climbing a wall or inflating a zeppelin on the rooftop, we would have been captured," Tomassevich explained, "but we did what the authorities never imagined.")

He arranged for four Movement agents to board Nicaragua's carriage en route; one, eighteen-year-old Nancy Ojeda Miranda, carried two pistols taped to her abdomen. Five guerrillas also volunteered to shave and infiltrate the train in civilian clothes. The undercover teams had never met, so to identify themselves they were given code words ("Frank," counterword "País") and tied red-and-black ribbons to their revolvers. They all planned to strike at the point where thirty guerrillas had blocked the tracks.

As the locomotive rattled through the night, many of the guards got drunk on cheap rum. Even so, they searched the teenage Nancy and her three companions when they boarded; the demure-looking teenage girl opened her bags with a shy smile, and the guards didn't think to frisk her loose blouse. The spruced-up guerrillas who boarded soon after were not so lucky. A soldier quickly found the revolver in one man's belt, with the telltale M-26-7 ribbon. A wild shoot-out ensued, sending passengers hiding under seats. Seconds later, the entire train was plunged into chaos when the driver stopped at the blocked tracks and guerrillas started firing at the windows. Nancy slipped her pistols to the undercover agents, who also started blazing. Glass flew, carriages filled with smoke. Nicaragua managed to free one hand from his cuffs and crawl out the train door, picking up an automatic rifle along the way. When he tried to join the fight, Tomassevich had to drag him angrily to safety.

By the time the shooting ended, eleven soldiers had been killed; the others had changed into civilian clothes and hidden. It was a bloody victory. The guerrillas had five dead, including three of their five disguised volunteers. Miraculously, only one passenger had been killed: an elderly man had been ordered by soldiers to take a message to the train driver and, when he had refused, was shot dead. As the guerrillas drove by jeep towards the mountains, Tomassevich looked back at the train. "The most gratifying image of the day," he says, "was the surge of [passengers'] hands waving in the air accompanied by affectionate smiles, as if a patriotic delegation was congratulating us."

CHAPTER 27

Hurricane Season

(August–October 1958)

T HE TOTAL WITHDRAWAL of the army from the Sierra Maestra had
surpassed the rebels' wildest dreams. Most observers assumed the
guerrillas would take a well-earned break and repair the havoc caused
to their mountain republic. Instead, Fidel decided to send Che and
Camilo Cienfuegos immediately on the offensive. He ordered each of
them to descend into the lowlands with a column of volunteers and
sneak along the length of Cuba. Their two forces would meet in the
island's geographical middle—the belly of the crocodile, as it were—
where another mountain range, the Escambray, hovered south of the
city of Santa Clara, cutting Cuba in two. As biographer Tad Szulc
aptly sums up, "It must have seemed like a demented plan." They
would be leaving the security of the Free Zone, with its natural defenses and finely tuned support networks, for total uncertainty and
exposure to attack. Recruitment for the missions was sluggish, possibly because Che declared that he expected a 50 percent casualty rate;
his blunt warning that volunteers should expect miserable conditions
with little or no food was less than encouraging. But the two leaders
of the mission seem never to have doubted that they would succeed.
Camilo left the Comandancia with eighty-two men (the magical
Granma number) on August 21, less than a week after the last soldiers

had abandoned the Sierra Maestra; Che left with 148 men ten days later.

On his last night, the bon vivant Camilo somehow obtained a good bottle of wine and tried to find Fidel for a farewell toast; he ended up drinking it with the journalist Carlos Franqui and leaving a cheerful note. Che had to say farewell to his lover Zoila before leaving. She begged to come along with him on the expedition, but it was too dangerous, Che insisted, and they kissed good-bye at the village of El Jíbaro. It was the end of their affair. As a consolation, Che left her his favorite mule Armando, who she had shod at their first meeting. ("I cared for him as if he were a real Christian," Zoila recalled.)

Che and Camilo's optimism would be sorely put to the test. The 350-mile trek was one of the most extreme experiences of the war. Their men were forced to trudge through desolate swamps, often at night, dodging an unreliable populace and the army snapping at their heels. Planes strafed them whenever they were caught in the open. For much of the time they were simply lost. To make matters even worse, it was hurricane season: every step was made more difficult by the tropical storms that pummeled the island with clockwork regularity.

Camilo had been gone for around ten days when Hurricane Ella hit the Oriente; Che was just preparing to leave and caught the brunt of the system. Rains had already been pounding down for days before the storm made landfall at Santiago on September 2 then hit the Sierra Maestra. Gale-force winds were measured at 115 miles per hour, flooding roads and tearing the thatch roofs from the Comandancia. The Bayamo River overflowed and swept away twenty-five houses. At least six people drowned, along with hundreds of livestock. The gales subsided on the 6th, but Ella was soon followed by Hurricane Fifi. Over the rest of the month, Tropical Storm Gerda, Hurricane Helene, and Hurricane Ilsa followed, each one bringing torrential deluges. (Che, with typical practicality, used the alphabetic order of the hurricanes' names to teach illiterate men their letters.) Devastating although they were, the storms often worked to the guerrillas' advantage: Batista's troops stayed in their barracks; aerial searches were grounded. Camilo and Che were able to melt into the sodden countryside for crucial days.

CAMILO RECALLED HIS harrowing expedition in religious terms as forty days and forty nights of famine. The first two weeks following the south coast were "disastrously bad," he admitted in his official report to Fidel, as his men slogged through marshland with water and mud up to their knees. In the first month they ate only eleven times; at one stage, after four days without a meal, they devoured one of their packhorses, "raw and unsalted." Their sixty-strong "cavalry" soon had to be abandoned. When they managed to commandeer some trucks, they became stuck in mud after only a few miles.

One flooded river was crossed with handmade rafts; to ford another, they strung up a rope and dragged themselves across currents surging up to their chests. ("When I reached the other bank, I kissed the ground," Camilo noted.) In the flat, unfamiliar landscape, they found they had sometimes wandered in circles. Reliable guides proved difficult to find among the sullen inhabitants; some scouts became lost themselves or turned out to be police informers. A lucky break occurred when they captured an army corporal with an excellent memory who revealed the only safe route through the obstacle course of army posts. As they headed west, Camilo was also encouraged to find that the few patrols who did spot the guerrillas would often try to avoid them. ("This is striking proof that Batista's army does not want to fight and its morale is getting lower and lower.") Still, there were accidental skirmishes. An unlucky lieutenant, Senén Mariño, was captured and tortured to death, but "he conducted himself like a true revolutionary and did not give our location away to the enemy."

It took Camilo's men six weeks to reach their goal, a feat of endurance worthy of the Victorian explorers. Only three of his eighty-two men were killed en route; five dropped out from physical exhaustion. Fidel was elated. "There are no words with which to express the joy, the pride and the admiration that I feel for you and your men," he wrote back to Camilo.

CHE WAS JUST as frank when reporting his own "truly horrible" trek. His column of 148 men was a disparate bunch, including El Vaquerito and his "suicide squad"; a gung ho American named Herman Marks who said he had served in the Korean War; and Lázaro, "El Negro," a hulking Afro-Cuban with a whimsical sense of humor who lugged a leather saddle on the entire expedition in case he found a horse to ride. (He never did.) Che also brought along his notorious disciplinary squadron to treat what he called *apendijitis*, or "yellowitis." (Che had not softened his Spartan severity. Several months earlier, some teens went on a hunger strike over the terrible food at his camp. At first he threatened to shoot the lot of them. Only after discussing the matter with Fidel did he relent and order them to go without food entirely for five days "so they could know what real hunger was.")

Che had hoped to start his journey in trucks, but the army intercepted the gasoline shipment. The rains from Hurricane Ella soon made the roads unpassable in any case, so he, too, resolved to hike cross-country. "I've been through enough mud and water to last me the rest of my life," he wrote to Fidel. With his usual poetic economy, Che conjured their journey: "Hunger, thirst, weariness, the feeling of impotence against the enemy forces that were increasingly closing in on us, and above all, the terrible foot disease that the peasants called *mazamorra*—which turned each step our soldiers took into an intolerable torment—had made us an army of shadows. It was difficult to advance, very difficult. The troops' physical condition worsened by the day, and meals—today yes, tomorrow no, the next day, maybe—in no way helped to alleviate the misery we were suffering." Flooded rivers were swum naked; to dodge one army patrol, they fled across a shallow lagoon filled with spiky plants, which shredded the feet of the men who had no boots.

The indifference of lowland farmers to their plight made a stark contrast to the Sierra Maestra. The army had spread word that Che and his guerrillas were Communists, which led many to turn against them. Paranoia set in amongst the rebel troop: "Every peasant looked to us like a possible informer." Even the local wings of M-26-7 were suspicious of the Argentine, responding to one request for food: "If Che asks in writing, we'll help him; if not, he can go fuck himself." In late September, disaster struck when one of Che's captains led his men into an ambush. He had commandeered two trucks and was foolishly driving at night through unknown territory. The army intercepted them and eighteen rebels were killed. Eleven more wounded were taken to a hospital until an officer arrived from Havana to take over. After handing out 1,000 pesos to the soldiers—Batista wanted to reward a rare military success—he ordered the rebel wounded put back in the trucks. He then tossed hand grenades inside, to make it appear that they had been killed in battle.

A subtler blow to the sentimental Che came when he lost the tattered canvas forage cap that had once belonged to his friend Ciro Redondo. From then on, Che took to wearing his black beret, originally with a crossed saber badge and later a brass star, which would soon become the Cuban Revolution's most famous fashion statement.

Finally, the Sierra Escambray mountains rose in a purplish haze on the horizon like El Dorado. But Che's exhausted men had arrived into a world of barely suppressed anarchy. It wasn't only M-26-7 leaders who saw the strategic value of the range. Located only a day's drive from Havana, the Escambray had become in recent months the refuge of three other guerrilla groups with radically different political views, including the Revolutionary Directorate, or DR—the conservative student group that had attacked the Presidential Palace—and the PSP, the Cuban Communist Party, which had finally decided to become involved in armed rebellion. Some leaders were operating like Afghan warlords, extorting "taxes" from farmers and rustling their cattle. In this quagmire of competing interests, Che used his authority as Fidel's emissary to argue that they should all put aside their political differences and work together under his overall command. It was not an easy task. At one stage Che was stopped by a resentful group of partisans who refused to let him advance because he didn't know their password. A shoot-out nearly occurred when a group from the DR who wanted to join Che were told by their superiors to surrender their arms. Even when an "operational agreement" was drawn up with the DR, their leader was insulted that the Argentine simply signed "Che," which he regarded as a sign of disrespect. ("This is a formal document," he protested, not the place for foreign nicknames.)

But Che had an aura the others could not resist. The men of the Escambray looked on him with a mix of admiration and fear: he was like a mysterious, otherworldly cult figure who had magically descended from the east, surrounded by teenage soldiers who were obsessively devoted to him. Once again, he began to create his own mini-society in the Escambray, with its own courts, bakeries, bomb factories, and a newspaper, *El Miliciano, The Militiaman*. To combat drunkenness, he ordered that every bottle of rum in bodegas be shattered. He also continued his obsessive reading, poring over a monumental history of the Roman Empire—evidently Gibbon's *Decline and Fall*—with such intensity that aides had to alert him when an air raid was under way.

Reports of Che during this period border on the surreal. One frigid, moonless night an M-26-7 organizer named Enrique Oltuski arrived at his camp and was surprised that the emaciated figure looked nothing like the photos in newspapers or wanted posters. Che was standing by a fire in his black beret with long hair and thin, scraggly beard, wearing a cape and with his shirt open to the waist. "The flames of the bonfire and the mustache, which fell over either side of his mouth, gave him a Chinese aspect. I thought of Genghis Khan."

Later, Oltuski found himself both horrified and fascinated by Che's hygienic habits. He watched Che settle down to a fireside meal of maggoty goat meat, downing the green chunks with filthy fingers. "Judging from the relish with which he ate, it tasted gloriously to him," Oltuski recalled. Che then smoked a rancid, cheap cigar, wheezing the whole time. (He "smoked and coughed, a damp cough, as if he was all wet inside.") El Chancho, "the Pig," was exceeding his reputation. "He smelled bad," Oltuski added. "He stank of decomposed sweat. It was a penetrating odor and I fought it with the tobacco smoke." And yet, he could not help admiring the strange Argentine, he confessed to a friend: "He knows what he wants better than we do. And he lives entirely for it."

A LITTLE STENCH clearly did not offend another who met Che at the time: the twenty-four-year-old *guerrillera* Aleida March. In the annals of revolutionary romance, their unlikely relationship holds a special place: while we know relatively few of the intimate details of Fidel and Celia's courtship, or Raúl and Vilma's, Aleida wrote a detailed memoir of their days together on the front lines of battle, *Remembering Che*—which also offers incidental insights into the daily challenges for a woman in the Rebel Army.

Their first meetings were not auspicious. A former schoolteacher who had become one of the most trusted operatives in Santa Clara, Aleida was assigned in October to courier crucial funds to Che in the Escambray, which she carried in an envelope that was duct-taped to her torso for safekeeping. She was the only woman in a group, and the trip was marred by pain from the tape and mild sexual harassment. When Aleida arrived at the camp, the male guerrillas crowded, panting, around her—an attractive twenty-four-year-old was a rare sight— and "some of the boldest of the group dared to ask if I was the girlfriend of one of the new arrivals."

When she was introduced to the legendary Che, she was as surprised as Oltuski by his appearance. Che seemed much older than his thirty years, weary, solitary, and thin—although his "penetrating gaze [was] rather intriguing," she admitted. A female lawyer who was also in the camp "commented on his beautiful hands, something I had not noticed at the time, but I did later on." Che was dismissive of the prim, petite bourgeois provincial Aleida; his first impression, he later confessed, was of "a little fair-haired girl, slightly chubby . . ." (Her hair was "fair" by Latin American standards; in photos it was dark brown.) In the following days, he actively avoided her, convinced that she had been sent from Santa Clara to monitor him.

Other guerrillas were more enthusiastic. When Aleida asked Che if she could get help removing the tape on her midriff, "in an instant there were quite a few eager volunteers." The drooling soon became annoying. "I was constantly pestered by various guerrillas trying to chat me up," she recalled. Eventually she befriended some of the less lecherous men, such as one of Che's teenage sidekicks, Rogelio Acevedo. She thought his long blond hair made him look like a girl, and amused herself by plaiting his locks.

The tensions with Che escalated when it was discovered that Aleida couldn't return to Santa Clara. SIM had smoked her out using her nicknames Cara Cortaga ("Scarface," referring to a small scar on her right cheek, the result of a dog bite as a child) and Teta Manchada ("Stained Breast," from a birthmark on her left upper chest). While Fidel was forming the Marianas, Che was still wary of women in his camp. He begrudgingly let Aleida remain as a nurse, ignoring her objections. She spent weeks doing chores and fending off lovesick *compañeros*. Things came to a head while she was riding in a jeep with three men sitting behind her. When one "accidentally" stroked her back, "I reacted so violently they never attempted to touch me again."

THE SPIKY DYNAMIC between Che and Aleida shifted in late November, when they were unexpectedly thrown together during an army offensive. It was a Hollywood moment. She was sitting on the side-walk with her bag just before dawn in the town of El Pedrero, when Che passed by driving a jeep and screeched to a halt.

"What are you doing here?" he asked, according to her account.

"I couldn't sleep."

Che said he was going to counterattack the army in Cabaiguán and invited her along "to shoot a few rounds." "Without a second thought, I accepted and jumped into his jeep," Aleida recalled. "And that was it. In a way, I never again got out of that jeep."

One of Che's hangers-on, Oscarito Fernández Mell, realized that "Suddenly, Aleida was with Che everywhere he went . . . They went around in the jeep together, she carried his papers for him, she washed his clothes." (Perhaps she was gently improving his notorious scent.) And yet the relationship was very much of the 1950s, developing at a languid pace closer to a Debbie Reynolds romance than a sultry Harlequin novel. Aleida wrote that their affair was not consummated un-til much later, and not just because they had an almost complete lack of privacy during the guerrilla war. In the beginning, she mostly saw Che as an older man "who would protect me from the advances of the other *compañeros.*" As December unfolded and she became Che's full-time assistant, Aleida sensed "sparks between us," but there was little opportunity to explore their attraction.

Reserved and distracted, Che chose improbable moments to ex-press his affection. One night, when they were occupying a tobacco factory, he started to recite a poem while standing behind her; for the first time Aleida glimpsed behind his cool exterior. Over coming weeks she grew less in awe of Che, but the pair were either too ex-hausted, busy, or famished to analyze what was happening. As they were preparing a major offensive, he started talking about his Peruvian wife, Hilda, and their daughter, Hildita, saying (with a slight bending of the truth) that he and his wife were "already separated" when he left Mexico two years before. As ever, Aleida was left to make of this snip-pet what she would as they raced together to the front lines.

※

WHILE CHE AND Camilo were slogging through the leech-filled swamps, life at the Comandancia de La Plata was something of an idyll. Fidel and Celia's serene aerie even welcomed a new cook who had defected from one of Cuba's finest provincial restaurants. Fidel could read with electric light produced by generators, listen to classical music, and entertain a stream of official visitors: Cuban politicians, journalists, editors, lawyers—all beat a path to his hut, until foot traffic became so heavy that it impeded the mule trains bringing supplies. Celia juggled Fidel's schedule and served refreshments to his guests while the Marianas stood watchful guard. Departing visitors would be taken to a safe farmhouse in the lowlands. While they bathed, their clothes were pressed and shoes polished to remove any telltale signs that they had been in the sierra. Then they were ushered back to Santiago in a freshly washed jeep.

An urbane staff writer for the *Washington Post*, Karl E. Meyer, was one who made the pilgrimage to "Castro's roost," mostly by horseback. He was dismayed to find that he had to tackle the steep final day's climb on foot: "Rain coats the rocks with slime," he complained, "and the last lap is shin-breaking clamber through nettled trees up an endless slope." Finally reaching the "rebel realm," he found Fidel sprawled across his bed like a pasha, surrounded by piles of half-open books and note jottings.

"Welcome to free Cuba," Fidel said, flourishing his cigar with supreme confidence. "You can see and report on anything you want here. Can Batista afford to make you the same offer?" While Meyer was there, a gift was borne triumphantly into the hut: a framed picture of the ten-year-old Fidelito Castro, scrubbed and with hair parted as if for his Confirmation. Fidel "grabbed the picture," Meyer wrote, "looked at it hungrily and explained, beaming, 'This is my son.'" Fidelito had just come back to Havana from a year in New York City with his mother, where he had attended PS 20 public school in Queens.

※

FEW REALIZED THAT a ground shift was now occurring in Cuba. The army was losing faith in itself, its spirit ebbing slowly but inexorably, like rice from a torn sack. The rebels' unexpected victory in the summer brought a sudden upswing in public support for M-26-7, and it was given added momentum by a moderate agreement between Cuban opposition leaders called the Caracas Pact, which focused on the one goal everyone could agree on: removing Batista. A respected judge in exile, Manuel Urrutia, was chosen as provisional president, and the middle class began to pump in donations. Fidel also stopped burning sugar fields and instead imposed a fifteen-cent tax on each 250-pound bag; even US-owned plantations found it easier to pay up, making M-26-7 flush with cash. A new influx of volunteers was arriving at Fidel's camps, including a stream of army deserters. There was even a small rebel air force coming together, piloted by airmen repelled by the orders to bomb their own countrymen.

Years later, the adventurous CBS TV reporter Robert Taber would write a book on unconventional warfare called *The War of the Flea*, trying to understand how small bands of rebels can undermine powerful governments. "This is the grand objective of the guerrilla," he wrote. "To create 'the climate of collapse.' It may be taken as the key to everything he does." In the fall of 1958 in Cuba, that climate—a sense of growing disorder, an impression that the country was slipping out of Batista's control—was becoming more tangible every day.

CHAPTER 28

Have Gun, Will Travel: The Gringo Guerrillas

(Fall 1958)

WHEN CHE HAD first approached the Escambray mountains in October, he decided to dismiss his most unpleasant recruit, the American Herman Marks. A native of Milwaukee, with the chinless, paunchy look of a suburban accountant before he grew the regulation beard, Marks had made his way to the Sierra Maestra six months earlier and offered his services as a supposed Korean War veteran. His presence was first mentioned by Raúl, who told Fidel in a letter on March 9, 1958, that he had been joined by a mysterious, twenty-six-year-old gringo—"He's brave in battle and gives military training to the *chicos*." Marks helped the men make Sputnik grenade-throwers and showed them how to use a car battery as a bomb detonator. It would later be discovered that Marks's war record was a complete fabrication. In fact, he was a draft dodger who had been arrested thirty-two times in the United States for crimes including armed robbery, theft, and statutory rape. His affinity for firearms had been developed while staging heists.

Nobody in the Rebel Army was prying. Marks transferred to Che's column during the summer offensive and acquitted himself so well that he was promoted to captain. It was only when he joined Che's autumn expedition across the island that his true nature began to come out. At the end of the ordeal, Marks was one of eight men Che asked to leave "in an attempt to clean out the scum of the column." He had been wounded in the foot and fallen sick, Che reported to Fidel, but the real reason was that he "fundamentally didn't fit into the group." Another guerrilla, Enrique Acevado, explained that Marks was "brave and crazy in combat, tyrannical and arbitrary in the peace of camp." Evidently his fondness for conducting executions—particularly the coup de grâce—bordered on the sadistic and disturbed other men.

By then, Marks was less of an exotic figure; American soldiers of fortune were floating all across Cuba. Only days after Che dismissed the perverse Marks, he encountered an even more surprising gringo soldier in the depths of the Escambray Mountains: William Morgan from Toledo, Ohio, who would soon become internationally renowned as Fidel's "Yankee *comandante.*"

AMERICANS WERE FASCINATED by stories of their own countrymen joining the guerrillas. According to US embassy estimates, there were some twenty-five young gringos bearing arms against Batista by late 1958. These would-be Lafayettes were an oddball bunch. Some, like the hardened Marks, are difficult to romanticize. But many others were genuine free spirits who longed to escape the leaden conformity of Cold War America. Cracks were already beginning to appear in the facade of suburban prosperity: Allen Ginsberg's *Howl* had been published the month before the *Granma* landing in 1956, Jack Kerouac's *On the Road* came out in September 1957 and became an overnight bestseller. At the same time, Martin Luther King, Jr. organized the Montgomery bus boycott in Alabama. The bearded Cubans tapped into the amorphous dissatisfaction many young Americans felt with society; "the sixties," in a sense, were gestating in the late 1950s.

In mid-1957, after the three teenage runaways from Guantánamo

Bay had their fifteen minutes of fame on CBS TV, a string of others developed addled plans to emulate them. (We know, for example, that a dozen UCLA students plotted to take jeeps via Key West to the Oriente.) But while the Gitmo boys became minor celebrities, most *yanqui* volunteers are today ghostly figures whose adventures must be pieced together from stray references. Some remain entirely anonymous. Raúl mentions a gringo "demolitions expert" with echoes of Hemingway's Robert Jordan; *Times* correspondent Ruby Hart Phillips met "a boy from Iowa" with Fidel in the summer of 1957; *Life* refers to an ashen-faced Chicagoan with polio who worked as a guard. Not all potential American volunteers were successful at reaching their goal. A Miami pipe fitter named Bill Leonard was reported walking into a Cuban police station in Oriente and asking for a "pass" to the Sierra Maestra so he could visit "his friend Chuck Ryan" who was fighting with Fidel. The astonished officers searched him, found a knife and tear gas gun, and—after letting him cool his heels in the cells—put him on a train back to Havana.

Many Americans who did make it into the mountains buckled under the hardship of guerrilla life. During the hostage crisis, journalists had met Charlie Bartlett, the Navy machinist's mate from California, who had joined Raúl after seeing Batista's soldiers beat up civilians. A few months later, Bartlett slipped back to the Navy base and was court-martialed. Even more feckless was Edward Bethune, a soldier of fortune from Knoxville, Tennessee, who hiked up to the Comandancia and was inducted into the Rebel Army, but left after only a few days complaining he had a "toothache." (Perhaps he couldn't face the pedal-operated dentist's chair.)

Other *yanqui* volunteers had more staying power. Perhaps the most likable was Neill Macaulay, a twenty-three-year-old history graduate from South Carolina, whose picaresque memoir of his guerrilla adventures, *A Rebel in Cuba*, is the military equivalent of Kerouac's footloose epic. In the summer of 1958 Macaulay dropped by the Movement's Manhattan office, an old brownstone at 305 Amsterdam Avenue on the Upper West Side, which was identified by a black-and-red banner hanging from the second-floor window. Filled with antique portraits of independence heroes and piles of leaflets, the "agreeably chaotic" office was run by a former basketball champion named José Llanusa and staffed with clean-cut young Cubans who had come to study in New York after the island's universities were all closed. The voluble activists fielded a steady stream of well-meaning gringo volunteers— many of them Columbia students who only wanted to fight during summer break—and politely told most that under US neutrality rules they could only accept financial donations, not recruits.

Unlike Herman Marks, Macaulay had really been in Korea for two years—as an Army postal officer. But he exaggerated his record so convincingly that he was given the contact details for an M-26-7 agent in Havana. After a $10 flight from Key West, upon which he evidently carried his pistols on board, Macaulay lived out the cliché of the self-absorbed American sightseer, getting a "monstrous hangover" from Cuba Libres at the Tropicana, and ending up at a low-budget brothel. Macaulay finally met his underground contact, a "willowy brunette" who had studied at Harvard Business School. A new uprising was starting in Cuba's fertile agricultural heartland, Pinar del Río, she explained. It was only an hour west of the capital, so Macaulay was taken there by taxi to meet its leader—a twenty-one-year-old former sculpture student known as "Captain Claudio." Claudio's mother gave Macaulay a brown paper bag containing a uniform and armband; his pointy shoes from Hong Kong, purchased when he was stationed in Korea, were admired by all. He had become a rebel overnight.

The guerrillas expected Macaulay to fit the stereotype of Americans, he says—that is, "hungry, strong, aggressive, brave, smart, jovial, instructive, and entertaining"—and he did his best to oblige. His rudimentary Spanish kept his *compañeros* in hysterics, as did his tales of the Lone Ranger (El Llanero Solitario) and Speedy Gonzales (El Rápido). His confusion of the Cuban nickname for hand grenades— *piñas,* or pineapples—with *pinga,* penis, was a perennial favorite.

There were drunken nights of bonhomie when the guerrillas taught Macaulay to swear in Spanish ("I am going to shit on your mother" was one Cuban classic from Claudio that silenced everyone). His proudest moment may have come when a commander praised him as *un americano con cojones*, "an American with balls." But the partisan war also involved brutal, raw encounters. There were bloody skirmishes in the verdant countryside around Viñales, long a popular tourist destination for its ravishing limestone protrusions called *mogotes*. Macaulay witnessed innumerable executions, usually by hanging to save ammunition—of *chivatos* ("snitches"), SIM officers, and, most difficult of all, three high school–age deserters.

FEW AMERICAN REBELS had political notions beyond a vague longing to be a "freedom fighter," conjuring Fidel's camp as a Latin revival of Valley Forge. One who did have a broader sense of politics was Don Soldini, a loudmouthed Staten Island kid from a radical family—his grandfather had been a Wobbly, a member of the militant International Workers of the World labor union—who bounced back and forth at a manic pace between the US and Cuba, getting into trouble at every stop. Soldini first won the rebels' trust by showering pro-Castro pamphlets over Yankee Stadium during a televised World Series game. At age eighteen he traveled to Santiago, where he joined riots after the murder of Frank País; by the spring of 1958 he made his way to the Sierra Cristal, where he fought with Raúl's column before being wounded in the neck. After that, he took up arms smuggling. He was soon apprehended by SIM in Havana, beaten up, then given a shovel and told to dig his own grave by the light of a squad car. He claims he was spared only by incessantly repeating that his uncle owned an Italian restaurant in New York and was a close personal friend of Batista.

Back in Manhattan again in late 1958, the irrepressible Soldini came up with a new plan when M-26-7 agents showed him the "avalanche" of letters from Americans now begging to join the war effort. He invited some seventy of the most promising candidates to Miami, where he began to organize his own "gringo column" along the lines of the Abraham Lincoln Brigade in the Spanish Civil War. Most of the volunteers were drifters and dreamers. "It was a bunch of assholes, really," Soldini later told the historian Van Gosse; his only real criterion for membership was that recruits could pay their own expenses. Like Soldini himself, they were drawn to Fidel's rebellion because its goals seemed so black-and-white: "I loved it. I truly loved it," he recalled of his time as a guerrilla warrior in Cuba. "With all the privations—hunger, thirst, dysentery . . . I mean, this [was] pure idealism, pure passion. Batista the bad guy, Fidel the good guy—I'm on the side of the good, how great can you go?" The "gringo column," sadly, never left Miami.

THE SPOTLIGHT OF history has fallen more directly on another yanqui soldier in Fidel's fold, William Morgan. Thanks to two biographies, a *New Yorker* article, a PBS television special, and a planned film produced by George Clooney, Morgan has today become almost as celebrated as he was in 1958, when US journalists first began to write him up and newspapers ran dashing portraits of him in rebel uniform. As writer David Grann observes, "with a stark jaw, pugnacious nose, and scruffy blond hair, he had the gallant look of an adventurer in a movie serial, of a throwback to an earlier age." One reporter at the time, impressed by Morgan's straight-talking manner, dubbed him "Holden Caulfield with a machine gun."

A more accurate literary reference may be Jay Gatsby, since Morgan's story is a parable of American reinvention. Until he shipped off to Cuba, he was a lost soul who failed at everything he did. Raised a Boy Scout in a middle-class home in Toledo, Ohio, Morgan could have grown into a pillar of the Midwestern community; instead, impetuous and restless, he took to stealing cars in his mid-teens, ran away from home, and drifted through a string of odd jobs on the fringes of the law. While serving in Japan as a GI, Morgan was arrested when he went AWOL to visit his local girlfriend, then broke out of military prison. He spent three years doing hard labor and was dishonorably discharged from the army—the very definition of a loser in the patriotic 1950s.

At this point Morgan's biography becomes hazy and fantastical. Working as a fire-eater in a Florida circus, he married the snake lady and had two children. Then at the age of twenty-nine he decided to shed his former life like an old skin. On the day after Christmas 1957, Morgan ran away again—this time to join the Cuban Rebel Army. His road to a new life was swaddled in lies. Wandering Havana disguised as a rich tourist in a white linen suit and shiny shoes, Morgan made up appealing stories about his military service—at one point saying he had been a World War Two paratrooper—and told underground contacts that he wanted to avenge a friend who had been murdered by Batista's men. Morgan was chubby, tattooed, and out of shape; he could also barely speak a word of Spanish. Nevertheless, an agent of the Revolutionary Directorate agreed to take him to join their forces in the Sierra Escambray, which could be reached in a day's drive.

The troop of thirty guerrillas Morgan found there were a scared bunch of near-adolescents with almost no combat experience. Their leader was a waifish, bespectacled ex-student named Eloy Gutiérrez Menoyo whose brother had died leading the attack on the Presidential Palace in March. At first the Cubans regarded the pudgy American with suspicion. They hazed him with brutal all-day hikes, leaving him sunburned, exhausted, and covered with scratches from hostile foliage. ("I am not a mule!" Morgan finally bellowed.) Morgan lost thirty-five pounds but stayed the course: he had been cashiered from one army, he would not drop out of this one. Before long, he was teaching his *compañeros* marksmanship, judo, knife throwing (a talent he picked up in the circus, not the military), and Boy Scout tricks like using a reed to hide underwater.

Morgan's rudimentary Spanish nearly got the whole group killed when he started firing prematurely on a passing army patrol. Vowing to improve, Morgan began pointing to every object and asking "*¿Como se llama en español?*" His next encounter was far more successful. When some two hundred enemy soldiers were spotted moving in single file, Morgan arranged the guerrillas in a U formation to ambush the advance guard. He then rallied the wavering rebels by marching at the enemy alone like John Wayne, his rifle blazing. ("We thought he was insane," one companion admitted.) The victory bolstered morale and won over local peasants. Morgan now found himself an esteemed member of the DR's dysfunctional family and began to rise through the ranks.

Rumors about the gringo guerrilla filtered out. Worried that he might be stripped of his US citizenship, Morgan wrote a florid statement entitled "Why I am Here" and sent it—needless to say—to Herbert L. Matthews of the *New York Times*. "Why did I come here far from my home and family?" he mused. "I am here because the most important thing for free men to do is protect the freedom of others." Morgan had seen wondrous things in Cuba, he said: "Here, the impossible happens every day. Where a boy of nineteen can march twelve hours with a broken foot over country comparable to the American Rockies without complaint. Where a cigarette is smoked by ten men." Matthews tidied up the letter and published parts of it in a story. He described Morgan with approval as a "tough, uneducated young American" and included a plucky snapshot of him posing with other rebels. It appeared just before Morgan's thirtieth birthday. At last he was a somebody, a contender.

In July, Morgan was promoted to *comandante*, the only foreigner apart from Che himself to reach the position. Not long after, Batista posted a $20,000 bounty on his head.

%

MORGAN'S RELATIONS WITH Che when he first arrived in the Escambray were frosty, to say the least. Like the other DR guerrillas, he was annoyed that the Argentine assumed he could simply take command. The two foreigners were also polar opposites: Morgan, the barely educated, happy-go-lucky Midwesterner, did not trust the monkish, cerebral Argentine. The "Second Front of the Escambray," as Morgan's DR group grandly called itself, was also politically conservative, and its leaders got into heated arguments with the radical Marxist interloper Che over such thorny subjects as land reform. There is one appealing report in the *Miami Herald* that Che and Morgan faced off in a mountain clearing with troops on either side, challenging one another to "draw," cowboy-style, but sadly it appears to be fiction. The closest the pair got to blows was when Morgan sent a letter demanding the return of some weapons; Che ignored it. Fidel's right-hand man regarded the DR with contempt as *comevacas*, "cow eaters," who preyed on helpless peasants. Nor did Che take the American's rank seriously, joking that there were more *comandantes* in the Second Front than there were foot soldiers.

Perhaps the only thing the two had in common was that they both fell in love with *santaclareñas* ("girls from Santa Clara"). One day, Morgan arrived in camp—riding a white mare and whistling the theme song from *The Bridge on the River Kwai,* no less—when he spotted a petite nurse named Olga Rodríguez. A former urban agent, Olga had been forced to flee disguised as a man, cutting her hair short and hiding her face beneath a cap like a Shakespearean heroine. Morgan came up behind her, drawled, "Hey, *muchacho*," and pulled the cap down over her eyes. Olga later confessed that she was impressed by the thickset gringo with his carefree swagger, even though his Spanish could still use serious work: for a time he called her Olgo, until she pointed out her name's feminine ending.

One day, out of the blue, William took her hand. She later recalled stammering: "I don't know you. I don't know anything about you."

He replied: "The past is already past."

"Now is not the time—or the place. We are in a war."

Her resistance did not last. He sent her bunches of wildflowers and love letters: "When I found you, I found everything you can wish for in the world," he wrote. "Only death can separate us." She slowed down her machine-gun-fast, argot-riddled Spanish and his language skills improved. They spooned during bombing raids and whispered to one another, "Our fates are intertwined." A single photograph survives of them together in the mountains, both cradling rifles and hugging one another casually with spare hands—Morgan with a dense beard, Olga now letting her hair grow wild. But she had dark intimations: "From the beginning, I had this terrible feeling that things would not end well." In November, orders arrived for Morgan to lead his guerrilla platoon into the plains. Olga had to stay behind, so they slipped off to a farmhouse to be married. Beforehand, Olga had her first bath in months and borrowed a fresh blouse; Morgan washed his clothes and shaved (something of a shock; she barely recognized him beardless). The farm owners laid out tropical fruit for the wedding feast.

In one of the most touching courtship gestures of the insurgency, Morgan fashioned Olga a wedding ring from a leaf. Before a handful of witnesses, the lovers promised to honor one another, "*Hasta que la muerte nos separa*," "Till death do us part." The marriage was consummated in a starlit field, and Morgan left a few hours later. "We barely had time to kiss," Rodríguez summed up. As a wedding present, Morgan left behind a parrot that he had trained to screech sweet nothings such as "*We*-liam" and "I love you!" But to Olga's distress, one day it flew off. It seemed an ill omen.

THERE WOULD HAVE been many more *yanquis* in Cuban battle lines had some of the zany pro-Fidel plots succeeded in the US. On March

28, 1958, for example, a Coast Guard gunship rammed a shrimp trawler leaving Brownsville, Texas, and boarded it to find thirty-four militiamen wearing uniforms with M-26-7 arm bands trying to emulate the *Granma* landing. They were all New Yorkers aged from seventeen to fifty-two, including a medic and a chaplain, under the command of a former construction worker named Arnold Barrow; also on board was a sporting goods store owner who had supplied the $20,000 worth of weapons loaded in the hull. As American citizens, they were all arrested under the Neutrality Act. "I feel our rights are being violated," Barrow complained. "We are fighting for democracy in Cuba and the United States should help us." A photo appeared in the *New York Times* of them sitting on a dock and waving cheerfully. All sat out the revolution in prison.

By late 1958, every major US city had its Movement sympathizers: gangs of bomb makers were busted in Brooklyn and Chicago; a group in Los Angeles was caught with machine guns. The going rate to hire a fishing boat to ship arms from South Carolina, a hub for America's gun culture, to Cuba, was $2,000. Many decided that a light plane was more efficient: Fidel now had several secret airstrips; Raúl had no less than seven.

The main locus of pro-Castro support now became Miami, which seethed like an Art Deco Casablanca. The tourist mecca was also a "plotters' playground," *Time* reported in September, "a hive of revolutionaries . . . where hardly a day goes by without at least one new plot brewing." Its 85,000-strong Latino community had its fingers in a smorgasbord of nationalist causes in Central America and the Caribbean, but it was the Cubans who were the busiest and most imaginative. They were drawn from every social class—one cell was said to be led by a restaurant busboy—and they took great risks, since the city was also filled with FBI agents and Batista spies, which led to shootouts and long-distance car chases. Cubans caught smuggling arms could have their visas revoked; luckily, Florida judges were sympathetic and resisted deporting activists to their deaths.

Haydée Santamaría was sent to Miami in April to beef up M-26-7 fund-raising efforts, slipping onto an Air Cubana flight from Havana in disguise. She was revulsed by Florida's "Magic City": "This is the most unpleasant place on earth," she wrote to Celia, "so much loneliness . . . at times I feel such a desire to be [home] that I have to control myself not to just run away." (The young Che had a similarly negative reaction when he was stuck in Miami six years earlier on his shoestring travels. Crashing on a friend's couch and working as a dishwasher, he bummed beers and french fries from fellow Argentines on the beach. But he left the US appalled at the South's racial segregation and resentful that Florida police were suspicious of him for his political views.)

Regardless of her objections to Miami, Yeyé proved to be an inspired fund-raiser, hosting Spanish classical guitar concerts and theatrical events with up-and-coming Cuban playwrights. Wealthy exiles opened their checkbooks; the less well-heeled bought portraits of Fidel for $1. By fall of 1958, she was raising between $12,000 and $15,000 per month, much of which was funneled to freelance arms dealers up and down the Florida coast. Miami had many assets for conspirators, she discovered: it offered a coastline porous with swamps and islands, dozens of private airstrips, and policemen keen to improve their meager $300-a-month salaries. For a modest payoff, law enforcement would, Yeyé discovered, "give us the *vista gorda*," the blank, unseeing eye. Its shores became as fertile a home for filibusters, or gunrunners, as it had been in the pirate era. Car trunks were filled with smuggled rifles; closets of holiday houses were piled high with grenades; ammunition caches were buried at remote beaches. The Trade Winds apartment complex in South Beach doubled as a dynamite storehouse; a police raid turned up nine hundred sticks. On the tourist ferry from Key West to Havana, ten men were arrested shipping arms in false gas tanks of secondhand Chevrolets. There is no record of how many arms slipped through the Coast Guard net, but *Time* magazine estimated $200,000 worth in September alone. That same month, a patrol boat chased down the *Harpoon* from Miami with thirty-two would-be militiamen on board until the captain ran aground in mangroves. The men put up a fight: one tried to fire his machine gun, but it jammed; another pulled the pin of a grenade but it blew up in his hand, taking a finger.

The FBI was less indulgent with the Cuban exiles than Miami police, enforcing US "neutrality" by harassing M-26-7 activists while leaving Batista's agents untouched. In February, the FBI even arrested the high-profile ex-president Prío for financing military expeditions. The elegantly dressed figure was walked in handcuffs from his penthouse in the Vendôme Hotel in Miami Beach to the police station, where he spent a night in the cells and was eventually fined $9,000. Latin Americans were outraged at Prío's humiliating treatment, especially since the US had just given asylum to a bloodthirsty dictator who had been forced to flee Venezuela in disgrace. It was yet another example of American double standards, it seemed.

CHAPTER 29

The Lightning Campaign

(December 1958)

A S THE SECOND anniversary of the *Granma* landing approached, Fidel was able to celebrate two days early. On November 30, a 2,500-strong Batista force abandoned Guisa, a strategic town in the lowlands of Oriente, to the Rebel Army, ending a ten-day battle. Cheered on by the townsfolk, the *barbudos* entered the blacked-out streets and went straight to a bodega, where Fidel purchased the entire food stock for his hungry troops. Sitting on a wooden crate by candlelight, he devoured two cans of Spanish tuna with his fingers, washed down with tinned fruit juice. As ever, Celia was by his side with a nylon bag over her shoulder stuffed with documents. On December 2, the *Granma* anniversary, Fidel spent hours answering written questions from international journalists about the sudden acceleration of the war. The rebels were doing what nobody had thought possible: taking the fight to Batista in the plains. Rumors spread among Santería believers that the rebels used voodoo to make bullets bounce from their bodies. Spent shells could be purchased for $10 each as good luck charms.

For a month beforehand, guerrillas had been spilling from the mountains. On November 3, Che and Camilo made forays from the Escambray to disrupt rigged presidential elections, although Batista's candidate romped home on fake ballots delivered around Cuba by the air force. Later in the month, Raúl and Almeida led troops from the Sierra Cristal. Finally, Fidel himself had said farewell to the comforts of the Comandancia and descended to the *llanos*. The quiet months after the army's failed summer offensive had allowed him to expand his force from three hundred to eight hundred. Although few of them had combat experience, they acquitted themselves well at Guisa against four times as many soldiers.

Five Marianas also joined the attack even though they had left their rifles back in the Comandancia; like the new male recruits, they were expected to seize weapons from the army. One, Ada Bella Acosta, carried an old revolver and used it to force a cowering soldier to surrender. In another set-piece moment for Cuban feminism, the soldier scowled at her: "If I knew you were a woman, I would never have surrendered." The fifteen-year-old Norma, who was by her side, suggested that Bella return the man his rifle "so he can battle it out with you." The soldier quickly backtracked, stam mering, "No, no, I've already surrendered now anyway!"

This larger-scale combat in the plains required new tactics. The guerrillas dug extensive trenches and handmade larger mines that could stop armored cars and Sherman tanks. They also excavated and covered holes in the few muddy roads, which could swallow heavy vehicles. While besieging the Guisa barracks, the guerrillas also became more creative in tormenting the enemy with loudspeakers after dark. In saccharine voices, they would mock the *casquitos* as Batista's dupes before letting off a fifteen-minute volley of gunfire. This would be followed by a hideously out-of-tune pop song, *Ahorita va a llover, ahorita va a llover. Ay, el que no tenga paraguas, el agua lo va a coger . . .* ("In a little while, it's going to rain . . . Whoever has no umbrella is going to get soaked . . .") Even on the first night, Lieutenant Reinaldo Blanco, at the ripe age of twenty the senior army officer, sighed: "They are going to drive us crazy in here." After holding out for eight nights, the nerve-racked Blanco received the order to withdraw:

"Burn the town, kill the prisoners and to hell with everything." (In fact he retreated peacefully and let his one captive free—an honorable act for which Fidel sent a personal letter of thanks.)

As the year drew to a close, everyone in Cuba was jumping on the Fidelista bandwagon. Respectable middle-class citizens were now openly pro-Castro. Donations flooded in from Cuban industrialists. Even the conservative Association of Cuban Landholders begged Batista to step aside. The highest levels of government were being pervaded by a sense of defeatism and impotence. After the defeat at Guisa, the army too slid into a defensive paralysis: their rural barracks now stood as isolated as medieval castles while the rebels prowled freely around them. A domino effect set in. Prisoners who surrendered at one stronghold would be handed over to the Red Cross, who transported them to the next barracks. The former captives would describe how well they had been treated by the rebels and convince their hosts to give up—and so on across eastern Cuba. By contrast, at each liberated village, a festive mood prevailed as locals posed with rebels for souvenir photos and feted them with lavish feasts. Long gone were the lean repasts of the sierra: Manuel Fajardo wrote a glowing letter to Celia about an unforgettable breakfast of fresh orange juice, two fried eggs, bread and butter, and *café con leche*. His men were having three square meals a day, he marveled, "all accompanied by dessert."

A PERCEPTIVE GLIMPSE of this new stage of the war comes from the legendary Dickey Chapelle (née Georgette Meyer), America's first woman war photographer, who spent three weeks on the front lines with Fidel in early December. A veteran of the Pacific War, Algeria, and the Hungarian uprising (where she had spent two months in a Russian prison), the hard-as-nails Chapelle got into Santiago by dressing up as a ditzy tourist in spike heels, dangle earrings, and a fluffy sky-blue shirt, chaperoned by a "girl courier" with enormous eyelashes. (Chapelle reports that her guide was later captured and murdered.) A police officer at first refused to allow Chapelle to leave the airport: "There is nothing for you here, nothing." When she bluffed that she was on her way to a forbidden love tryst with a Marine from Guantánamo Bay, the official relented and let her pass "with a fourteen karat leer." She spent a day trying to find camera gear and film—she had given her Leicas to M-26-7 agents to smuggle in, but they had disappeared. Other foreign journalists had already given up on the Cuba story, Chapelle discovered: she ran into Andrew St. George on his way back to the US for the holidays because Fidel's offensive had "stalled." "I probably was in the wrong place at the wrong time," she lamented.

As a feminist pioneer, Chapelle had more reason than most to be fascinated by the Marianas she soon encountered in battle. "I was never more proud to be a woman than when I marched with Fidel Castro's Cuban guerrillas," she wrote in *Coronet* magazine. "I saw members of my sex perform breathless deeds of valor—squirming through roadblocks with ten grenades hooked to their belts and fighting alongside the Fidelista troops, an 11-lb rifle in their manicured hands." Chapelle was famous for her distinctive sartorial style, sporting cat-eye glasses and pearl earrings even during the battle of Iwo Jima. In Cuba she related in particular to the well-groomed Celia, who, Chapelle noted, "could deploy mortars like a man yet clung to her femininity," having designed her own uniform of "green twill tapered slacks and V-necked over-blouse." She was also struck by her fellow MIT grad, Vilma: "While snipers exchanged shots, she and Raúl would neck in foxholes," she wrote. "Yet I rarely saw Vilma without an automatic rifle, and she practically cooed when Raúl brought her a new, European-made paratrooper's gun with a special folding stock."

Her sojourn with the guerrillas was action-packed. When the clutch of a jeep she was traveling in gave out, one of the passengers was killed by a flying petrol drum, but Dickey somehow escaped with only a sprained ankle. Chapelle rescued other injured men on horseback then photographed them recuperating in the field clinic, a former coffee-drying shed. Chapelle was also present at the "family reunion" when Fidel and Raúl met up after nine months apart. Any differences between the brothers over the hostage crisis were forgotten thanks to Raúl's enormous recent success in seizing the Oriente's north. "Fidel, tremendous in wet and muddy fatigues, laughed deeply as he swung back and forth in a hammock," she wrote. "Raúl spoke shrilly and incessantly of his victories." Celia, meanwhile, "hovered . . . thin and febrile." Chapelle found that the "emotional tension" surrounding Fidel never stopped as he paced back and forth and barked orders. ("It was nearly impossible to photograph him.") Any good news prompted bear hugs with his men; setbacks were greeted with an "earthquake loss of temper." "He reacted with Gargantuan anger to every report of dead and wounded," she recalled, and insisted that she photograph rebel corpses "so their martyrdom will not be forgotten by the world." Fidel's "incisive mind" was at odds with his bottomless hunger for conflict, she concluded, reflecting a "psychopathic temper." The placid Midwesterner Chapelle found the perpetual whirlwind of emotion exhausting, and discovered that she could only get any of the guerrillas to listen to her by feigning a volcanic "Latin" fury.

In battle after battle she saw how Batista's vastly superior army—which "by all military theory since Hannibal . . . still held the advantage"—would crumple before the rebels. The reason, Chapelle explained in a long technical article in the *Marine Corps Gazette*, was the guerrillas' iron determination and their simple tactic of shooting nonstop. Fidel's men, now flush with ammunition, fired their guns at the enemy without a second's respite. Unwilling to die for Batista, soldiers fled in the face of this "unfaltering hail of lead," even if a small effort might win the day. Whenever they surrendered, Raúl would give them a speech promising that, even if they took up arms again, they would be released unharmed. "The utter contempt for the fighting potential of the defeated had an almost physical impact. Some actually flinched as they listened."

%

AS THE SITUATION in the Oriente degenerated, rumors spread in Havana that Batista was mentally disturbed. He now rarely appeared in public, shuffling in a bulletproof black Cadillac (license plate 1) between the Presidential Palace, where his office windows were now covered by steel plates to deter snipers, and his fortress-like rural estate Kuquine, whose landscaped grounds were complete with sumptuous swimming pool and private zoo, were patrolled by machine-gun–toting guards.

Even the president's closest aides had little idea what was really going through his head, since he maintained the icy, emotionless exterior that had served him well since he first took power. As later recounted by his press secretary, Batista's habits were becoming more compulsive. He abandoned the larger matters of state to minions and obsessed over minutiae, pondering for hours the correct punctuation of private letters or standing in front of a mirror tying and retying his Italian silk neckties. Foreign reporters were still told that Batista had a seventeen-hour workday, but the reality was the opposite: he spent most of his time listening to the taped telephone conversations of both enemies and friends, trying to glean a deeper meaning; sometimes his assistants read out the juicier parts of transcripts concerning the private lives of politicians, which they called "the novel." Servants saw the dictator eat huge meals, then quietly go into the garden, where he would vomit behind a tree in quick explosions. Horror movies remained his favorite distraction, with Boris Karloff and *Dracula* now almost on a perpetual loop. No matter how Cuba's crisis deepened, he continued to invite acquaintances to Kuquine every Sunday night to play canasta. Although the sums were small, $10 to $50, Batista would cheat; waiters tipped him off with secret signals, as in *The Sting*. These games often went on for hours while crucial military decisions were put on hold. Indeed, his press secretary later said bitterly that Fidel's greatest ally was canasta.

Despite the anarchy in eastern Cuba, money continued to flood in to Batista's private coffers. Meyer Lansky's men dropped off a briefcase bulging with Mob cash every Monday at noon, with the dictator's cut from casinos, bars, and brothels now $1,280,000 monthly. (Nobody has ever confirmed Batista's true wealth squirreled away offshore in Miami and Zurich banks, but it has been estimated at between $200 and $300 million.) Of course, his expenses were also enormous: $450,000 monthly was earmarked for "publicity" alone. Every week brown envelopes would flitter through Havana bulging with bribes for local journalists. Batista was now existing in a fantasy world, cushioned from reality by his own censorship laws. Even his army officers would hide the truth from him. He had followed the summer offensive on an antique map that had blank spaces in the Sierra Maestra—aides had difficulty at first convincing him that anyone even lived in the remote mountains—and in a sense had never taken Fidel and his young upstarts seriously. So long as his tanks were amassed in Camp Columbia, the dictator felt safe; he worried more about a palace coup than the insurgency.

A sudden reality check was provided on the night of December 17 when Batista agreed to a secret meeting with one of his most loyal supporters, the US ambassador, Earl Smith. After the first winter rain storm, Smith arrived by limousine in Kuquine and was led into the library. This was where the dictator still liked to meet official guests amongst tacky marble busts of his heroes—along with Ben Franklin, Gandhi, and Joan of Arc, Smith recalled seeing Churchill, Dante, and Field Marshal Montgomery—each one on an individual pedestal. (Of course, Abraham Lincoln was still Batista's idol; Vice President Nixon had even once toasted him as Abe's modern successor.) A rare 1822 edition of Napoleon's memoirs stood on its own table.

Over the previous few months, Smith had done everything he could to help Batista, lobbying the State Department to restart arms shipments and denouncing Fidel as a Communist. To his frustration, the dictator had made himself more abhorrent by the day, refusing to consider reforms or curtail his police. Now Smith had been instructed to say that the US could no longer support Batista or his puppet successor, Andrés Rivero Agüero, who was regarded by Cubans with derision. In his memoirs, Smith recalled that he tried to break the news gently, rattling on about how great a friend Batista had been to the US over the years. It was "like applying the Vaseline before inserting the stick." Then Smith broke the bad news, adding that Washington "would view with skepticism" the idea of Batista continuing to live in Cuba. Smith thought he heard Batista's breath change, letting out a wheeze "like a man who was hurt." Even worse, retirement to Daytona Beach was no longer an option. Spain would be better. Washington could not force Batista to resign but had given him a serious push.

A few days later, Batista told his trusted military liaison officer that he wanted to draw up a list of who should be alerted "in case we have to leave Cuba." The young man, Brigadier General Francisco "Sillito" Tabernilla, the son of the armed forces chief, was stunned. "Why don't we fight to the last man?" he asked. After all, the rebels still only controlled a small portion of the island, and not a single city.

"Sillito," Batista sighed, averting his eyes. "That's not possible."

Three DC-4s were put on constant standby at his sprawling main base and command center Camp Columbia on the western edge of the city. Pacing back and forth in his office beneath photos of his greatest successes, Batista dictated a string of names from memory. It was crucial that the list be kept secret, he stressed. Any word that the president was even considering escape would lead to a total collapse. On his way out, Batista gave Sillito a brown paper envelope. "This is for you," he smiled. It contained $15,000 cash.

CHRISTMAS CAME EARLY for M-26-7. On December 23 a major sugar company with strong ties to Batista decided to hedge its bets and pay Fidel's "war tax." In Havana's colonial Old Town, a lawyer with

Movement ties was ushered into an elegant office, where an elderly executive was waiting at a desk piled with 100 peso notes. After the April strike, the rebels had only mustered $700 in monthly donations in the entire capital. In November they had received $30,000. Now the lawyer was being offered $450,000 in one drop. Making this "contribution," the executive said carefully, "was the right thing to do at the right time." He then asked for a receipt.

For other *habaneros*, the next night, Nochebuena, or Christmas Eve, went ahead with an eerie sense of normalcy. The Tropicana nightclub offered a dinner choice of all-American stuffed turkey with cranberry sauce or Cuban roast suckling pig. Newspapers were filled with positive news—"Rural Outlaws Express Regret for Taking up Arms"—while the *New York Times* had recently run a story by Ruby Hart Phillips on the upcoming winter tourist season that might have been penned by the Cuban chamber of commerce. Frank Sinatra and assorted Hollywood moguls were financing a new hospitality concept for Havana, an all-inclusive resort called the Monte Carlo, with 656 hotel rooms, a private marina, interior canals, a golf course, and helicopter pads.

In Santiago, cut off from all transport by the guerrillas, the mood was more somber. At dusk, a giant red-and-black M-26-7 flag was unfurled over a nearby hill, and residents came out to stare. Rumors spread of an imminent rebel assault. Fidel and Celia felt so secure in the countryside that they traveled to Birán to spend Christmas Day with Fidel's mother, Lina, and his older brother, a farmer who sat out the war. Señora Castro burst into tears when she first saw her illustrious son, who had brought $1,000 to pay for a feast for local villagers. "Oh, what a party we had that night!" she recalled.

The season was more dramatic for Camilo. His advance had ground to a halt before a barracks in Yaguajay, an otherwise nondescript provincial town on the edge of a coastal swamp. As a Chinese-Cuban officer and his men held out day after day against his sixty men, Camilo became so frustrated that he designed a "war machine" that seemed inspired by his favorite novel, *Don Quixote*.

Nicknamed "Dragón I," it has gone down as one of the great guerrilla brainstorms. A fourteen-ton Caterpillar tractor was encrusted by local handymen with sandbags and metal plates. Two heavy machine guns were mounted on the sides along with the pièce de resistance, an improvised "flamethrower" made from a fumigation spray gun that shot a cocktail of motor oil and petrol. The lumbering assault vehicle was a cross between a World War One tank and a siege engine from the Dark Ages. (Its impressive name "quite contradicted its rather rudimentary design," noted Aleida March when she saw it.) Driven by three men, Dragón I enjoyed mixed results. On its first surprise attack at 4:00 a.m. on Christmas Eve, it sprayed flames for thirty feet—an intimidating sight in the darkness that reportedly caused teenage soldiers to scream, "It's a monster! The monster is coming!" After heavy fire forced its retreat, it returned with reinforced armor on Christmas Day. This time, the Dragón turned too sharply and its engine stalled. The soldiers then scored a direct hit on it with a bazooka; the drivers were unhurt but forced to reverse to safety.

Dragón I's main impact was psychological, adding to the usual torments by loudspeaker. For their Christmas broadcast at Yaguajay, rebels smacked their lips and gloated over the food they had seized from air force parachute drops: "We are eating your holiday dinner and loving it. What's this? A leg of lamb? And here is some rice. And black beans. And roast pork. And look what we have here for dessert!" (The hungry soldiers, meanwhile, were surrounded by "the odors of stale sweat, death and feces," since they were trapped with overflowing latrines and decaying corpses.) The siege dragged on, until the madam of the town brothel even promised a free night for the rebels if they would capture the barracks. It would take another week for the army commander, Captain Alfredo Abon Lee, to surrender. There is no record of anyone designing a Dragón II.

※

Batista watched horror movies; Camilo created his mechanized monster; Fidel prepared to besiege Santiago. But the fate of Cuba, it turned out, would be decided by Che. After bursting out of the Escambray Mountains, he descended on Santa Clara—a flat, featureless provincial city that was strategically placed at the island's geographical center and the hub of its transport network. If Santa Clara fell, Cuba would be cut in two. But it was an enormous "if." Che had only 340 men, including a few wild card DR veterans like William Morgan; his only heavy weapon was a single bazooka. They were going up against 3,500 soldiers with a dozen tanks entrenched in a city of 150,000 people, ten times larger than any the guerrillas had ever taken. Che seems not to have given it a second thought. In fact, instead of attacking by night, he decided to fight in broad daylight.

At dawn on December 27, Che arrived at the local university and declared that it would be his HQ; he was guided by the *santaclareña* Aleida, who had studied at the same campus. A geography professor provided city maps. According to Che's biographer Jon Lee Anderson, Aleida's college friend Lolita and her father arrived to welcome the guerrillas but were shocked to find how "dirty and messed up" they were. The pungent Che was even nursing a broken arm; he had tripped over a fence while trying to avoid a B-26 bombing, and now carried it in a black sling made from Aleida's scarf. Lolita's father whispered: "*These* guys are going to take Santa Clara?" One young rebel asked the pair how many troops were amassed against them. Lolita guessed there might be as many as 5,000. The rebel shrugged at the odds: "Good, with our *jefe* that's no problem."

They fought for Santa Clara block by block. By radio Che appealed for help from the citizens, asking them to overturn cars in the streets as barricades. He ordered his men to infiltrate the most densely populated neighborhoods, which limited the army tanks' movements and range, as the gunners tried not to hit civilians. (The air force was less discriminate, bombing and strafing the population randomly.) Locals took up the rebel cause, tossing Molotov cocktails from their windows and opening their doors so guerrillas could duck to safety. As the battle raged, the wounded began to pour into the field hospitals, civilian, military, and rebel. A classic "Che moment" occurred when he visited one clinic and recognized a young recruit on his deathbed. A few days earlier Che had stripped him of his rifle for accidentally firing off a round, and told him ("in my usual dry way") to "head back to the front lines and find yourself another gun . . . if you are up to it." Now the man proudly told Che that he had rejoined the fight. The pair had a short conversation. "A few minutes later, he died, and it seemed to me that he was happy to have showed his bravery," Che intoned. "Such was our Rebel Army."

ONCE AGAIN A single creative action by the guerrillas would produce outsized results. Early on December 29, Che commandeered two yellow tractors from the university agriculture department and sent them to tear up the railroad tracks running through the center of town. (Aleida, whose job it was to locate the vehicles, recalled an absurdist moment when Che used the English name Caterpillar to describe the vehicles—she thought he said in Spanish, *catres, palas y pilas*, beds, shovels, and batteries. The confusion was only cleared up when he looked at her notebook. The phrase *catres, palas y pilas* became a running joke between them from that moment on.)

The target was the army's fabled Tren Blindado ("Armored Train"), a twenty-two-carriage rolling fortress filled with weapons and ammunition. For the last two months the supply train had been thundering between military flash points around Cuba like a creation out of Jules Verne. When Che sent El Vaquerito and his elite "suicide squad" to attack the railway depot, panicked soldiers piled into the supposedly invulnerable citadel-on-wheels and left at high speed—straight into Che's trap. The locomotive and the first three cars overturned in a chaos of twisted metal and shrieking soldiers; the survivors found themselves pinned down by a handful of guerrilla snipers, who then tossed petrol bombs into the carriages. "The train became, thanks to the armored plating, a veritable oven for the soldiers," Che wrote with his usual clinical detachment. The entire force of over three hundred surrendered. To the awestruck rebels, each carriage was an Aladdin's Cave of military gear, overflowing with shiny bazookas, antiaircraft guns, and a million rounds of ammunition, much of it still in original factory crates marked U.S. ARMY. For the first time, the guerrillas had more hardware than they could possibly use. Once again the psychological blow was the most resounding part of the victory. The capture of the Armored Train seemed to symbolize the entire war, with a clumsy relic from another era rendered useless in one clean stroke. A sense of imminent disaster began to ripple from Santa Clara to the higher army echelons around Cuba.

Even so, bitter fighting plowed on, street by street, for the next two days. The battle was filled with tragic scenes. On December 30, Che and Aleida were both stopped in their tracks when they saw El Vaquerito being carried by four friends, his long hair dripping blood. He had been running over rooftops to seize a police station when a sniper hit him in the forehead. Che ordered him to be taken straight to the clinic. "I asked Che if he was dying," Aleida recalled, "because the poor young man was having convulsions." He was still breathing and had a faint pulse, but Che knew there was no chance of recovery. He cursed: "They have killed me a hundred men."

It was now, surrounded by bloodshed and tragedy, that Che realized he was in love with Aleida. When she had to dash across a street exposed to fire from an armored car, he was stricken with fear until he located her again. Che told her his feelings during a rare private second. ("Of course," she noted, "that was hardly the ideal moment for such a confession.") It is perhaps no coincidence that Che gave Aleida her first rifle in Santa Clara: an M1 Garand, the revolutionary equivalent of an engagement ring.

CAUGHT IN THIS helter-skelter struggle were a number of Cuban business travelers who had the bad luck to be passing through Santa Clara for the holiday season. One nail-biting drama occurred at the historic Gran Hotel on the leafy central plaza, which was seized by the military for its commanding views over the downtown area. Ten SIM snipers had stationed themselves in the tenth-floor penthouse and were holding down movement for blocks around. They had also destroyed the elevator and jammed furniture in the fifth-floor stairwell, trapping dozens of hotel guests. While the fighting dragged on below, some played poker; others gathered in the bar and drank in silence; a teenage clerk named Guillermo Domenech rationed out the last food. After dark on December 31, a call arrived from a rebel lieutenant saying he was in the lobby and needed help to reach the snipers. He asked the guests to quietly remove the furniture in the stairwell or he would have to burn it.

Neither option worked. The furniture was wedged tight, and all the fire did was fill the hotel with smoke. The manager worried that the SIM men might now use the guests as human shields to escape. The hotel electrician then had an inspiration. He remembered that one of the fifth-floor rooms opened within five feet of a cinema next door; he gambled that if he stood on the air-conditioning unit, he might jump the remaining distance. The foothold stayed firm: he was able to kick in a cinema window and make it across the fifty-foot drop above a concrete back alley. In hushed silence, guests lined up to sit on the AC unit to be pulled across, starting with the manager's Rubenesque mother-in-law. ("If the A-C can hold her, we will have no problem with anyone," the clerk Domenech muttered uncharitably to a chorizo salesman.) A sleeping baby was also passed across, wrapped in a blanket. The young clerk was one of the last to leave: finding himself in the cinema's projection room, he ran into a smiling *barbudo*, the first rebel he had ever met.

Suddenly everyone realized it was New Year's Eve. It was time to celebrate.

Part Four

HONEYMOON WITH CHE

CHAPTER 30

Compañeros Versus Mafiosi

(New Year's Eve 1958)

THE SCENE IS so vividly conjured in *The Godfather: Part II* that it has become part of popular culture. On New Year's Eve, well-dressed Cuban and American revelers, including a bevy of Mafiosi, led by Michael Corleone and his brother Fredo, gather at an aristocratic reception with Batista and his family. Midnight tolls, the champagne flows, the crowd rejoices. Outside, fireworks are let off and rich Cubans party as if they don't have a care in the world. But then Batista quiets the room to make a shocking announcement: he is fleeing the country. The rebels have won. Even as the dictator is talking, members of the audience start to slip out. When news reaches the streets outside, the partygoers turn angry, looting casinos and attacking parking meters. As panic spreads through the city, rich Cubans with their suitcases rush the yacht marinas in a desperate attempt to escape before the guerrillas arrive like avenging angels.

The reality of that cataclysmic night was somewhat different—and in many ways more gripping. It is true that Batista fled Havana like a cowardly comic-book villain, surprising even many of his closest confidants. But the details later became so confused—and buried beneath Coppola-esque mythology—that a timeline is needed to follow the convoluted ups and downs of the night. Piecing together newspaper reports and eyewitness testimony, the most dramatic twelve hours in Cuban history had a dreamlike pace:

10:00 p.m.: A sense of anxiety has already ensured that this will be a New Year's Eve like no other. The rebels have given the codename "03C" to the evening—*cero cine, cero compra, cero cabaret* ("zero cinema, zero shopping, zero cabaret"). Word of the boycott has spread under the authorities' noses: For days, cryptic ads have been appearing in newspapers with no text other than those three letters. They were paid for by a sympathetic American businessman, who told gullible censors that it was a teaser for a new hair tonic. "03C" meant, he said, "zero *calvicie* (baldness), zero *caspa* (dandruff), zero *canas* (gray hairs)."

Radio Rebelde then provided the real explanation: "What is 03C? What is 03C?" one announcer asked. "Pay attention! Because 03C is a matter of life or death for you. 03C is the watchword for public shame! Zero cinema, zero shopping, zero cabaret." The musical Medina family then burst into song:

If all of Cuba is at war,
Don't you go to the cabaret!

Although the guerrillas have disavowed terrorism, rumors have spread that they might target nightclubs. Many middle-class Cubans decide to party at home. Even so, the tourist hotels are hopping with affluent foreigners, including hundreds of Americans from two large cruise ships docked in port. The Cuban-owned Tropicana always seems to be above politics, luring braver *habaneros*; a line of cars keeps its four valets dashing nonstop. Instead of joining the festivities at his own Riviera Hotel, Meyer Lansky is dining with his mistress in the modest, low-profile Plaza Hotel downtown, joined by his trusted driver, Armando Jaime. He has put the word out at the Riviera (and to his wife) that his ulcers have kept him in his twentieth-floor suite.

Tradition is modified in Batista's circle, too. For decades, the dictator has hosted a lavish New Year's Eve party at his ample apartments in Camp Columbia, complete with live bands, feasting, and dancing. Instead, earlier in the afternoon, his secretary has invited about seventy intimates to join him for a simple midnight toast.

In the faraway Oriente, Fidel is in the América sugar mill planning the attack on Santiago with his staff. The Hollywood actor Errol Flynn (of all people) has been with him throughout the day.

Around Cuba, any M-26-7 supporters trying to find updates about the revolution were glum. Radio Rebelde is silent (it is moving studios), so the only information comes from US broadcasts, which are filled with terrible news. On his New Year's Eve roundup on CBS, Ed Murrow reports that Che's guerrillas have been forced back in Santa Clara. An announcer in Texas goes one further, declaring that the Cuban army has "smashed the rebel offensive and sent Castro's bearded warriors fleeing back to their mountain hideouts." Batista's US spokesman also confidently confirms that Fidel has been beaten and "the two-year-old Cuban civil war [is] nearing its end." Few are optimistic that the conflict will conclude any time soon.

11:00 p.m.: Lansky is absent, but his chic Riviera Hotel is playing host to the venerable *New York Times* journalist Herbert L. Matthews, who is visiting Havana by chance with his wife, Nancie; Ruby Hart Phillips and other American expats join them for dinner. The mambo band is spirited, the paper party hats colorful, and the cuisine—a set menu of turtle soup, filet mignon, and Baked Alaska—top-notch. The evening is going well until a guest whose house overlooks Camp Columbia casually mentions that he saw cars heading to the base filled with women, children, and valises. This puzzling news has Matthews and the reporters acting "like cats on hot bricks," Nancie notes.

11:30 p.m.: At the Tropicana, the cabaret show *Rumbo al Waldorf* begins. A dance number called "What a Thrill to Fly Cubana Airways!" includes film footage of a passenger plane taking off from Havana. It is followed by the theme song from *The Bridge on the River Kwai*, (William Morgan's favorite, aka the "Colonel Bogey March"), set to a cha-cha rhythm.

In an uncanny echo, the three DC-4 airplanes lined up on the tar-mac at Camp Columbia are ready with their engines idling. The pilots have been pulled from their family New Year's Eve celebrations but given no idea where they will be flying or why. At the other end of the enormous complex, Batista's guests have arrived at his headquarters, a Spanish Gothic mansion with stained glass windows, for the down-sized fiesta. As they await the president in the second-floor ballroom, conversation is strained. Chicken with rice is served on bone china. Some guests pensively sip champagne but most take coffee.

11:45 p.m.: Five hundred miles away, an exhausted Fidel retires with Celia to his quarters in the América sugar mill and falls asleep immediately.

11:50 p.m.: Batista's cavalcade roars up to the doors of his hushed soiree. He mingles with guests, calmly offering pleasantries; in his pocket he is carrying his list of names. (The night before, two of his sons, aged eight and eleven, were flown to New York City with ser-vants and bodyguards, to be installed in a Waldorf Astoria Hotel suite.) In the seconds before midnight, an aide hands Batista a cup of coffee laced with brandy.

Midnight: *"Cinco, quatro, tres, dos, uno . . . Feliz Año Nuevo!"* The champagne corks pop all over Havana. Many revelers, following Spanish tradition, eat a dozen purple grapes with each stroke of the clock for good luck; those celebrating at home also toss buckets of water from their balconies. Cheers ring out. Firecrackers explode in Old Havana.

In the América sugar mill, some cheeky rebel soldiers disobey Fi-del's orders and shoot off their guns. Other guerrillas listen to the Women's Platoon sing the "26th of July Hymn" and "Silent Night." When bearded well-wishers knock at their door, Celia apologizes that Fidel cannot join them because he is already sound asleep. The newly engaged Vilma and Raúl toast with shot glasses filled with Coca-Cola, overlooking the soft drink's imperialist overtones.

12:35 a.m.: In Camp Columbia, Batista takes his highest-ranking guests away from the main party downstairs to his airless office. Without preamble, he reads in a detached monotone a two-page statement announcing his resignation, referring to himself in the third person. The group's reaction is disbelief mixed with dread: Batista is washing his hands of Cuba and leaving thousands of his supporters to their fates. He names General Cantillo, the leader of the failed "Operation Fin de Fidel," as head of the armed forces, and an elderly supreme court judge as new president. An aide then reads the list of passengers who have seats in the escape planes; among them is the president-elect from the recent sham vote, Andrés Rivero Agüero, who has not been informed of Batista's departure until now.

Guests in the main party only learn of the drama when someone dashes upstairs gasping: "Batista is leaving." A few supporters elbow their way into the dictator's office, where the grim news is confirmed. "When we leave this room," the strongman advises them calmly, "grab your wives. Get in your cars. Don't tell your chauffeurs or bodyguards anything. Get in the planes. The engines are running. This is the most dangerous moment of all." A rush for the door begins; everyone is shouldering their way out to the garden. Men jump into their limousines shouting, "To the airfield!" Women trip over their long gowns and lose high heels. Batista's bodyguard later compares the scene to "a stampede of cows in a Western movie."

Military officers who live on Camp Columbia are able to rush home and grab jewels and cash; the civilian passengers are forced to leave Cuba with what they have on them. As he reaches the airfield, Agüero bitterly counts 215 pesos in his wallet. The execrable Havana police chief, Colonel Ventura—"the assassin in the white suit"— cannot understand why Batista did not warn him in advance to bring his wife and children with him to the party. "This is cowardice and a betrayal," he stammers to Batista. On being assured that his family will follow in a plane the next day, he reluctantly climbs aboard. Soldiers taunt the departing officers from the darkness: "Viva Fidel!" comes one distant cry. Then: "You should have left sooner!"

12:45 a.m.: Phillips and Ted Scott, editor of the English-language *Havana Post*, drop off Matthews and Nancie at their usual haunt, the Sevilla-Biltmore Hotel, then go to their office and call Camp Columbia. There is no answer. As Phillips drives home, the streets are deserted; even the police have vanished.

1:30 a.m.: The American-style shindig at the Plaza Hotel, complete with inebriated renditions of "Auld Lang Syne," is in full swing when Meyer Lansky is approached in his booth by one of his sidekicks, who whispers in his ear. Lansky's expression does not change. He stands up, apologizes to his mistress, and walks out with his driver. He orders Jaime to speedily make the rounds of his casinos before news of Batista's exit leaks out. "Get the money," Lanksy says. "All of it."

2:40 a.m.: From the doorway of a DC-4, Batista shouts "*¡Salud! ¡Salud!*" without apparent irony to a crowd of abandoned supporters, then disappears inside. One by one, the three aircraft roar off into the moonless night. An army officer left behind mumbles, "God help us."

Residents of the upscale suburbs of Marianao and Playa nearby have their celebrations interrupted by the din of the planes banking out over the ocean. Many think they are going to crash or that the pilots are intoxicated. The timing is unusual: commercial flights almost never leave Havana at that hour. CIA agent David Atlee Phillips is sipping champagne in a lawn chair when he sees lights receding in the sky like UFOs. He calls his case officer in Washington and says, "Batista just flew into exile." The reaction: "Are you drunk?"

At the Tropicana, a phone call comes in for a rich Batista crony. He has passed out at the roulette table, so the croupier passes the receiver to the man's wife. She blanches and gasps: "*¡No me digas!*"—"Don't tell me!" —then asks the dealer to carry her husband to their car. From that moment, Rosa Lowinger writes in the memoir *Tropicana Nights: The Life and Times of the Legendary Cuban Nightclub*, "like the first fat raindrops of a tropical thundershower, the rumors started."

4:00 a.m.: On board Batista's escape plane, the president casually informs passengers that they are flying to the Dominican Republic, not Florida as they had all assumed. He does not explain that the US had denied him asylum. The silence, one passenger says, is "funereal"; Agüero later compares the plane to "a huge casket carrying a cargo of live corpses." Still, there is a moment of black humor. As they pass over the Sierra Maestra, a senator wonders aloud what sort of reception they would get from the Rebel Army if they crash-landed.

5:00 a.m.: Word of Batista's cut and run filters thought Havana; telephone calls multiply, families wake each other with cries of *"¡Se fue!"*—"He's gone." Phillips calls up Matthews with the news, and soon he is on trunk calls to New York. As the sky pales, *habaneros* leave their houses, cheering, banging cymbals, drums, and kitchen pans in an instant Carnival. Convoys of cars honk horns through the city. Church bells ring. The years of frustration spill out: crowds attack parking meters with baseball bats and sledgehammers, sending rivers of coins onto the sidewalks. (The meters are despised symbols of corruption in auto-loving Havana, since the proceeds went straight to Batista's chums.) Shop windows are shattered. Then the casinos are targeted.

6:00 a.m.: Hollywood actor George Raft, who has been employed as MC at the Mob-run Capri Hotel—an inside joke for Americans, since he often played gangsters on-screen—is slipping between the silk sheets with his inamorata when he hears gunfire. He phones the front desk and is told, "Mr. Raft, the revolution is here." He throws on some clothes and dashes downstairs to find pandemonium. A hundred furious Cubans are destroying the lobby. One even lets loose with machine-gun fire at the bar, disintegrating the liquor bottles and mirrors. According to his own account, Raft climbs onto a table and shouts, "Calm down! For chrissake, calm down!" Miraculously, the crowd leader recognizes him and yells: "It's George Raft, the movie star!" Improvising wildly, Raft says that everyone is welcome to food and drink if they leave the hotel alone. After some "lightweight looting," most of the Cubans happily depart. Other casinos fare worse. The Plaza, where Lanksy was dining, is trashed. At the Riviera, farmers will soon arrive to let loose a truckload of pigs in the lobby, stomping mud over the carpets and defecating in the casino.

The malevolent Rolando Masferrer, chief of the Tigers death squad, throws 20,000 pesos into a bag and orders supporters to meet him on a former US Coast Guard vessel, the *Olo-Kun II*, which he has converted for just this emergency. They speed directly north to Florida. Top naval officials pile onto Batista's private yacht, the *Marta III*, and cast off.

7:00 a.m.: Matthews and Nancie venture out of the Sevilla-Biltmore to find the capital "a madhouse." While Matthews will knock out a front-page report for the *Times*, the most candid account comes from Nancie, who jots a detailed letter to their son Eric on scraps of paper and hotel stationery. No sooner have they stepped out the door than they run into "villainous-looking" armed throngs and are forced to drop to their stomachs to avoid stray bullets; police watch the looting from a distance, aware they will be lynched if they intervene. Scrambling back inside the hotel, they find that the lobby has been wrecked—"a mass of broken glass, overturned [tables]" and "full of Americans stranded." As at the Capri, the bar has been a target. "We couldn't even get a beer, much to Daddy's disgust who certainly does like his little drinks."

By now Batista has landed in the Dominican Republic, where he gives the pilot and copilot $1,000 in cash each. The second plane arrives within half an hour. The third, carrying several of Batista's children and other collaborators, lands in Jacksonville, Florida, where the fifty-two passengers are stuck in the airport for hours. Miami was deemed too full of pro-Castro exiles to be a safe destination, but even here the new arrivals are taunted in a terminal café. "Torturer," one Cuban yells at a SIM officer. A silver-haired man sitting next to him adds: "You're a killer . . . And we're going to kill *you*."

8:00 a.m.: The first American tourists from the cruise ship *Mauretania* land in Havana Harbor for shore excursions, unaware that the city is teetering on the edge of chaos. As they set off in convertible taxis, few wonder why the national radio station has canceled regular programming and is playing Beethoven's Ninth Symphony over and over again. Far away in the Oriente, with no telephone or telegraph service, Fidel and his rebels greet the New Year no better informed about the earth-shattering events of the night before.

CHAPTER 31

In (Cuba) Like Flynn

(New Year's Day 1959)

THE BOLSHEVIK REVOLUTION had John Reed as eyewitness chron- icler; the Cuban Revolution got Errol Flynn. Thanks to a murky series of events, the burned-out actor, his career in tatters, addled by vodka and morphine, talked his way onto the front lines of the guer- rilla war as a special correspondent for Hearst newspapers; now, on January 1, he became the only member of the press to be with Fidel at the moment of victory. The resulting five-part series for the high- circulation *New York Journal American* under the sensational head- line "I FOUGHT WITH CASTRO" (offering "a startled Flynn's-eye view of women without men and men without liquor") was lost for decades until the clippings were rediscovered in the archives of the University of Texas in 2009.

The idea of Flynn as a foreign correspondent was not so much of a stretch as it may seem. Although he is considered by most today as a hedonistic satyr who specialized in melodramatic, men-in-tights cos- tume dramas, the Australian-born Flynn had been a writer long be- fore he was an actor, filing columns in his early twenties from New Guinea for the *Sydney Bulletin*. Even as a Hollywood idol, he pined for the literary life, writing enough magazine stories to fill an anthology, dispatches on the Spanish Civil War for Hearst, and two bestselling novels. His final, soul-searching autobiography, *My Wicked, Wicked Ways*, would be compared to Casanova's for its heady mix of libertinism, gossip, and philosophical musings. Flynn had also been coming to Cuba since the mid-1930s, when he arrived in a yacht purchased with proceeds from the pirate film *Captain Blood*, so he knew the island—at least, its debauched underbelly—intimately.

In retrospect, there is a pleasing symmetry to the encounter between the aging thespian and rising star Fidel. The pop-culture vision of the guerrilla chief as a new Robin Hood mirrored Flynn's most celebrated screen role as the Prince of Thieves in 1938. Flynn felt the fictional Robin Hood expressed his real-life affinity for the downtrodden. ("Ever since boyhood, I have been drawn—perhaps romantically— to the idea of causes, crusades," he wrote self-deprecatingly. "When I see a poor land that wants its due, why then, I am willing to lend a hand—even if, as some say, it is only to reach out for a glass.")

As the historian Van Gosse notes, Flynn's Cuban adventure was "a last, too-good-to-be-true epilogue to the story of how Fidel Castro's revolution was aided from the US." It was also a poignant final act for the forty-nine-year-old Flynn himself. Doctors had told Flynn several years earlier that his liver was decomposing and he did not have long to live. Now he plunged into the front lines of Cuba like one of his own swashbuckling cinema creations. Fidel's victory was also Errol's swan song.

FROM THE START, the assignment had elements of farce. Flynn arrived in Havana with his sixteen-year-old girlfriend, the platinum-blond Beverly Aadland—registered as his "secretary" to quiet wagging tongues—and spent nearly a month holed up in the cocktail lounge at the swank Hotel Nacional angling for safe passage to Fidel's camp. A message abruptly arrived on Christmas Eve telling him to head with his photographer to the airport the next morning. Leaving Aadland behind, he filled an old briefcase labeled FLYNN ENTERPRISES with essentials—a bottle of vodka, tangerines, and toilet tissue—but its locks broke, so he tied a rope around the bag and stuck it in a pillow-case. Despite this hobo-like appearance, he told airport police that he was scouting film locations in the Oriente.

Even in his bloated twilight, Flynn was a celebrity. When they landed in Camagüey, he had to fend off autograph hunters in the bar before meeting his star-struck Movement contact, the American air-port manager. The next day he was smuggled onto a small plane to fly into rebel-controlled territory; he was then taken on an all-day "cement-mixer" of a jeep ride to the rebel base in the América sugar mill. He arrived at dusk on December 27, just as Che was preparing his assault some 350 miles away on Santa Clara.

Flynn's series for the *Herald Journal* offers a beguiling if wildly impressionistic snapshot of Fidel and his troops in the last days of 1958, unaware that they were on the cusp of victory. He found the *comandante en jefe* in his usual relaxed sprawl on the bed, absorbed by the radio news with Celia standing guard at his side. (Flynn as-sessed her as "36–24–35.") When Fidel got up to greet him, he "had grace, agility of movement and a simplicity of manner which I hadn't quite expected," Flynn wrote. "It simply wasn't the imperial thing I thought I might encounter, the manner of a man who commanded." The actor thought Fidel was still more of a lawyer than warrior. ("His face looked soft. So did his hands.") He noted one lovely detail about the revolutionary couple: While Fidel spoke, Celia took off his glasses, polished them, and put them back on his face without him noticing— moving "attentively but subtly, not getting in his way."

Errol still had a good deal of charm. According to his account, he joked with Fidel about booze: "Do you mind if I take a delicious draft of the wine of your land [rum] so as to make a revolutionary situation a little more viable?" Fidel told him to go ahead but refused to partake himself, musing that he might be allergic to spirits. "I have the same thing," Flynn laughed, "and by dint of great discipline have managed to overcome it." He then offered some unsolicited advice: the guerrillas should call themselves "patriots" rather than "rebels" to sound less lawless to American audiences. The word "rebel," Flynn suggested, had a negative Jesse James ring. Fidel shrugged off the advice but gave him a red-and-black M-26-7 scarf as a souvenir.

Flynn spent five days in Fidel's orbit, much of the time squeezed between two soldiers in the back seat of his jeep. He was surprised that Celia sat in the middle next to the driver and Castro by the door, exposed to possible snipers. For his part, Fidel seemed tickled to have a Hollywood actor with him, even though many rural Cubans did not recognize him at first. One asked Flynn flatly: "How can you look so young in the movies and so old now?" ("That hurt a little . . . I gulped some rum.") Another asked why he didn't make movies instead of drinking so much. He was billeted in a small church with a fine view of Santiago, where a portly priest (naturally dubbed "Friar Tuck") gave him a rare hot bath and a ripe tangerine for dinner. Breakfast was a banana and a slug of rum; lunch was *arroz con pollo*, although the chicken, Flynn said, was hard to find.

By day, he lingered around Fidel's HQ while negotiations for Santiago's surrender were brokered by Catholic bishops. Not surprisingly, the old roué Flynn was fascinated by the Marianas; indeed, he was already planning to make a feature movie, *Cuban Rebel Girls*, with Beverly in a lead role. "I learned they were armed with bras, low-heeled shoes, no makeup and guns," he wrote. "They had to put aside bobby pins, curlers, all the gadgety stuff that women everywhere find vital. I can't say that this made exactly a bevy of chorus-style beauties of the gals, but they had something that was pretty wonderful, a camaraderie, and fine faces"—even if he found their stories of murdered lovers and brothers, which had inspired them to join up, a little "grim."

One night he was awakened at 3:00 a.m. to watch Fidel berate his troops for lapses in discipline, drinking beer, and running around with girls who weren't in the Movement. ("You are failing yourselves!" Fidel thundered. The bemused debauchee Flynn noted: "I hadn't been so close to so much virtue in a long time.") Flynn had joked about giving Fidel tips on public speaking, but conceded he didn't need it: "Castro has as much power in his voice as anyone I ever heard say lines for the screen or the theater."

Then, on New Year's Day, the permanently hungover actor woke up in his church billet to cries of *"¡Se fue!"*—"He's gone!"

LIKE MOST OTHER Cubans, Fidel heard the news on the radio.

The first day of 1959 began with business as usual. Fidel awoke at sunrise in the sugar mill, dictated letters to Celia, and grumpily threatened to court-martial the men who had celebrated the night before with midnight gunfire. Then, a few minutes after 8:00 a.m., he sat down for breakfast: his usual chicken with rice and *café con leche*. A visiting Cuban journalist suddenly burst in and declared that Havana radio was announcing that "something important" had happened in the capital. Fidel immediately suspected a US-brokered military coup. "This is a betrayal," he bellowed. "A cowardly betrayal. They want to steal away our victory."

He learned the truth from a teenage villager who rushed in a few seconds later: American radio stations were saying that Batista had fled. Others followed with more snippets. There was a new army chief. A judge had been chosen to be the new president. All this only made Fidel more furious. As news spread throughout the HQ, guerrillas burst into shouting and singing, but those outside Fidel's office were surprised to hear their leader spouting a lurid stream of curses. It was exactly what he had feared: that others would step in to seize power when the dictator caved, leaving the Rebel Army out in the cold. He would march on Santiago immediately, he declared, and make a radio announcement calling for a general strike.

"Comandante," an aide begged, "I think you should wait at least fifteen minutes."

Fidel wouldn't hear of it. He was already making notes for an address to the nation. Victory had been snatched from Cubans back in

1898, he argued, when the *yanquis* swept in to "liberate" the island; he would not allow history to repeat. If the establishment kept control, their rebellion would have been for nothing.

For the true veterans, Batista's flight was bittersweet. In Miami, Haydée Santamaría sank into melancholy when she heard, remembering the loss of so many young lives in the struggle. It was only then, she later admitted, "that I truly realized [my brother] Abel was dead, that they were all dead." The medic-turned-guerrilla Manuel Fajardo felt a similar wave of sadness when he heard the first shouts of "He's gone!" He was about to attack a small military barracks and hung his head, lost in thought, until a local woman asked him what was wrong. He told her that he could not rejoice, since "the blood of our dead comrades was not dry." Two army sentries in the village would have more cause to celebrate. Fajardo barely stopped his snipers from opening fire on them. "Those two guys were saved by only five minutes!"

IN SANTA CLARA, where Che's men were still locked in battle, the army defense collapsed almost immediately when the news spread that morning. At the Gran Hotel, the ten SIM snipers in the penthouse finally surrendered and were led out through jeering crowds. (They were executed that afternoon.) Rank-and-file soldiers dropped their guns and embraced the rebels as if they were lifelong comrades. The army commander, Colonel Joaquín Casillas, was one of Batista's most detestable enforcers; he tried to flee the city in civilian clothes but was caught. It was soon heard that Casillas had been killed in an "escape attempt," quite probably on Che's orders.

The situation in Havana, meanwhile, was sliding into anarchy. The airport counters were mobbed with men in tuxedos and women in sequined gowns who had not had time to change. The last flight to the United States left at 9:19 a.m. when a police officer forced the pilot into the cockpit at gunpoint. Batista's minister for transportation was

among the ninety-one on board. After that, rebel agents drove trucks
to block the runways. A plane coming from Miami with pro-Castro
exiles was turned back, forcing a collective groan in the cabin.

RADIO REBELDE HAD been silent on New Year's Eve, but now Carlos
Franqui set up a new broadcast studio in the town of Palma Soriano
near Santiago, in a cavernous room with French windows. In mid-
morning Fidel recorded one of his most famous speeches, starting
with an ultimatum that the Moncada garrison must surrender by 6:00
p.m. He called a general strike across Cuba and asked citizens to resist
the urge to take vengeance on Batista's henchmen. (He was harking
back to Cuban history: when the dictator Machado fell in 1933, lynch
mobs tore through the streets of Havana; more than 1,000 people
were killed.) Lastly, he ordered Camilo and Che to speed to Havana to
take control of the city's two military fortresses, where thousands of
troops were stationed. The struggle was far from over, Fidel roared,
departing from his script. There would be no compromises, no wheel-
ing and dealing with the shabby remnants of Batista's regime. "The
Rebel Army will continue its sweeping campaign! Revolution, *yes*;
military coup, *no!*"

Afterward, Fidel allowed himself a brief moment of celebration. A
photo survives of him and Celia at a simple wooden bar surrounded
by *barbudos*. Fidel has a bottle of beer in front of him; Celia has what
looks like a glass of red wine. A pretty female admirer has come up to
pat Fidel on the shoulder and offer congratulations.

IN HAVANA, TELEVISION stations broadcast confirmation of Batista's
flight at noon. The volatile crowds roaming the streets now became
larger, and bonfires of slot machines and roulette tables raged on corners. Opposition activists began turning up at the TV studios to offer
firsthand accounts of the regime's horrors: viewers watched with grim

fascination as one man took off his shirt to reveal his back freshly covered with cigarette burns.

Movement leaders also headed to the TV stations to appeal for calm. As Fidel's radio speech was broadcast over and again, militiamen with M-26-7 armbands began to emerge. They soon patrolled the city in cars with loudspeakers, warning looters: "Get off the streets or be killed!" That afternoon, volunteers from civic clubs went to protect the casinos. Boy Scouts manned roadblocks and directed traffic. By nightfall, order had miraculously been restored to Havana. There were some isolated shoot-outs between rebels and police; some Batista supporters had their houses sacked; a SIM informer was strung up from a light post near El Principe prison. But only thirteen people were killed that day, Associated Press reported.

Meanwhile, hotel staff all over the city obeyed Fidel's call to go on strike, leaving hundreds of American tourists to line up for hot dogs passed out by management in the foyers. (Contrary to rumors that he fled for his life, Lansky stayed in Havana for a week to help serve at the Riviera.) Cruise line guests on shore excursions, some of whose taxis had been stuck in crowds chanting anti-*yanqui* slogans, made their way safely back to their ships. One seven-year-old, Dick Tannenbaum from Long Island, was reported in the *New York Times* summing up the historic day in his diary: "Left *Mauretania*, saw revolution, came back."

In Santiago, the Moncada garrison threw down its arms just before the 6:00 p.m. deadline. It was time for a symbolic rewrite of the Spanish–American War. "The history of 1898 will not be repeated," Fidel promised the nation, alluding to the humiliating memory of the US Army forbidding Cuban soldiers to attend the Spanish surrender. Raúl was dispatched in advance to accept the formal capitulation while Fidel followed at a more regal pace. In a sign that feminism would still face challenges in Cuba, Vilma begged to join her fiancé on his mission; it would be unforgettable for her, she said, to be present when the bastion of repression in her hometown capitulated. Raúl refused. It would be too dangerous, he said.

Vilma was incensed. "What am I doing here?" she snapped to Fidel as they watched Raúl roar off.

He shrugged. "Why didn't you go with him?"

Vilma stormed off—"really burned up," she recalled.

Errol Flynn and his photographer climbed into a jeep to join the rebels' triumphant procession, a two-mile-long line of cars and motorbikes festooned with flags on poles. The vehicles inched ahead while campesinos lined the road cheering them on. Fidel stood in a jeep so he could commune with "the people." At times, delirious crowds spilled onto the road to touch the *comandante en jefe*, slowing progress to a complete halt.

In Flynn's confused newspaper account, possibly lubricated by quantities of rum, his driver tried to skirt the traffic jam by taking a detour through the hills. When his jeep ran into a burst of gunfire, most of the passengers dove for cover into a ditch. Flynn dashed for a stone wall, where a sharp object slashed his shin—either a ricocheting bullet, he says, or flying piece of mortar.

Fidel's motorcade did not make it to Santiago until midnight. Ten thousand adoring *santiagenos* packed the plaza, hanging from rooftops and street lamps. "What an uproar!" Vilma recalled. "Everybody was in the streets, women in hairnets, men in pajamas. People were running out of houses crying and carrying us on their shoulders." At 2:15 a.m. Fidel emerged on the balcony of the town hall to cacophonous cheers. He spoke for over two hours, rejoicing that Cubans were finally fulfilling their destiny: "The revolution is now beginning . . . For the first time, the people will have what they deserve . . . This war was won by the people!"

CHAPTER 32

The Caravan of Victory

(January 2–8, 1959)

DESPITE THE EUPHORIA over Batista's midnight cut and run, Cuba's future was anyone's guess. Power was not about to fall like a ripe fruit into Fidel's hands. Some 40,000 government troops were still armed. Exiled politicians were flocking to Havana, as were rival guerrilla groups from the Escambray Mountains. In fact, the island was awash with weapons and could easily descend into civil war. Finally, many Cubans were worried that the US might send in the Marines. On January 1 Eisenhower had already dispatched three destroyers and two submarines from the Key West Navy base "to protect American lives and property."

The rebels kept up their momentum with more acts of bravado that no standard military textbook would have advised. At dawn on January 2, Camilo and his three hundred men were already speeding along the main highway to Havana, where they intended to seize Camp Columbia. At a roadside truck stop, he telephoned the ranking officer, Colonel Ramón Barquín—an anti-Batista figure from within the officer corps who had been released from prison only the day before—and breezily informed him that he had orders to "come in and take command" of the 5,000 soldiers there. Barquín knew that he had the option to resist, but the idea seemed fanciful. He was in charge, he felt, of "a dead army." The colonel simply sighed in resignation: "Well, if you have orders, then come on in." Officials in the US embassy, who were handing out turkey sandwiches and coffee to tourists, were baffled when they heard the news. The massive Cuban army was simply capitulating. A CIA agent was sent to Camp Columbia to meet Colonel Barquín and suggest that he hold out and perhaps help form a moderate new government for Cuba, but he shrugged: "What can I do? All they left me with is shit." Another US diplomat summed up the Americans' feelings: "It's just crazy."

There was a dreamlike air when Camilo's men pulled up at the Camp Columbia gates around 5:00 p.m. in their dusty trucks and jeeps. Their progress had been slowed by rapturous crowds who flocked to see the handsome Havana boy with his flashing smile, cowboy hat, and two pistols slung insouciantly on his hips. Having been by Fidel's side since the *Granma* landing, Camilo was an instant hero. One reporter thought he looked like Robinson Crusoe; Carlos Franqui, noting his exuberant beard, more memorably compared Camilo to "Christ on a spree." The sight of 5,000 troops surrendering to a few grimy guerrillas was, Franqui noted, "enough to make you burst out laughing." When Camilo wondered in bemusement how his few men would disarm so many soldiers, Colonel Barquín assured him they were too depressed to resist. The colonel agreed to stay on and help run the camp during the transition. Lodging was found for the new arrivals in the barracks, and bar privileges at the elite officers' club, a whitewashed manor with crenellated walls, were opened to the *barbudos*. They could sign for drinks or cigars at no cost, Barquín told them, and attend free films at the regimental theater.

By CONTRAST, CHE arrived at 4:00 a.m. on January 3 to a dark and silent city, riding along the empty Malecón sea wall in his battered old jeep with Aleida by his side. Like the majority of his men, he had never seen the Cuban capital before, and he gazed like a sightseer at the moonlit mansions of Old Havana with their intricate colonial facades, the gorgeous brocade of carved curlicues, heavy oak portals, and wrought iron balconies, evoking an abandoned opera set. His parade of trucks then rumbled through the tunnel under the harbor to the Spanish fortress of La Cabaña.

As ever, Che's emotional life echoed the campaign. Earlier on that same momentous evening, he had declared his love to Aleida again while they were refueling at a gas station. They were sitting in the jeep when he said that seeing her in danger in Santa Clara made him realize what she meant to him. "I was exhausted and half asleep, so I was hardly listening to what he was saying," Aleida confessed. "I didn't even take it very seriously . . . But that was it. The others piled back into the jeep, and we were soon on our way again."

Taking control of La Cabaña was "surreal," Aleida said. In the darkness the guerrillas marveled at its ten-foot-thick walls of coral stone, the rusty cannons that had once fired on English pirates, its palm-filled gardens and sweeping ocean views. "We, the dispossessed, for the first time felt ourselves masters of our own destiny," she wrote. Che and his officers bunked down in the commanding officer's quarters, many of them passing out on the floor. Aleida and the other women went through his wife's wardrobe looking for a change of clothes. She was given her own small room for privacy, since she and Che were still courting at an Edwardian pace.

Then they waited tensely for Fidel.

THE DAY BEFORE, on January 2, the *comandante en jefe* had begun his slow progress from Santiago to Havana. Instead of flying directly to the capital, Fidel decided to allow his dramatic instincts full rein by traveling the length of Cuba in a "caravan of victory," which echoed the triumphs of conquering Roman generals. The journey would take nearly a week along a route literally strewn with flowers. At every provincial town along the way, the *barbudos* were greeted as heroes by euphoric crowds, who implored Fidel to pause and give a speech. At some point along the way, he stopped wearing his spectacles, noting that "a leader does not wear glasses."

The 1,000-strong guerrilla force expanded at every stop, starting on the first day in Bayamo, where an entire army column swelled the ranks to 3,000. The rebels now rode fourteen tanks like carnival floats, with the Marianas atop the first, winning hearts along the way. Men shouted, "Look, here are the most beautiful women in Cuba!" One member, Rita García, remembered: "The women asked us, 'You fought? You shot a gun?' And when we said, 'yes,' many of them embraced us, crying." Women also wanted to see Celia, the Maid Marian of the revolution, who stayed as busy as ever: somehow en route her aides purchased quantities of toys which an air force pilot dropped in the Sierra Maestra on Three Kings' Day, the traditional Spanish gift-giving feast. It was an act of thanks for the *guajiros'* help in the war and a signal that a new era was beginning.

Meanwhile, young provincial guerrillas were able to see their families en route; many had not heard news from their rebel sons for months and did not know whether they were alive or dead. The *chicos* posed for photos around cakes and flowers with proud parents and neighbors, then left again at dawn. Not surprisingly, this festive victory tour often made only fifty miles a day. Fidel was soon hoarse and bleary-eyed from sleeping only two hours a night; his men fared little better. The standing joke became "I haven't slept since 1958." But each stopover added to Fidel's power and prestige. He was cementing his support along the spine of Cuba. By the time he arrived in the capital, he would be unstoppable.

WHILE THE CARAVAN crawled ahead, Havana remained in lockdown. The general strike kept stores closed; staple foods were in short supply. Some neighborhoods took on a postapocalyptic air, with garbage piling up in empty streets and only the occasional car speeding past in a cloud of debris. The Movement set up operations at the new Sports Palace, a circular covered arena whose Jet Age design resembled a white flying saucer, and piled up sandbags around the entrances. A parade of captured SIM officers accused of "war crimes" was brought in and locked in the athletic changing rooms. In the heat of the moment, overzealous *habaneros* made citizen's arrests of neighbors they believed were Batista sympathizers; most had to be released. The two prison cells at Camp Columbia, designed for sixty prisoners, soon held six hundred. The overflow was sent to La Cabaña.

Che and Camilo were slowly disarming the eight thousand-odd soldiers under their command and locking up their arsenals. Nobody knew quite how to behave at the old Batista fortresses: nervous army officers would stop and salute *barbudos* whenever they passed, which only confused the guerrillas, who had no military formalities or even officer insignia. A more serious threat to M-26-7 was the Revolutionary Directorate. Hundreds of armed students and insurgents from the Escambray had taken over Havana University, where the leader Faure Chomón presided in a massive wooden rector's chair. His supporters even took over the Presidential Palace for a while, risking shoot-outs with M-26-7 cadres, but begrudgingly left when Fidel's choice as interim president, the respected judge Manuel Urrutia, flew into Havana and wanted to move in with his wife.

When Fidel lifted the general strike on January 5, the tense mood in Havana evaporated overnight. The caravan of victory had made it as far as the port of Cienfuegos, only 150 miles away, and was due to arrive in the city any day. The airport reopened; groceries reappeared on the shelves. Music was also back on the streets, with buskers coming up with new patriotic songs such as "Just Like Martí Dreamed It" and "Wings of Liberty." Many of Che and Camilo's guerrillas were forced to camp out in hotel lobbies, to the bemusement of tourists; the Havana Hilton's glamorous ballroom was turned into a mess hall. Girls would follow the rebels around like rock stars. "Here were these baseball-playing, roguish, sexy guys who roll into town and chase the bad guys off," says Che biographer Jon Lee Anderson. "By all accounts, it was an orgy. If you were a *barbudo*, you were having a very good time." Many of the country-raised guerrilla boys were in a state of shock at the openness of Havana. The Tropicana reopened, and booze and cocaine were available on every corner. "Most of the women, and also many of the men, went wild over these hairy fellows," recalled the future poet and gay activist, Reinaldo Arenas, "everyone wanted to take one of the bearded men home." Newspapers, reappearing without censorship restrictions, poked mild fun at the sudden popularity of facial hair in Havana. One cartoon showed a man with light stubble on his cheeks being asked: "Señor, how long have you been with the rebels?" "About 24 hours," he replies. For those billeted at La Cabaña, the favorite trysting spot was beneath the giant white statue of Christ until Che put his foot down. He ordered a mass wedding to make illicit liaisons "official."

Che had his own fan club. When the American guerrilla Neill Macaulay visited him on official business, he had to fight past a block-long line of admirers "composed mostly of upper-class ladies and their teenage daughters." Che had pushed a big desk up against the door to keep all the "elegant, ecstatic females" at bay, and when they opened the office window shutters, "three shrieking teenage girls tried to climb through the window." Photographs also show Che surrounded by attractive European female journalists. His "secretary" Aleida soon gained a reputation for being unusually strict on Che's schedule with women.

On a darker note, *Bohemia* magazine published special issues documenting the dictatorship's excesses. Page after page was filled with grisly images of murdered young men, many in their underwear and savagely tortured. A nationwide search for mass graves began, and photo spreads soon showed dozens of shallow death pits picked over by vultures. Across Cuba, a longing for vengeance was building. In Santa Clara, where the fighting had been freshest, rebel officials were already carrying out summary executions in a field on the edge of town. Crowds gathered to watch. Entrepreneurs rented folding chairs. Ice cream trucks appeared. After the first shootings elicited cheers, the commanding rebel officer felt things were getting out of hand. "Ladies and gentlemen, this is not a circus," he said, moving the proceedings to the garrison.

Retribution came more slowly in Santiago. A few arrests of Masferrer's Tigers occurred, but the cruelest SIM agents were still at large. Vilma brought in a delegation of mothers to see Raúl, complaining that the men who had murdered their sons were walking free. "Trust us," Raúl assured them. "We will not disappoint you."

By THEN, THE only foreign guest in Santiago's Casa Grande Hotel was Errol Flynn, who spent his time drinking on the patio and listening to sporadic shooting as his shin became infected. His whimsical observations continued: he joked that nobody could get a haircut in the city—even the barbers were growing their hair like the *barbudos*. But when a portly tourist guide offered to show him the city sights, Flynn decided he'd had enough. He made his way to the airport to talk his way onto a rebel flight, turning up the charm for the airport agent. "I promised her everything except a starring role in my next movie . . . I held her hand. I beamed at her like the warm Cuban sun." By the time he was back in Havana, there were already rumors that he had never left the hotel bar. Perhaps as a joke, a theatrical agent sent him a cable: IF YOU WIN THE WAR HAVE POSSIBILITY TOP NOTCH BROADWAY SHOW CONTACT IMMEDIATELY UPON RETURN TO NEW YORK.

For more regular foreign correspondents, a race now began for the first interview with Fidel. On January 3, helpful rebel agents arranged a plane for Herbert L. Matthews to fly directly to catch Fidel in the provincial city of Holguin, but it developed engine trouble after takeoff. Much to his chagrin, he was scooped by Jules Dubois of the *Chicago Tribune*, who had chartered a Piper Apache in Miami. "You can be sure that we will be friendly towards the United States, as long as the United States is friendly to us," Fidel told Dubois. The US in fact recognized the new government on January 7, the second country to do so; the USSR followed suit on the tenth.

Getting Fidel on US television screens was another, more complicated race. The resumption of commercial flights from New York to Havana inspired the CBS entertainer Ed Sullivan to fly there in secret to land the first video interview. Despite the staggering popularity of his variety show, Sullivan dreamed of being taken seriously as a reporter. He told a young cameraman from *The Phil Silvers Show* that they were flying to the Dominican Republic, and only admitted the truth about their mission once they were already on the plane. They arrived at the Havana airport after dark on January 7 and wrestled their way to meet Sullivan's friend and fixer Jules Dubois. Unfortunately, Fidel had been delayed yet again, Dubois explained; his caravan was still in Matanzas, a town sixty miles east. But some friendly guerrillas arranged a taxicab for them, with a guard cradling a machine gun in the front seat. The headlights lit up the empty highways as they passed one rebel checkpoint after the next—"a real war scene," Sullivan melodramatically recalled.

When they rolled into Matanzas at midnight, Fidel was finishing up yet another three-hour speech from the town hall balcony to a spellbound crowd. Celia gave the go-ahead for the interview, so the cameraman set up the gear in the reception hall after a frantic search for a decent power outlet. Around 2:00 a.m. Fidel swept into the room with his host of *barbudos*, filling it with smoke, sweat, and noise. No sooner had Fidel and Sullivan shaken hands than the air was split by a thunderous crack, sending Ed ducking for cover and guards waving cocked weapons. One of the guerrillas had knocked over a camera light.

Afterward, Sullivan's posse drove into Havana at dawn, stopping at a roadside cart for chorizo and cheese sandwiches for breakfast. At the airport, his rebel escort forced a path to the check-in counter through the throngs of Batista supporters trying to leave. In line, Sullivan recognized the actor George Raft, who said his bank account had been frozen; Sullivan lent Raft the cash for a ticket out.

THE CLIMAX OF the revolutionary war was almost as improvised and spontaneous as its birth. A color Super 8 film taken by an anonymous Cuban film buff survives of the caravan of victory roaring into the outskirts of Havana that afternoon. One after another, trucks, jeeps, buses, and beaten-up jalopies sped along the waterfront under the brilliant blue Caribbean sky, guerrillas hanging from the sides, waving enormous M-26-7 flags and holding their fingers in V signs. Fidel himself arrived riding a tank on a flatbed and chomping a cigar while Sikorsky helicopters hovered protectively overhead. By his side was his nine-year-old son, Fidelito, dressed up in a crisp olive-green mini-uniform. They had detoured to pick the boy up from relatives at a Shell gas station en route.

By the time the caravan reached the Malecón, it was mobbed. Tearful throngs threw confetti from wrought iron balconies; black-and-red crepe paper rained down. Exultant guards shot their rifles in the air. Two Cuban warships steaming into the harbor set off a salute as air force planes shot by. As a CBS newsman reported: "It looks like Ike and MacArthur coming home."

Fidel took one moment for personal reflection when he spotted the impounded *Granma* in the port. Fidel ordered his driver to stop and pushed his way over. "That boat is like a piece of my life," he declared. Fidel later said that he felt a premonition of the changes that were to come. He was about to leave behind the simplicity of the guerrilla war, with its pure, straightforward goal of eliminating the dictator, for the morass of actual government.

There were also brief reunions. The socialite-turned-underground-agent Naty Revuelta, who had been Fidel's lover in Havana before he went into exile in Mexico, was standing in the crowd with a flower in her hand. She had not believed she would see Fidel alive again and had never told him that she had borne his child. Now a friend pushed her forward to the tank. Fidel spotted her, beamed down, and said, *"Ay, Naty, que bueno."* Then he was gone; she carried the flower with her to Camp Columbia to hear his speech.

Fidel still had his telescopic rifle on his shoulder when he and Celia entered the gaudy Presidential Palace to join the new president, Manuel Urrutia, and his wife for a press conference. After enjoying several glasses of Coca-Cola in the Hall of Mirrors, Fidel went to address the crowd. In an early sign that Fidel would not fit the classic Latin American mold for revolutionaries, who after their moment of triumph would slowly be co-opted into the system, he expressed his dislike for the palace and said he wanted to make a complete break with the past. He then walked through the silent crowd back to his vehicle, which opened up without the need for guards; it was like Moses parting the Red Sea, one awestruck journalist noted.

The driver to Camp Columbia took the wrong entrance, and in an unplanned detour the whole guerrilla leadership—Celia, Raúl, Vilma, Juan Almeida, and other *comandantes*—went to an empty officer's house and, exhausted, stole a few minutes siesta. When they emerged, they realized that the fastest way to the makeshift podium was by climbing over a fence; Celia used a tree branch. At 9:00 p.m., 40,000 people packed the grassy parade ground to hear Fidel speak with the heroes lined up behind him. But it was the unscripted moments that would pass into legend. At one stage Fidel interrupted himself to turn to Camilo.

"Am I doing OK, Camilo?" he asked.

"You're doing OK, Fidel!" Camilo smiled, to roars of approval.

At his most crucial speech, Fidel's genius as an orator was now revealed. As his voice rose from a barely audible rasp to a thunderous roar, his body began to sway, and he started to move his arms "like a bronco rider," according to Spanish journalist Ignacio Ramonet, waving his index finger at the spellbound audience. ("A great orator to the masses," Ramonet adds, "must master the gestures of a lion tamer.")

Even a skeptic like Ruby Hart Phillips could not help but be impressed. "As I watched Castro I realized the magic of his personality, the fanatic loyalty of the insurgents," she wrote. "He seemed to weave a hypnotic net over his listeners."

The most riveting moment came when someone in the audience released three white doves, the symbols of peace. Two of them fluttered down to land on the podium; the third landed on Fidel's shoulder and remained there for the duration. To Cubans, it was like a divine benediction. Soldiers took off their caps, women crossed themselves, the pious went down on their knees, Santería worshippers muttered invocations.

Conspiracy theorists would later say that the presence of the doves was a trick, their stomachs weighed down with lead pellets or their wings clipped. In fact, nobody seems to know how they got there. A front-page newspaper editorial in Havana expressed the general feeling that their behavior was no coincidence: "We believe it is a sign from the Lord who is sending us the universal symbol of the peace which we all desire."

The doves only added more power to the moment when Fidel assailed the "private armies" who had seized arms in Havana and were not giving them up, a thinly veiled reference to the Revolutionary Directorate. "*¿Armas para que?*" "Arms for what?" he asked. "To fight against whom? To blackmail the president of the republic? To threaten the government?" The crowd took up the chant: "*¿Armas para que? ¿Armas para que?*" Even before his speech was over, the DR sent word that it would surrender its guns.

"The audience could say that the curtain had descended," Phillips reported of the night in the *New York Times*, "the play was over." As it turned out, nothing could be further from the truth, but in that moment it seemed that anything was possible.

CHAPTER 33

Days of Rum and Roses

(January 1959–October 1960)

THUS BEGAN THE "honeymoon phase" of the revolution. At the start of 1959 Havana was an open city, and everyone with a sense of adventure wanted to be there. A traveler could fly from New York or Miami on a bargain Cubana Air charter, then take a room in one of the Art Deco hotels at massively discounted rates. From the moment they left the airport in a shark-finned taxi, visitors would be swept up in the popular fervor. Volunteers were raising money in the streets for the new government, famous Cuban musicians gave free concerts, and armed militia roamed the plazas singing patriotic anthems. (Someone came up with the catchy "With Fidel, with Fidel, always with Fidel," sung to the tune of *Jingle Bells*, which became a popular hit at rallies.) The revolutionary-chic address of choice was the Havana Hilton, soon renamed La Habana Libre, where Fidel and Celia had taken up residence in the penthouse, a sumptuously furnished suite with wraparound views of the city. Dozens of guerrillas took lesser rooms, often baffling maids by continuing to sleep on the floor. Che's parents flew in from Buenos Aires and stayed at the Hilton before heading off on a tour of their son's battle sites. The obsessive secrecy of the guerrilla days was a thing of the past: Fidel could be seen prowling the hotel at night to get a chocolate milkshake from the snack bar. Camilo took to turning up in the early hours at the Tropicana nightclub, where he had once worked in the kitchen, to dine on shrimp and chat up sequined showgirls.

There was a tentative return to normalcy. After waiters staged a protest march, the casinos were reopened under tight restrictions. ("We are not only disposed to deport the gangsters," Fidel remarked of those with US Mafia connections, "but to shoot them." The brothels stayed closed, however, and Superman was forced to find other employment.) Visitors could sit alongside *barbudos* on city buses, which they rode for free, since they had no money. The politics of beards continued, with the length now measuring political commitment: men with three-day growths might be angrily ordered to remove their M-26-7 armbands by the more hirsute. A Cuban cartoon showed a clean-shaven man jumping on a bus and refusing to pay: "I'm undercover," he explains.

Ever at the center of the action, Errol Flynn also took a room at the Hilton with the bubbly Beverly Aadland to work on a documentary about the revolution, *A Cuban Story,* and his feature film, *Cuban Rebel Girls.* The renowned Hollywood screenwriter Budd Schulberg, who had won the Academy Award for *On the Waterfront* in 1954, spotted Fidel and Flynn in the lobby walking "arm in arm," he told an interviewer in 2005. He knew Flynn from California. "So I went up to the room with them—Errol served up a tall vodka—and got to talk to Castro. The whole world wanted to talk to him." When he suggested that the story of the Castro brothers might make a good film, Raúl joked that he wanted Brando and Sinatra for the parts. On a less glamorous note, Flynn had to be rescued after he set fire to the mattress in his hotel room, having passed out with a lit cigarette. He was also briefly arrested by the tourist police for being in possession of narcotics, but managed to find a prescription.

Some 350 international journalists shuffled through the hotel in early 1959, including the roustabout American from CBS TV, Robert Taber. Intoxicated by the rebel victory, Taber signed up as a columnist for the Movement's new official newspaper *Revolución* and became a familiar figure on Havana streets, where locals greeted him as *"El Comandante"* because he wore a Colt .45 strapped to his hip.

Romantic dreams were now fulfilled. Che and Aleida went arm in arm on sightseeing strolls around the capital, joking that they were worse than provincial yokels when they got lost in colonial back streets or became confused by traffic lights. Like the other guerrilla women, Aleida recalled the strangeness of shedding her fatigues for the traditional Cuban feminine look, with flower-patterned frocks and ornate hairstyles. Their relationship still moved at a glacial pace by modern standards. On January 12, Che asked Aleida as his "secretary" to read a letter to his wife, Hilda. He was asking for a divorce so he could marry a Cuban woman he had met during the war. Aleida asked who the woman was. "He looked at me with surprise and said it was me . . . I wondered why he hadn't ever mentioned this." Che's next smooth move came when they took a trip together to a beach resort and he held her hand in the back of the car. "I felt my heart would jump out of my chest," Aleida wrote, and she realized she really was in love. "Not long after that, on a memorable January night, Che came into my room in La Cabaña and we consummated an already strong relationship." Che joked with her that this was "the day the fortress was taken." She said it "'surrendered' without resistance."

The first celebrity marriage was between Raúl and Vilma, the lovebirds who used to neck in foxholes, less than four weeks after Batista fled. It was a happy mix of Santiago high society and guerrilla celebrities, Old Cuba and New: she wore a meringue-white wedding dress and carried a bridal bouquet, while Raúl kept his rebel uniform with .45 on a holster and his hair tied back in a ponytail. The reception was held at the fashionable Rancho Club, founded by the Bacardi rum magnate (and Fidel fan) Pepín Bosch, the tables groaning with flowers and forty crates of champagne. *Life* magazine covered the wedding under the headline "Raúl Castro Is Captured," a joking reference to his habit of kidnapping US citizens only half a year earlier.

On a more risqué note, Fidel moved a new lover into the Havana Hilton: Marita Lorenz, a nineteen-year-old German-American woman he had met on a visiting cruise ship. Celia was busy setting up an apartment nearby on Calle Once (Eleventh Street), which would become the nerve center of government, where he would work every day. "Celia didn't resent me," Lorenz later recounted to a *Vanity Fair* journalist. "She was happier to have only one girl than to have him flying around." Marita herself soon found she also had to be tolerant of Fidel's flings. "Every day letters came in from women all over the world, offering to do anything to meet him."

THE FIRST DISCORDANT notes in this happy pageant came as the executions of Batista's henchmen gained pace. Only four days after Fidel's victory speech, on January 12, Raúl made good on his promise to avenge the mothers of Santiago when more than seventy detested SIM officers were gunned down before an open trench. (Reports filtered out describing the disorganized scene, where only half of the condemned men got blindfolds and one broke for the nearby woods but was dragged back. A lieutenant charged with fifty-three murders received a four-hour reprieve when a Cuban TV crew requested the firing squad wait for better light.) In Havana, executions were conducted in La Cabaña under Che's orders, including members of the CIA-funded death squad BRAC (Bureau for the Repression of Communist Activities). There was not a whiff of sympathy for the victims from Cubans, but international observers, especially in the United States, expressed outrage; one US congressman denounced the executions as a "bloodbath."

Cubans were just as offended by the criticism. The US government had remained silent during the long years of Batista's brutality, so the indignation seemed like rank hypocrisy. The charges against 1,000 or so officers were a fraction of the reprisals against Nazi collaborators in France, Cubans pointed out. On January 21 a million people joined a Havana rally in support of the trials, waving banners such as "Women Support the Execution of Murderers!"; "Let the Firing Squads Continue!"; and "We Want No Foreign Interference!" Fidel vowed to bring justice, although it did not calm matters that he was overheard saying: "If the Americans do not like what is happening, let them send in the Marines! Then there will be 200,000 dead gringos."

Fidel was making a rare PR blunder. When the first public trial was held the next day, it was a mockery. Three of Batista's vilest offenders were brought in handcuffs to the Sports City stadium, where a crowd of 18,000 greeted them with jeers of "Kill them!" and "To the wall!" Speaking before the tribunal, one defendant, Jesús José Blanco, compared the blood-crazed proceedings to the Roman Colosseum, but his words were drowned out by shouts as witnesses stepped forward to recount his grisly crimes. Women broke down in tears. A twelve-year-old boy pointed an accusing finger. Two prisoners were nearly seized by the angry throng as they left. The foreign press reveled in comparisons to the howling Parisian mob at the guillotine. *Time* reported that it all revealed "the Latin capacity for brooding revenge and blood purges."

From then on, trials were removed to the relative seclusion of La Cabaña fortress. In an ironic twist, given the outcry from the US, the shooting squads were overseen by an American. Herman Marks, the sadistic ex-con from Milwaukee whom Che had dismissed from his column the October before, had come back out of the woodwork in Havana to offer his distinctive talents. For a period "Captain Marks" became one of the most notorious *yanquis* in Cuba, profiled in *Time* as Fidel's "Chief Executioner" and nicknamed by unlucky inmates El Carnicero, "the Butcher." He was known for emptying his revolver clip into a victim's face during the coup de grâce so relatives could not recognize the corpse. He claimed to be respected by Cubans for doing a difficult but necessary job, and would be given the best tables at the Riviera and Plaza when he went out to dine.

Marks's presence even attracted a morbid tourism, with Americans surreptitiously asking him if they could attend an execution. The young writer George Plimpton met him in the Floridita bar while drinking with fellow literati, the playwright Tennessee Williams and English critic Kenneth Tynan. When Marks offered to bring them along that night, Plimpton and Williams guiltily accepted, while Tynan, stammering badly, promised to turn up and denounce the proceedings as immoral. Later that day Hemingway encouraged Plimpton to go, since "it was important that a writer get around to see just about anything, especially the excesses of human behavior, as long as he could keep his emotional reactions in check." Whatever the loss for literature, the macabre rendezvous fell through when the execution was delayed.

The English writer Norman Lewis also met Marks, who told him that most of the condemned men liked to give the order to fire themselves. The American said he took pride in his work. "As a technician—that's how I see myself—I hate to see a bungled job," he said. "Sleep well? I sure do." Lewis learned that Marks had cuff links made from the firing squad's spent rifle shells and gave them as presents to friends.

Perhaps the most humane account comes from Errol Flynn. In an unpublished typescript "How to Die" he wrote: "I have witnessed many gruesome sights in my life, but none more so than a human being facing the firing squad. I don't care how much he deserves it, it made me vomit—and I couldn't have given a damn when I saw the expressions of faint amusement on the faces watching the hero of a thousand screen battles, Flynn, so white and [about to] heave his brave guts up. Brave? Guts? I puked—close to the feet of a guard, spilling on the end of his hardworn boot, and there was a faint amusement in the faint flicker of the smile he had."

Friends said that Flynn would return from these ceremonies looking gray and swearing to cut down his drinking: "I'm down to two bottles of vodka a day."

※

IN OTHER REGARDS, Fidel remained a picture of moderation, promising that democratic elections would be held within eighteen months, denouncing communism, flaunting his religious medals, and in general assuring the world that Cuba was on track for a Caribbean version of Roosevelt's New Deal. Segregation rules were done away with in bastions of privilege such as the Havana Country Club. Cuban business leaders were so supportive that they agreed to pay taxes in advance. Esso and Texaco even advertised in *Revolución*.

The American infatuation with Fidel as folk hero reached such a pitch that the revered newsman Ed Murrow agreed to interview him relaxing in silk pajamas in his Hilton penthouse. In a bizarre celebrity puff piece for the CBS series *Person to Person*, Fidel looks like a grown-up surprised on a sleepover as Murrow banters about the most crucial subject for US audiences: When does he intend to shave? "My beard means many things to my country," Fidel explained, glancing at the collection of armed *barbudos*, whom the producer asked to stand off-camera. "When we have fulfilled our promise of new government, I will cut my beard." Soon after, "Fidel Junior" is introduced with an adorable puppy and asked about his public school spell in Queens. "Were you as good-looking as your son when you were his age?" Murrow inquires flirtatiously of Fidel.

IN MID-APRIL, FIDEL accepted an invitation from the American Society of Newspaper Editors to speak in Washington, DC, which turned into a triumphant tour of the northeastern United States. He set off "full of hope," wrote his press secretary Teresa Casuso (the Cuban novelist who had hidden weapons for him in Mexico and returned to join the revolution), and was welcomed as the second coming of Simon Bolívar, with the largest crowds that any foreign leader had ever attracted. To cash in on his popularity, a toy company made 100,000 fake beards and forage caps marked "El Libertador" to be sold along-side Davy Crockett coonskin hats. Fidel had hired a Manhattan PR agent, Bernard Relling, who advised him to cut the guerrillas' hair and have them wear suits; the Cuban team should be university-educated and English-speaking. Fidel ignored the suggestions. He knew the power of their shaggy-haired image at a time when almost all American men stuck to a clean-cut look straight out of *My Three Sons*; in the 1950s, anyone who dressed otherwise risked alienating themselves from the establishment at best, at worst (in the more red-neck parts of the South) receiving a hiding from police and spending a night in the cells.

Fidel was mobbed as he went for photo ops at the Lincoln Memorial in DC and an excursion to Mount Vernon. He spoke to legions of ad-miring students at Harvard and Princeton, who knocked down police barricades and rushed him. (Casuso found them "seemingly crazed.") But the biggest frenzy occurred in New York City. When his train pulled into Penn Station, a crowd of 20,000 gave him a "tumultuous welcome"; it took twenty-four minutes just to cross the avenue to his hotel, most of the time carried on the shoulders of his admirers. He met Mayor Robert F. Wagner in City Hall, took in the view from the Empire State Building, and visited the Bronx Zoo, where he charmed reporters by hopping the fence and sticking his hand in the tiger cage. While eating a hot dog, he declared the zoo "the best thing in New York." (Carlos Franqui had tried to get Fidel to visit the Museum of Modern Art instead but failed.) On his last evening he gave a speech in Spanish to an estimated 40,000 people at the Central Park band shell, and was presented with the symbolic keys to the city.

To the horror of the NYPD, which fielded the largest security detail in its history, Fidel repeatedly insisted on pushing past his bodyguards to shake hands. ("He has to greet his public," Celia explained.) On one Manhattan drive, Casuso was terrified that their car might be over-turned by crowds trying to get closer to their hero. Another night Fi-del left his hotel without warning and ended up at a Chinese restaurant, chatting with students. "I don't know if I'm interested in the Revolution," one New York woman told Cuban reporters, "but Fidel Castro is the biggest thing to happen to North American women since Rudolph Valentino."

On the surface, the visit was a smashing success. Newspapers embraced Fidel as representing Americans' better selves. He came "out of another century," the *New York Times* fluttered, "the century of Sam Adams and Patrick Henry and Tom Paine and Thomas Jefferson," and "stirred memories, long dimmed, of a revolutionary past." But behind all the grinning faces was a less happy story. President Eisenhower was miffed that the Cubans had defied diplomatic protocol and visited without an official invitation, and had even suggested that Fidel be denied a visa. Instead he made sure he was away on a golf trip when Fidel was in DC; the Second World War hero was not going to sit down with an upstart guerrilla. (He had become Prime Minister in February and remained head of the armed forces, making President Urrutia a virtual figurehead.) Fidel was forced to settle for a meeting with Vice President Nixon. The two men disliked each other on sight. "That son-of-a-bitch Nixon," Castro reportedly said. "He treated me badly and he is going to pay for it." Fidel had instructed his Cuban negotiators not to beg for US aid, and nobody offered it.

Fidel's deepest wish had been to commune directly with the American public, just as he did with Cubans. Calling his visit "Operation Truth," he appeared to be genuinely certain that, if only the political situation on the island was properly explained, Americans would be won over to the revolutionary cause. One night he did a jig in his hotel room, singing: "They are beginning to understand us better!"

In fact, Americans were not really listening.

The American public's mood swing was apparent during Fidel's next visit to New York a little over a year later, in late September 1960, when he was a delegate at the United Nations. Teresa Casuso describes a gloomy car ride along the same Manhattan streets where they had been mobbed the year before: "Instead of the acclamation of thousands of people crowding the sidewalks, and the joyful faces of the automobile's occupants, there were now only whistles and angry shouts as we crossed the city, and the sad silence of the passengers. I know what Fidel must have been suffering at seeing himself so utterly rejected." This time, Fidel was mocked by the *Daily News* as "El Beardo." Editorials ran with titles like "Spoiled Brat with a Gun," which quoted Senator Barry Goldwater saying that the "knight in shining armor" had turned out to be "a bum without a shave." The once-raffish Cubans were now wild-haired, unwashed degenerates: "Girls, girls, girls have marched into the Cubans' suites," tut-tutted the *News*. "There have been blondes, brunettes, redheads and—a detective said—many known prostitutes. Along with the girls have gone booze, booze, booze . . . Fidel himself had a visitor from 2 a.m. to 3:30 a.m. yesterday—an attractive bosomy blonde." Instead of kids running around with toy Fidel beards, some Long Island residents burned him in effigy.

When the manager at the upscale Shelburne Hotel in midtown demanded a $10,000 cash security deposit from the Cubans, alleging that they were killing and cooking chickens in their rooms, Fidel packed his bags and marched his entire menagerie of seventy to the United Nations Secretariat, the sleek Modernist skyscraper that looms like a tombstone over the East River. There he explained to mild-mannered Secretary-General Dag Hammarskjöld that the Cubans would prefer to sleep in Central Park if need be, since they were "mountain people" and happy to be *en plein air*, than suffer such insults. Suddenly, they all hopped into cars at midnight for Harlem, the "capital of black America," where the thirteen-story Hotel Theresa on 125th Street had offered to put them up.

It was a deft stroke on the eve of the civil rights movement. In 1960, Harlem was a "city within the city," an isolated African-American enclave in uptown Manhattan that was culturally rich but economically depressed, its once-splendid streets of brownstones in decay, plagued by crime and drugs. Unlike the Jazz Age 1920s and '30s, when nightspots like the Stork Club and Apollo were world-famous, only the most bohemian white New Yorkers were seen there after dark. No world leader had ever stayed in Harlem.

Fidel's gesture of solidarity did not come out of nowhere. He had long encouraged African-Americans to come to Cuba to see the revolution for themselves, and even celebrated New Year's Eve 1959 in Havana with black civic leaders from across the US with the boxer Joe Louis at his side. On his first night in Harlem, Malcolm X arrived and was photographed embracing Fidel in the hotel lobby. Every day, huge crowds of well-wishers from the Harlem community gathered in the streets. Two thousand rallied from the Nation of Islam. Photo ops included Fidel's staff eating at a Chock full o' Nuts and Juan Almeida, his Afro-Cuban military chief, bantering with waitresses in a diner. The puckish Soviet premier Nikita Khrushchev also made the pilgrimage uptown to pay homage, and was photographed almost enveloped in a bear hug by the towering Fidel.

Fidel now stole headlines every day. When Eisenhower held a luncheon for Latin American leaders without inviting him, the Cubans hosted a rival meal at the Theresa with the black hotel staff. As Fidel sat down to steaks and beer alongside a bellboy, he declared himself most at home among "the poor and humble people of Harlem." The group Fair Play for Cuba, which had been founded by Robert Taber and Richard Gibson, the first African-American reporter for CBS, then hosted a soiree that was the precise opposite of the UN's stiff black-tie affairs. In an early example of "radical chic," the gathering attracted a mixed-race group of leftist politicians, civil rights activists, and bohemians like poet Allen Ginsberg and photographer Henri Cartier-Bresson.

It was the perfect backdrop for Fidel's speech at the United Nations on September 26, denouncing US imperialism. Clocking in at four hours and twenty-six minutes, it is still the longest address ever given to the body. When the Cubans were ready to go home, they found the US had impounded their planes. Khrushchev lent them a Soviet one.

WHAT HAD GONE wrong in between the two Manhattan visits? In retrospect, the American public's feverish joy during Fidel's 1959 tour turned out to be puppy love; the infatuation was superficial. White middle-class Americans did not want a genuine revolutionary. They expected Fidel to turn into a clean-shaven, well-behaved supporter and, above all, someone who could be controlled. When he went home to Cuba and enacted his first land reform bill in May, with genuinely radical changes that threatened the enormous American-owned sugar plantations, the affection evaporated. From then on, at every sign of Cuban independence, the US reacted like a jilted lover. As Herbert L. Matthews observed, Americans had been romanticizing Fidel as a hero who was going to "save" Cuba but let their wildly unequal economic relationship proceed as usual: "In reality, Americans were welcoming a figure who did not exist, expected what could not and would not happen, and then blamed Fidel Castro for their own blindness and ignorance."

By early 1960, a tit-for-tat standoff was in full swing as Congress stopped Cuban sugar imports and Fidel and Che (who had been elevated to oversee the economy) began nationalizing American assets. Behind closed doors, Washington quickly gave up on peaceful coexistence. In March, six months before Fidel's Harlem visit, Eisenhower had already approved a secret plan to get rid of him either by assassination or invasion. The argument over whether Cuba was pushed or jumped towards the Eastern Bloc may never be fully settled, but British Intelligence was already warning the US that its punitive actions were forcing Fidel into ever more radical positions and ensuring the island would be "lost." The CIA began to destabilize Cuba by supporting anti-Castro rebels in the mountains. Bombs went off in the cities. The largest department store in Havana was torched; a French freighter in Havana Harbor exploded with massive loss of life. Fidel clamped down on dissent at home, and wealthy Cubans who had supported him began to flee. The country was becoming dour and humorless. Color began fading from Havana like bleached coral.

When the CIA-backed Bay of Pigs invasion occurred just after midnight on April 17, 1961, the Cuban population was already armed with Soviet-made weapons. Some 1,500 soldiers of fortune, mostly Cuban exiles, landed on the south coast; within three days 115 had been killed and the rest surrendered. It was a resounding defeat. Soon afterward Che sent a message to the White House through intermediaries, thanking JFK for organizing the botched invasion attempt, which had galvanized the Cuban population behind the new regime's most extreme measures. "Before the invasion, the revolution was shaky," he wrote. "Now, it is stronger than ever." On May Day 1961, Fidel declared that Cuba was officially a socialist country in the Soviet camp.

The "honeymoon period" was not just over; it was such a distant memory that the two countries would forget that it had ever occurred. The long, acrimonious divorce had begun.

COULD THINGS HAVE gone otherwise? We will never know what Fidel was really thinking in the heady early days of 1959—and it is hard to imagine that he would have given up power once he had it, given the megalomaniacal tendencies he was already showing. But the course of the revolution was far from fixed when he first swept into Havana. Many around Fidel observed that he had no concrete plan for government. As Celia admitted, the *barbudos* were surprised to find that they had been handed such complete control of Cuba; M-26-7 had always thought it would share power. Overnight, they were running the country much as they had run the guerrilla war: by making things up as they went along.

Few observers at the time dreamed that Cuba would turn into the Soviet Union's tropical satellite. Almost none of the men who landed in the *Granma* regarded themselves as Communists—including

Fidel. Every CIA investigator had agreed that he had no real interest in socialist ideas; at heart he was a left-of-center nationalist whose burning desire was for Cuba to gain genuine independence. And yet, an air of inevitability hangs over the confrontations that unfolded. In 1959, American businesses owned almost every economic asset in the country, including the best land, the oil and telephone companies, power stations, and train lines. Fidel knew that Cuba would always be under US domination until the stranglehold was broken. By 1960, Fidel could see that a confrontation with the US was coming and began to seek out a new patron. The Soviet Union was eagerly waiting in the wings to buy Cuba's sugar and offer economic aid. With its Sputniks soaring across the sky and industrial strength apparently surging ahead, the USSR was then regarded a viable alternative to the capitalist West. Soon Fidel and Che were requesting Soviet military assistance to fend off the coming invasion.

It may be idle to speculate, but a more flexible attitude from the United States in 1959—and an attempt to understand what independence really meant to Cubans—might have taken advantage of the enormous reserves of goodwill that remained between the two countries. Instead, Washington insisted on its right to control the island. We will never know where a more creative approach might have led— if, for example, the US had offered a generous loan and aid package to Cuba, as it did with almost every other new Latin American government. The result could hardly have been worse for America's larger diplomatic goals than the hostile policy begun by Eisenhower and followed by JFK, leading the world to the brink of nuclear holocaust in the Missile Crisis of October 1962.

Another what-if proposition is more certain: history would surely have been different if Washington had not backed Batista throughout the 1950s. Cubans could never understand why the United States would abandon its noblest founding ideals to support a dictator who terrorized his own people. If the US had taken a more principled stand after his 1952 coup—if it had withdrawn military aid immediately, pushed for democratic elections, and criticized the regime's most fla-grant abuses—it's quite possible that Batista would have stepped aside and change would have come to Cuba through peaceful means. There would have been no need for Fidel to start a revolution in the first place. It's a dismal pattern that has been repeated over and over again in the decades since Batista fled, with the United States propping up a string of appalling dictators in Iran, Vietnam, Chile, and Panama, to name a few. The tragedy is that it has almost always led to disastrous results. By betraying its own principles, the United States has also managed to defeat its most basic strategic goals.

Epilogue:
Last Kids on the Bloc

I guess really good soldiers are really good at very little else . . .
—ERNEST HEMINGWAY, *FOR WHOM THE BELL TOLLS*

TODAY IT'S NOT hard to see why the Comandancia de La Plata was never found by Batista's patrols. Getting to the guerrilla HQ still feels like a covert mission. The Sierra Maestra remains free of road signs, so I had to ask for directions from passing campesinos on horseback while zigzagging between wandering livestock and potholes that could swallow a Cadillac. In the hamlet of Santo Domingo, an official guide filled out paperwork in quadruplicate to secure access permits before ushering me into a creaky state-owned four-wheel-drive van. The vehicle proceeded to wheeze its way up roads at gradients so steep, it felt like a cable car should be installed.

The guide, Omar Pérez, then took me along a steep hiking trail ascending for a mile into the tropical forest. Rains had turned stretches into muddy streams, and the intense humidity had us soaked with sweat after only a few steps. A spry local farmer, Pérez pushed ahead with exhortations of *"¡Vámanos, muchachos! ¡Adelante!"* like Fidel at the Moncada. By the time I spotted Che's field hospital, I looked like a half-wild guerrilla myself.

In any other country, the Comandancia might have made an excellent eco-lodge, but in Cuba it has been maintained as the revolution's most intimate shrine. Despite repairs for hurricane damage over the decades, the sixteen structures look much as they did when Fidel left in November 1958, each one lovingly labeled with a wooden sign. Paths lead past the Press Office and the Marianas' cabins to the summit, where the Radio Rebelde hut still contains original transmitters and the antenna that was raised and lowered by hand.

The main attraction, La Casa de Fidel, the cabin designed by Celia, still looks as if the revolutionary power couple have just popped out for a cigar. The large windows remain propped open to let in the cool breeze and the sound of the stream tinkling below. Their gasoline-fueled refrigerator is there in the kitchen, complete with bullet holes. The only change is in the bedroom, where the couple's original mattress is now covered in thick protective plastic. It's not permitted to enter the cabin, but when Pérez meandered off, I climbed the ladder and slipped inside unseen. I lay down on the bed to channel 1958, gazing up at a window still filled with flowers and foliage.

But even the hallowed Comandancia is now enveloped by a sense of broken dreams. After the collapse of the Soviet Union in 1989, Cuba fell into an economic crisis from which it has still not escaped; although the socialist system is slowly being modified, it remains isolated by the US trade embargo, a last fragment of the Cold War adrift in the tropics. As we hiked back down the mountain, Pérez explained that he had landed his job as a tourist guide in part because his grandfather had helped the rebels and knew them personally. Although he has a university degree in agricultural engineering, he made far more from foreign travelers than he could on a state-run farm—14 CUC (US $16) a month, but bolstered, he added pointedly, by *propinitas*, "little tips."

All over Cuba, the memory of the revolutionary war is very much alive: everywhere the guerrillas went has a lavish memorial or a quasi-religious museum offering artifacts like Che's beret, Camilo's tommy gun, or leftover Molotov cocktails—not to mention oddities such as the darned socks, hair combs, and the toothbrushes of vanished heroes. Even the more cynical younger generation likes to remain on a first-name basis with the rebels. Cubans remain extremely proud of the uprising's against-all-odds victories as well as revolutionary achievements such as creating free education and health care systems that rival the finest in the First World.

But the idealistic aura has become almost painfully poignant as the socialist system decays, and the shrines are less and less visited. Hardly anyone tracks down Haydée's small apartment in Havana where the *chicos* plotted the Moncada attack, or the prison cell on the Isle of Pines (now called the Isle of Youth) where the rebels' beds are lined up beneath faded photo portraits. Even fewer find Frank País's family home in Santiago, where the gramophone that once played jazz to drown out subversive conversation still sits in his bedroom.

Perhaps the most forlorn memorial of all is where the drama began in 1956, the *Granma* "invasion" site. The coastline near Playa las Coloradas is still so pristine that it is part of a national park, although in the 1970s, a 1,300-yard concrete walkway was laid across the mangroves to reach the exact landing spot. When I arrived, the lone guide could not hide her surprise: she averaged one visitor per week. A jovial woman with a PhD in history, she led me along the sun-blasted path as crabs scuttled underfoot. Every year on December 2, the anniversary of the landing is celebrated here with the singing of anthems and "acts of political solidarity," she said. The highlight is when eighty-two young men and women chosen for their patriotic bona fides jump out of a *Granma* replica and reenact the rebels' arrival. "But we don't force them to wade through the swamp," she confided.

OLD REVOLUTIONARIES DON'T quietly fade away. The subsequent stories of almost everyone involved in the Cuban uprising are filled with operatic drama:

The first tragedy occurred in October 1959 when the idolized, wisecracking Comandante Camilo Cienfuegos vanished at sea in a Cessna flying to Havana. When the news broke, Cubans burst into tears in the street, and the memory still causes anguish among older citizens. Parts of the plane were recovered and the reason for the crash was almost certainly mechanical failure, but this has never been proven, leading to conspiracy theories that Fidel was behind it. Today, Camilo's swaggering image, his smile extending from ear to ear, is still emblazoned all over Cuba, although few foreigners recognize him.

Che Guevara and Aleida March were married in June 1959—photos show Che beaming maniacally at the camera—and had four children in quick succession. But he became increasingly impatient with domestic life and the demands of his desk jobs. First he set off on a guerrilla venture to the Congo. Then, in 1967, with a shaved head, false teeth, and horn-rimmed glasses, he slipped into Bolivia and tried to foment revolution in the dirt-poor Andes. The peasants were indifferent; after a manhunt that continued for months, he was captured by CIA-backed troops on the verge of starvation. The last photographs of Che are shocking: the Adonis-like hero of the Sierra Maestra looks a ruin, with long matted hair and a haunted, vacant expression. He was executed on October 9. His last words to the man who volunteered for the job were, "I know you are here to finish me. Shoot, coward, you are only going to kill a man." He was thirty-nine years old. Ironically, the officers who tracked him down had very likely read his book *Guerrilla Warfare*, which their CIA trainers used for reference.

Che's martyrdom guaranteed his fate as an international superstar. Shortly before he died, the Cuban photographer Alberto Korda gave a portrait called *Guerrillero Heroico* (*The Heroic Guerrilla*) to a left-wing Italian businessman who was visiting Havana. The image of Che staring beatifically into the distance was soon reproduced in Europe as a silkscreened poster and has become one of the modern era's most reproduced images. (Korda liked to complain that he never received a centavo in royalties.)

In 2005, Che's remains were rediscovered in a mass grave in Bolivia and sent back to Cuba, where they were interred with much fanfare in Santa Clara, the site of his greatest military success. The mausoleum is now guarded by cadres of young women dressed in khaki mini-skirts and aviator sunglasses, who loll about by the eternal flame like Che groupies. An attached museum offers some poignant exhibits from Che's childhood in Argentina, including his leather asthma inhaler and copies of schoolbooks "read by young Ernesto." They include *Tom Sawyer, Treasure Island,* and *Don Quixote.* Fifteen years after his death, Aleida became director of the Center for Che Guevara Studies in Havana "to promote the study and understanding of Che's thought." Their four children are active in progressive social causes in Cuba and abroad.

Although their romance faded, Celia Sánchez remained for two decades Fidel's most trusted confidante. Her Havana apartment on Calle Once became, in Carlos Franqui's words, the *comandante en jefe*'s "home, office, and working quarters," and she traveled with him to every important engagement. Celia personally received campesino visitors from the sierras in need of aid—they would often come straight from the bus station—making her one of the most beloved figures of the revolution. In 1964 she also realized her dream of setting up an archive, the Office of Historical Affairs, filled with the documents she saved in the guerrilla war. By the late 1970s her constant workload and chain-smoking led to a diagnosis of lung cancer. After she died on January 11, 1980, at the age of fifty-nine, the nation went into mourning. In scenes reminiscent of the passing of Evita Perón, thousands traveled from around Cuba for the funeral, and Fidel stayed up all night as she lay in state. A family friend reported: "When you see any man cry, it is very impressive, but to see Fidel Castro cry . . . He was very red, like a pomegranate. And tears flowed down both sides of his face." The funeral procession was led by a giant wreath covered with orchids, bearing the words: "For Celia from Fidel." He never spoke about her publicly.

No sooner had Batista fled than Haydée Santamaría abandoned the Miami she loathed for Havana. Within four months she had set up the Casa de las Américas, a cultural center that promoted exchange around Latin America, with its own publishing house, concert halls, and literary prizes. But she continued to be plagued by the depression that had deepened with the murder of her fiancé and brother years before. In an open letter sent to Che after his death, she wrote: "I think that I have already lived too much. The sun is not as beautiful, I don't feel pleasure in seeing the palm trees. Sometimes, like now, in spite of enjoying life so much, knowing that it is worth opening one's eyes every morning . . . I have the desire to keep them closed, like you." Not long after Celia's death in 1980, she took a pistol and killed herself—on July 26, the anniversary of the Moncada. She was fifty-seven.

Most other members of the Movement had more cheerful lives. Juan Almeida, the former construction worker and lovelorn poet from Havana, maintained a leading role in the armed forces from 1959. He wrote a string of memoirs and poetry volumes, and became one of the world's few military leaders to have hit love songs to his name, including *"Dame un traguito"* ("Give Me a Drink"), *"Mejor Concluir"* ("We'd Better Part"), and *"Déjale que Baile Sola"* ("Let Her Dance Alone"). Almeida died in 2009 at the age of eighty-two.

Haydée's *compañera* at the Moncada, the lawyer Melba Hernández, kept a lower profile but held a string of government posts, including managing the prison system and serving as president of the Pro-Vietnam Committee. She died in 2014, age eighty-two.

Vilma Espín remained in the inner circle of government her whole life. She was a tireless promoter of women's rights—"the revolution within the revolution"—bringing women into the workforce and creating childcare centers across Cuba. She also backed a controversial law in 1975 that forced men and women to share housework fifty-fifty. After Celia's death, she became the unofficial first lady of Cuba, accompanying Fidel on many overseas trips. She had four children with Raúl, although their marriage was volatile and there were reports that they had secretly divorced. She died in 2007, age seventy-seven.

The self-taught journalist who had been born in a cane field, Carlos Franqui, became the first editor of *Revolución,* which allowed him to travel widely in Europe and hobnob with Picasso, Miró, and Calder. Within Cuba, he was friends with the greatest artists of the era, including the writer Guillermo Cabrera Infante and the painter Wifredo Lam. He left Cuba in the mid-1960s and finally broke with Fidel over his support of the Soviet invasion of Czechoslovakia. As his criticism became more vocal—and his recollections became more fanciful—Franqui was accused of being a CIA agent and airbrushed out of many early photographs of the guerrilla war, inspiring him to respond with a poem:

> *I discover my photographic death.*
> *Do I exist?*
> *I am a little black,*
> *I am a little white,*
> *I am a little shit,*
> *On Fidel's vest.*

Franqui died in 2010, aged eighty-eight.

The socialite-rebel Naty Revuelta briefly allowed herself to dream that she might become the first lady of the new Cuba. Soon after the victory, Fidel came to visit her in her mansion and met his young daughter Alina, then a toddler, but explained that marriage to an aristocratic woman was impossible in the new society he was creating. Still, the visits made her surgeon husband suspicious, and in 1961 the couple divorced and he left for Miami. Naty remained in Cuba and became an exemplary revolutionary, joining labor brigades, spurning the black market, and working in government offices. She died in 2015, age eighty-nine.

THE FATES OF the more nefarious figures in the story were no less dramatic. For a quarter century after his ignominious exit, Fulgencio Batista became the epitome of a disgraced ex-dictator, drifting in comfortable exile with the fortune he had pillaged from Cuba. He lived in an opulent hotel on Portugal's island of Madeira surrounded by watchful bodyguards and writing five self-serving memoirs, then moved to the seaside in Franco's Spain, where he brokered real estate deals in cheesy resorts on the Costa del Sol. Although he always feared an assassin's bullet, he died there of a heart attack on August 6, 1973, at age seventy-two.

Many of Batista's most vicious minions lived to ripe old ages in Miami, including the psychopathic Havana police chief, Esteban Ventura, "the assassin in the white suit," who used his skills to found a successful security firm and died quietly in his bed in 2001 at age eighty-seven. The bloodthirsty leader of the Tigers, Rolando Masferrer, became involved in a string of anti-Castro plots in Florida, and even funded his own newspaper, *Libertad*. In October 1975 he wrote that bombing and assassination were legitimate political tools and—in poetic justice—was killed by a car bomb a week later. The murder is still unsolved.

The American Mafiosi did not last long in Havana. The US-run casinos and hotels were nationalized in October 1960, ending Meyer Lansky's dreams of a Caribbean Monte Carlo. His succinct verdict was: "I crapped out." The "Jewish godfather" continued to be hounded by the FBI but was never prosecuted. When he died in Miami in 1982 at age eighty-two, his personal fortune was found to be a modest $57,000. The dead-eyed gangster Santo Trafficante Jr., who owned the Capri Hotel, had the roughest exit from Havana. He spent months in a detention center on the Malecón in 1960; convinced he was on the execution list, he bribed his way out. His name would recur in US mob prosecutions until he died of a heart attack in 1987, age seventy-two.

The Tropicana nightclub was also nationalized, even though it had put on a floor show in mid-1959 called "Canto a Oriente," "Song for the Oriente," which sung the praises of Fidel's land reform law. Today the cabaret is still performed for tourists and hordes of *jineteras*, female hustlers.

※

SYMPATHETIC AMERICANS CAUGHT up in the revolution were al-most destroyed by the association. Herbert L. Matthews was one of a dozen American journalists presented with gold medals by Fidel during his 1959 visit to Washington. Within a year he would be de-rided as a Communist dupe and pilloried by the conservative press. Bitter and frustrated, he retired to live with his son in Adelaide, Aus-tralia, although he continued to defend his famous 1957 scoop from the Sierra Maestra. He died in 1977 at age seventy-seven. Another of Fidel's gold medalists, Jules Dubois, wrote a quick book praising Fidel in 1959 but later recanted; he died of an unexpected heart attack in 1966 at the age of fifty-five. The only woman in the press group, war photographer Dickey Chapelle also went back on her initial, cautious enthusiasm for the revolution by the time she wrote her disarmingly frank 1962 memoir, *What's a Woman Doing Here?: A Combat Report-er's Report on Herself.* She continued working with the Marines and went on assignment in Vietnam, where she was killed by shrapnel from a booby trap in 1965. She was forty-five years old.

Ed Sullivan was equally embarrassed by his positive TV coverage of Fidel and said that he regretted comparing him to George Wash-ington. Still, he liked the interview enough to include it on his "best of" fifteenth anniversary special in 1963. Sullivan was never elevated to the ranks of CBS foreign correspondents; his boss Ed Murrow found the idea ludicrous. His variety show lasted until 1971.

Robert Taber, the bank robber turned reporter, became one of the revolution's most persistent American supporters. He wrote books on M-26-7 and guerrilla warfare and translated Fidel's classic pamphlet, *History Will Absolve Me*, into English. Returning to New York in 1960, he became alarmed by the plans openly being laid for a US-backed invasion of Cuba. He and his CBS coworker Richard Gibson formed the Fair Play for Cuba Committee, and ran (apparently with Cuban funding) a full-page open letter supporting Fidel in the *New York*

Times, signed by such luminaries as Norman Mailer, Truman Capote, Jean-Paul Sartre, and Simone de Beauvoir. CBS soon forced Taber and Gibson to resign.

Trading in his pen for a machine gun, Taber fought on the Cuban side at the Bay of Pigs and was badly wounded. Two years later, disillusioned with both the US and Cuba, he slipped out of a communist conference in Czechoslovakia by hiking into Austria. He was brought before Senate Committees after the assassination of JFK. (It had turned out that Lee Harvey Oswald had been a member of the FPCC, and wild accusations flew that the pair had met in Havana.) Taber's career as a journalist was seriously affected for the rest of his life, and at one stage the only work he could get was as a copy editor at the *Bergen County Record* of Hackensack, New Jersey. He retreated to Maine and refused repeated requests for interviews. He died peacefully in his sleep at age seventy-six in 1995. "It's not what you would have betted the end of his life would be," said his son Peter.

OF THE AMERICAN soldiers of fortune, the luckiest managed to get out of Cuba within a year or two. The loudmouthed Don Soldini had a small cameo on *The Jack Paar Tonight Show* with Fidel when it was taped in the Havana Hilton in January 1959; he ended up a successful businessman in Fort Lauderdale and was interviewed by the *Miami Herald* a quarter century later driving a Rolls-Royce Corniche convertible. Neill Macaulay stayed in Pinar del Río for several months, helping to train firing squads, although with much less relish than Herman Marks. (Macaulay refused to give the order to fire, he said.) He successfully raised tomatoes for a season but returned home when export controls were tightened in 1961. As professor of Latin American history at the University of Florida, he authored his Cuban war memoir and a string of well-received books.

The three runaway teenage "Navy brats" from Guantánamo who joined Fidel all eventually enlisted in the US military. The youngest,

Victor Buehlman, had watched the rebel victory on TV while in high school in Jacksonville, Florida. He somehow managed to call the Havana Hilton and get Camilo on the line, who told him to come on down and "join the party." ("I couldn't," he lamented. "I didn't have any money. I was just a kid.") Chuck Ryan was sent to New York in 1958 to speak at M-26-7 fund-raisers, but he soon dropped out. He did a tour of duty in Vietnam in 1966. The third, Mike Garvey, became a paratrooper; during the 1962 Missile Crisis, he was worried that he would be sent to Cuba and forced to fight his old guerrilla comrades.

The trio lost touch until 1996, when CBS reporters tracked them down and Fidel invited them to Havana as his personal guests at his seventieth birthday party. Ryan and Garvey accepted. (Buehlman had by then become violently anti-Castro.) They reminisced with the Maximum Leader for over five hours. Afterward, the three American veterans had their life stories optioned for a film titled *The Boys from Guantánamo*. Buehlman died in 2010, Ryan in 2012. The film has yet to be made.

The "Yankee *comandante*" William Morgan reveled in US press coverage after the 1959 victory and became one of Fidel's confidants when he worked as a double agent to expose a coup plot organized from the Dominican Republic. Electing to stay in Cuba and run a frog farm with Olga, he became increasingly disenchanted with Fidel's left-wing leanings. In late 1960 Cubans charged him with running guns to the CIA-backed rebels in his old haunt, the Escambray Mountains. Although he protested his innocence, Morgan was executed at La Cabaña on the night of March 11, 1961, in a gruesome scene: when he refused to kneel, he was shot in both knees and left to squirm in agony before his body was riddled with bullets. Olga was also arrested, and spent ten years in prison before being released to live in Morgan's hometown of Toledo, Ohio.

By then, executions were no longer being run by the malevolent American ex-con Herman Marks: "the Butcher" was already off the

scene. In May 1960, stories of his vile treatment of prisoners—some
were allegedly bayoneted to death—led Fidel to transfer him to the
Isle of Pines; he escaped on a fishing boat with a young American
freelance journalist he had seduced, traveling to Mexico and then illegally back into the US. There he fought for several years to avoid
deportation on the grounds that he would be killed in Cuba. In the
mid-1960s he disappeared from sight and is thought to have lived to
old age in Florida.

ERNEST HEMINGWAY FINALLY made a public statement about the
Revolution on his last visit to the island in November 1959, when
Prensa Latina journalists met him at Havana airport. The FBI report
says that Hemingway declared it "the best thing that had ever happened to Cuba." Adding that he hoped he would be regarded not as a
yanqui but as a Cuban, Ernesto walked over and kissed the national
flag. He met Fidel only once, at a fishing tournament in 1960, and
presented him with a trophy; the pair evidently talked about marlin.
Hemingway left the island later that year and, ever more depressed
from electric shock therapy, killed himself in Ketchum, Idaho, in July,
1961. His wife donated their house to the Cuban government to maintain as a museum; today, it is one of the most popular tourist attrac-
tions in the country, with Hem's fishing boat, the *Pilar*, mounted
in the former tennis court, and the pet cemetery boasting a tomb-
stone to his beloved Black Dog.

Errol Flynn somehow managed to make his two movies in Havana.
His documentary using footage of Fidel's arrival in the capital was
shown in Russia, then lost, resurfacing in a Moscow archive only in
2001. *Cuban Rebel Girls* was his last released feature film, with himself playing a war correspondent and Beverly Aadland as a ditzy New
Yorker who becomes a guerrilla. It was panned by critics and remains
difficult to watch. ("When I first got here, I didn't know what the word

'liberty' meant," Aadland's character squeaks. "I read about it in books and stuff, but it took this trip for me to find out the meaning.") In the last scene, Flynn gazes out over a parade from his hotel balcony. "Well, I guess this about winds up another stage in the fight to rid Latin America of tyrants, dictators," he mumbles. "But the spirit started by this handful of wonderful rebels is spreading and growing stronger every day. And all you young men and women fighting for political freedom and your beliefs everywhere, I wish you good luck." Flynn died a few months later, of a heart attack; he was in Vancouver, trying to sell his yacht before the IRS repossessed it. His Cuban years were dramatized in the 2013 biopic *The Last of Robin Hood* starring Kevin Kline as Flynn and Dakota Fanning as Aadland.

DESPITE 638 ATTEMPTS on his life, Fidel Castro went on to become the world's longest-serving leader, outlasting ten US presidents and gaining an aura of immortality. (A Cuban joke from around 2000: Fidel is offered a Galápagos turtle as a pet but turns it down when he learns that it lives for only three centuries. "What a pity," he says. "You just get used to a pet and it dies.") For decade after decade, he was one of the world's most vocal and divisive leaders, keeping Cuba in the world's eye as he delighted in taunting the United States. But time caught up even with Fidel. Just before his eightieth birthday in 2006, he withdrew from public life after emergency surgery for intestinal bleeding and in 2008—forty-nine years after the revolution rolled into Havana—stepped down from active public office. Despite his absence, news of Fidel's death on November 25, 2016, sent Cuba into shock. In a symbolic mirror image of his 1959 "caravan of victory," Fidel's ashes were taken by cavalcade from Havana back to Santiago, with crowds of tearful, flag-waving Cubans lining the way. His remains were interred in the Santa Ifigenia necropolis next to the tomb of his hero José Martí and within sight of a wall dedicated to the "martyrs of the revolution." His tomb is a giant granite boulder with a simple metal plaque that reads: "Fidel."

Fidel's "relief pitcher," Raúl Castro, emerged from the shadows when his brother first fell sick and in 2008 assumed the presidency. Three years later, Raúl ushered in far-reaching reforms to open up the Cuban economy, including legalizing private employment for nearly two hundred jobs. The restoration of diplomatic relations with the US, the easing of travel restrictions, and President Obama's visit to Havana in 2011 led to a promising thaw in relations with the Monster of the North—but the mood of optimism quickly dissolved when President Trump took office in 2017 and moved to return Cuba to its Cold War isolation.

Fidelito grew up to be a world-respected nuclear physicist, but became depressed after his father's death and killed himself in 2018, age sixty-eight.

A Note on Sources

The key archive for anything to do with the Cuban Revolution remains Celia's Oficina de Asuntos Históricos (Office of Historical Affairs) in Havana. The staff were initially wary of a *neoyorquino* digging into their sacred trove, although learning about my Australian origins did wonders to allay Cold War suspicions. After a dozen or so visits—and a string of beery lunches with the archivists—they began to produce all sorts of treasures: Celia's financial accounts from the early days of the struggle, Juan Almeida's unpublished journal, handwritten notes between Fidel and Che in the Sierra Maestra, and the Super 8 color movie shot by a Cuban camera buff of Fidel's arrival in Havana on January 8, 1959, to name a few. Raúl's first five war journals are also there, having been unearthed intact from the rice field where Celia buried them in a sealed bottle in 1957. (His later volumes are sadly unreadable, since the protective bottle cracked and they were soaked. In the 1980s, the surviving fragments were sent to the Soviet Union for restoration, without success; more recently, Cuban conservationists have been using laser technology in an attempt to resurrect the lost text.)

The Office staff also invited me to "revolutionary events" such as the annual memorial service for Celia in the Colón necropolis in Havana, which was attended by every living guerrilla hero. It was here that I met the legendary Teté (Delsa Puebla), still in her military uniform glittering with medals, and Celia's right-hand man from Manzanillo, Felipe Guerra Matos. I later interviewed the hospitable "Guerrita" in his cozy Miramar residence, which sits (surreally enough) in the shadow of the swank new Sheraton Hotel.

Although he was in his mid-eighties, he nearly drank me under the table with 15-year-old rum.

Other breakthroughs were serendipitous, in a very Cuban way. Working at the archive, for example, I ran into an elderly gentleman in an olive-green uniform shuffling along the corridors. He turned out to be Delio Gómez Ochoa, who rose from the ranks to become second in command of Fidel's core column in 1958 and then *comandante* of the "Fourth Front" in Oriente. Under his arm was the manuscript for his new book on the Marianas with whom he fought in the last days of the guerrilla war. Pushing ninety, Ochoa still had a photographic memory and confirmed many key details.

The recollections of many other elderly guerrillas were hazy, but looking at old photographs hanging on their walls often jogged their memories. Luckily, almost everyone in Cuba who was involved in the war also wrote a memoir. Most prolific was Juan Almeida, who knocked out a string of books with derring-do titles such as *The Sierra Maestra and Beyond* (Havana, 1998), *Against Water and Wind* (Havana, 2002), and *Pay Attention! I'm Recounting!* (Havana, 1993). Che Guevara's writings are still enormously readable, including *Guerrilla Warfare: Episodes of the Revolutionary War* (New York, 1968), *Diary of a Combatant: From the Sierra Maestra to Santa Clara, Cuba, 1956–58* (New York, 2013), and his practical handbook *Guerrilla Warfare* (New York, 1961). Even so, the most intimate vision of Ernesto, which casts a light behind the legend, was written by his widow, Aleida March: *Remembering Che: My Life with Che Guevara* (Melbourne, Australia, 2012).

Many of Fidel's own writings have been translated, including *The Prison Letters of Fidel Castro* (New York, 2007) and *History Will Absolve Me* (New York, 1961). Fidel granted hours of interviews to Spanish journalist Ignacio Ramonet, resulting in *Fidel Castro: My Life: A Spoken Autobiography*. Other key memoirs include Felipe Guerra Matos with José Antonio Fulgueiras, *El Marabuzal* (Havana, 2009) and Raúl Menéndez Tomassevich's *Rebeldía* (Havana, 2005). Additionally, many of the most important documents from the late 1950s are reproduced in Carlos Franqui's *Diario de la Revolución Cubana* (Barcelona, 1976); a slightly abridged version appeared in English as *Diary of the Cuban Revolution* (New York, 1980).

Finally, contemporary newspapers and magazines give an irreplaceable sense of how the war was received (and how improbable victory looked at the time). The *New York Times* offered the most consistent Cuba coverage, but wonderful glimpses are provided by the *Washington Post*, the *Chicago Tribune*, and a host of monthly photo magazines: *Life, Look, Coronet, Reader's Digest*, and, in Europe, *Paris Match*. In early 1959 the Cuban magazine *Bohemia* issued a string of commemorative issues chronicling the crimes of the Batista regime.

SECONDARY SOURCES: GENERAL

Within Cuba, whole libraries have been written on the nuts and bolts of the war, although many texts are hard to find in the outside world. (Single copies of some can be tracked down at New York University or in the Fifth Avenue branch of the New York Public Library, as if smuggled into the US by academic operatives.) The most significant is a day-by-day account of the conflict, *Diario de la Guerra*, currently in three volumes—the first written by Pedro Álvarez Tabío (Havana, 1986), the second coauthored by Álvarez with historian Heberto Norman Acosta (Havana, 2010), the third by Norman alone (Havana, 2015). Norman has also produced works with a level of detail that would overwhelm the most passionate Cubaphile. They include two hefty volumes on Fidel's exile in Mexico, for example, normally considered a footnote to history: *La Palabra Empeñada: El Exilio Revolucionario Cubano, 1953–1959* (Havana, 2006).

In English, several fundamental works are the foundation for any book on the revolution, starting with Hugh Thomas's magisterial 1,700-page tome *Cuba: the Pursuit of Freedom* (New York, 1971). *Fidel: A Critical Portrait* by *New York Times* reporter Tad Szulc, published in 1987 and updated in 2000, remains the most perceptive book on Castro himself. (Almost as valuable are transcripts of Szulc's many interviews kept at the University of Miami and available online.) Jon Lee Anderson's *Che Guevara: A Revolutionary Life* (New York, 1997; updated 2010) remains the gold standard on the poster boy for the Rebel Army. An excellent supplement is *Fidel and Che: A Revolutionary Friendship* by Simon Reid-Henry (New York, 2009).

The definitive biography of Celia, *One Day in December: Celia Sánchez and the Cuban Revolution* (New York, 2013) by Nancy Stout, is filled with vivid personal data about all the participants, including the best study of Frank País. Stout's interviews with Cuban participants (particularly women in the underground) shed crucial light on many episodes, particularly in chapters 7, 8, 14, and 26. Many of Haydée's writings are collected in Betsy Maclean (ed.), *Rebel Lives: Haydée Santamaría* (Melbourne, Australia, 2003). Attention to Camilo Cienfuegos is more quirky: See William Gálvez, *Camilo: Señor de la Vanguardia* (Havana, 1979); Carlos Franqui, *Camilo Cienfuegos* (Madrid, 2011); and *Camilo Cienfuegos y La Invasión: Rumbo a Occidente* by Sergio del Valle (Havana, 2011).

For Vilma Espín, the commemorative volume *Vilma: Una Vida Extraordinario* (Havana, 2013) collates press reports and letters over the decades. On the Bacardi rum dynasty, for which Vilma's father worked, see Tom Gjelten, *Bacardi and the Long Fight for Cuba: the Biography of a Cause* (New York, 2008).

※

WHILE THE ABOVE books were used throughout, there were also specific references:

PROLOGUE: FIDELMANIA

Ed Sullivan's bizarre 1959 CBS TV interview with Fidel can be seen in the Paley Center for Media in midtown Manhattan. Its background is described in James Maguire, *Impresario: The Life and Times of Ed Sullivan* (New York, 2006). For post-victory ambiance, see Van Gosse's *Where the Boys Are: Cuba, Cold War America and the Making of a New Left* (New York, 1993), the classic overview of the revolution in its early days; the first editions of *Bohemia* magazine in Havana in early 1959; and Jean-Paul Sartre, *Sartre on Cuba* (New York, 1961).

PART ONE: THE CUBAN "MADNESS"

For added detail on the Spanish–American War, see Evan Thomas's *The War Lovers: Roosevelt, Lodge, Hearst, and the Rush to Empire, 1898* (New York, 2010).

The only account of Batista's early life is Frank Argote-Freyre's *Fulgencio Batista: From Revolutionary to Strongman* (New Brunswick, NJ, 2006).

On Fidel's childhood, *The Boys from Dolores: Fidel Castro's Schoolmates from Revolution to Exile* by Patrick Symmes (New York, 2007) is a marvelous, sprawling survey. The last word on the myth of Fidel's youthful baseball prowess (and supposed offers from American pro teams) comes from the Society for American Baseball Research: https://sabr.org/bioproj/topic/fidel-castro-and-baseball.

On the Moncada, see Haydée Santamaría, *Moncada: Memories of the Attack That Launched the Cuban Revolution* (New York, 1980); more recent studies are Antonio Rafael de la Cova, *The Moncada Attack: Birth of the Cuban Revolution* (Columbia, SC, 2007), and *El Moncada: La Respuesta Necesaria* (Havana, 2013). Also useful are Juan Almeida's memoirs *Prison* (Havana, 1986) and *Exile* (1987); Fidel's letters from the Isle of Pines have also been published in English and Spanish.

The best surveys of Havana's decadent underbelly in the 1950s are T. J. English's page-turner *Havana Nocturne: How the Mob Owned Cuba . . . and Then Lost It to Revolution* (New York, 2008); *Tropicana Nights: The Life and Times of the Legendary Cuban Nightclub* by Rosa Lowinger and Ofelia Fox (New York, 2005); Peter Moruzzi's *Havana Before Castro: When Cuba Was a Tropical Playground* (Layton, UT, 2008); and Cuban author Enrique Cirules's

Mafia y Mafiosos en la Habana (Havana, 1999). Contemporary guidebooks for American tourists also provide fascinating firsthand details; they range from *Norton's Complete Hand-Book of Havana and Cuba*, published in 1900 during the US military occupation, to Basil Woon's loopy Prohibition era tome, *When It's Cocktail Time in Cuba* and the naughty *Cabaret Quarterly* issue of December 1956, which gives readers a rundown of the most wicked venues.

PART TWO: THE AMATEUR GUERRILLAS

The *Granma* expeditionaries' fates are recounted in *Diario de la Guerrilla* and Norman's other detailed works, particularly *El Retorno Anunciado* (Havana, 2011), a three-hundred-page epic devoted solely to the month of December 1956.

Indispensable on the crucial Herbert L. Matthews interview is *The Man Who Invented Fidel: Cuba, Castro, and Herbert L. Matthews of the New York Times* by Anthony DePalma (New York, 2006). On doctors in the Rebel Army, see Eugenio Suárez Pérez (ed.), *Médicos de la Guerrilla: Testimonios 1956–1958* (Havana, 2014).

American eyewitnesses to the war also produced key memoirs. The CBS journalist Robert Taber wrote several books sympathetic to Fidel, including *M-26: Biography of a Revolution* (New York, 1961) and *The War of the Flea: A Study of Guerrilla Warfare Theory and Practice* (New York, 1970). Biographical details on Taber were generously supplemented by interviews with his son Peter Taber.

Other firsthand American accounts include: Dickey Chapelle, *What's a Woman Doing Here?: A Combat Reporter's Report on Herself* (New York, 1962); Jules Dubois, *Freedom Is My Beat* (New York, 1959); Herbert L. Matthews, *The Cuban Story* (New York, 1961); and Ruby Hart Phillips, *Cuba: Island of Paradox* (New York, 1959). The best recent overview on US attitudes is *Fighting Over Fidel: New York Intellectuals and the Cuban Revolution*, by Rafael Rojas (New York, 2016).

The key work on insurgents in the cities—including the April 1957 strike—is Julia E. Sweig's *Inside the Cuban Revolution: Fidel Castro and the Urban Underground* (Cambridge, MA, 2002). On José Antonio Echeverría, see Ernesto Alvarea Blanco, *Subiendo Como un Sol las Escalinata* (Havana, 2009). For urban gay support to the rebels, see Lourdes Arguelles and B. Ruby Rich, "Homosexuality, Homophobia, and Revolution: Notes Toward an Understanding of the Cuban Lesbian and Gay Male Experience, Part I," *Signs* 9, no. 4 (Summer 1984), pp. 683–99.

The death of Hemingway's dog is recounted (unexpectedly) in *Hemingway's Cats: An Illustrated Biography* by Carlene Fredericka Brennen (New York,

2006); see also Brennen's book with Hilary Hemingway, *Hemingway in Cuba* (New York, 2003) and Enrique Cirules, *Hemingway en Cuba* (Havana, 1999).

For details on the nomadic early days of the guerrilla war: Luis Baez, *Secretos de Generales* (Havana, 1996); Juan José Soto Valdespino, *Mártires del Granma* (Havana, 2012); Carlos Franqui, *The Twelve* (New York, 1968); H. P. Klepak, *Raúl Castro and Cuba: A Military Story* (New York, 2012); and *Epopeya de Libertad* (Havana, 2007).

PART THREE: REVOLUTIONARY ROAD

For the 1958 summer offensive (aka "Operation Fin de Fidel") and the final push to Santiago, see Fidel's own enormous two-volume account, *La Victoria Estratégica: Por Todos los Caminos de la Sierra* and *La Contraofensiva Estratégica: De la Sierra Maestra a Santiago de Cuba* (Havana, 2010). The best account of the hostage crisis (and relations between the rebels and US generally) is Thomas G. Paterson, *Contesting Castro: The United States and the Triumph of the Cuban Revolution* (New York, 1994), although the vivid eyewitness accounts can be culled from contemporary newspaper and magazine stories.

The role of women in the war has inspired a flurry of recent books, most notably Lorraine Bayard de Volo's *Women and the Cuban Insurrection: How Gender Shaped Castro's Victory* (New York, 2018). Teté's extensive interview with Mary-Alice Waters is in *Marianas in Combat: Teté Puebla and the Mariana Grajales Women's Platoon in Cuba's Revolutionary War* (New York, 2003). See also: Alexis Leanna Henshaw, *Why Women Rebel: Understanding Women's Participation in Armed Rebel Groups* (New York, 2016); Linda A. Klouzal, *Women and Rebel Communities in the Cuban Insurgent Movement, 1952–1959* (London, 2008); Ileana Rodríguez, *Women, Guerrillas and Love: Understanding War in Central America* (New York, 1996); Karen Kampwirth, *Women and Guerrilla Movements: Nicaragua, El Salvador, Chiapas, Cuba* (Philadelphia, 2002); and Lois M. Smith and Alfred Padula, *Sex and Revolution: Women in Socialist Cuba* (New York, 1963).

On Americans in Cuba: William Morgan now has two full-length biographies, *El Americano: Fighting with Castro for Cuba's Freedom* by Aran Shetterly (New York, 2007) and *The Yankee Comandante: The Untold Story of Courage, Passion and One American's Fight to Liberate Cuba* by Michael Sallah and Mitch Weiss (New York, 2015). Even so, the most readable account remains David Grann's story in the *New Yorker*, "The Yankee Comandante" (May 28, 2012). The largely unknown story of Herman Marks is culled from contemporary press reports. Neill Macaulay's memoir is *A Rebel in Cuba* (New York, 1970). References to other Americans crop up in the *New York Times, Life, Look*, the *Miami Herald*, and even *Man's Magazine*.

PART FOUR: HONEYMOON WITH CHE

My account of Batista's final days relies heavily on *The Winds of December* by John Dorschner and Roberto Fabricio (New York, 1980). The gossipy insider story of the dictator's personality disorders is *El Gran Culpable: Como 12 Guerrilleros Aniquilaron a 45,000 Soldados?* by Batista's disillusioned press secretary, José Suárez Núñez. The US ambassador Earl T. Smith produced a heavily biased memoir of the last days, *The Fourth Floor: An Account of the Castro Communist Revolution* (New York, 1962).

The best Errol Flynn biography is Thomas McNulty, *Errol Flynn: The Life and Career* (New York, 2004). His original reports on Castro for the *New York Journal American* I tracked down at the University of Texas. Extra details were gained from interviews with Kyra Pahlen, daughter of Victor Pahlen, who directed the documentary *Cuban Story* with Flynn in 1959, and former showgirl Ida Carlini, who met Flynn and Beverly Aadland while she was working in Havana clubs. Flynn's memoir, *My Wicked, Wicked Ways*, provides more color. His report on 1959 executions is from a private letter that was published in the Australian magazine *Bulletin* when it came up for auction. His documentary *Cuban Story* (which contains valuable footage) and the regrettable *Cuban Rebel Girls* are both available on DVD.

See also: Carlos Franqui, *Family Portrait with Fidel: A Memoir* (New York, 1985); Joseph E. Persico, *Edward Murrow: An American Original* (New York, 1990); Roberta Ostroff, *Fire in the Wind: The Life of Dickey Chapelle* (New York, 1994); and George Plimpton, *Shadow Box: An Amateur in the Ring* (New York, 2016).

EPILOGUE: LAST KIDS ON THE BLOC

The only detailed analysis of Fidel's 1959 trip to the US—and what went wrong soon after—is Alan McPherson's perceptive essay "The Limits of Populist Diplomacy: Fidel Castro's April 1959 Trip to North America," *Diplomacy and Statecraft* 18, no. 1 (2007), pp. 237–68. Fidel's press secretary, Teresa Casuso, was present at both the 1959 and 1960 Harlem visits, recounted in *Cuba and Castro* (New York, 1961).

Acknowledgments

The idea for this project was born over several mojitos in a West Village bar, just before I made my first return trip to Havana after the Obama-era travel thaw in 2016. I asked my friend Julia Cooke, author of *The Other Side of Paradise: Life in the New Cuba*, to recommend a good book about the early revolution—something entertaining and readable, unsaturated by ideology, not an eight hundred page brick.

"It doesn't exist," she said. "You should write it!"

It seemed a crazy idea. For one thing, the prospect of getting into Cuba's historical archives made my forays into the Vatican Library sound like child's play. But then I made my trip to Havana—on the first private jet to fly directly from Miami in over five decades—and it began to feel slightly less daunting. My first visit to Cuba had been more than two decades earlier, during the Special Period of the mid-1990s, when I could only get there by giving $1,000 cash to a man in the Bahamas known only as Lionel to fly in a Russian prop plane that looked like it had seen service in the siege of Leningrad. The Cuba I found in 2016 was like a different country.

I took a step closer that summer, when the visionary editor of the *Smithsonian* magazine, Michael Caruso, assigned me to trace the guerrilla war's route, which led me to such lovingly preserved sites as the Comandancia de La Plata in the Sierra Maestra. On my return to New York, my agent Henry Dunow saw the potential and helped me hone a proposal that would expand the feature story into a full-length book. I must also thank my editor at Penguin, Jill Schwartzman, for agreeing that the idea might actually work. (No doubt I should also thank her aunt, who met Fidel in a New York elevator when she was seven years old, and transmitted the personal connection.) Her ever-patient assistant Marya Pasciuto gave invaluable attention to the manuscript in the following months.

Research in Havana would have been impossible without the assistance of historian Nancy Stout, author of *One Day in December: Celia Sánchez and the Cuban Revolution*. After explaining the inner workings of the Office of Historical Affairs, she put me in touch with the local archival curator, Nelsy Babeira, who in turn introduced me to the helpful director, Dr. Eugenio Suárez Pérez, the sub-director, Dr. Jorge Luis Aneiros, and their assistant Armando. Over Heinekens in the nearby Swiss restaurant, Cuban historian Herbert Norman Acosta kindly straightened out countless details.

Thanks also to Collin and Michael Laverty of Cuba Educational Travel for tips on Havana nightlife; early readers Brian Turner and Robyn Fookes; moral supporter Bonnie Blue Edwards; the *librero* Alian Alera, who could track down any book ever published in Cuba, no matter how long out of date; art dealer Bryant Toth; and everyone who worked at Bar Roma, which made my stays in Havana many times more pleasant than they otherwise would have been.

Index

About the Author

TONY PERROTTET is the author of five books: *Off the Deep End: Travels in Forgotten Frontiers*; *Pagan Holiday: On the Trail of Ancient Roman Tourists*; *The Naked Olympics: The True Story of the Ancient Games*; *Napoleon's Privates: 2,500 Years of History Unzipped*, and *The Sinner's Grand Tour: A Journey through the Historical Underbelly of Europe*. His travel stories have been translated into a dozen languages and widely anthologized, having been selected seven times for the Best American Travel Writing series. He is a regular television guest on the History Channel and a contributing writer at *Smithsonian* magazine; his work has also appeared in the *New York Times*, the *Wall Street Journal Magazine*, *Condé Nast Traveler*, *Travel + Leisure*, *Outside*, *Surface*, and the *London Sunday Times*. He lives in the East Village of Manhattan.